Asher 2017

The Sensory Processing Anthology

The Sensory Processing Anthology

A Comprehensive Guide for Parents and
Caregivers of Sensational Kids

Martha Ohler-Guerrero

Acknowledgements

I am grateful for this opportunity to bring this message of compassionate, nurturing, and loving approaches to children with sensory processing disorder.

It is with significant gratitude that I thank Heidi Clopton, OTR/L, Dr. Jason Clopton, FCOVD, Jeanane Ferre, PhD, Dr. Neil Margolis, FCOVD, Beth Osten, OTR/L, Margot Touris, PhD, and Cynthia Ingle, PhD. These talented professionals graciously afforded their time and effort toward this project for which I will be forever indebted. I would especially like to thank Mrs. Heidi Clopton, OTR/L, Director and Owner of the Center for Development in Cookeville, Tennessee, for the oversight of the entire project; without her, this book would not exist!

To Dr. Lucy Jane Miller, I owe many thanks for permission to use some of her material in this book. Also, I would like to thank all the wonderful therapists at Beth Osten and Associates who answered my neverending questions over the years.

I would like to thank the CreateSpace team and editor Emily Autenrieth for providing wonderful ideas and revisions. In addition, I would like to thank Tali Eingel, OTR/L for encouraging me to write this book many years ago.

Lastly, I would like to thank my fabulous children for providing the inspiration for this project!

Contents

Introduction

Did you know that it is estimated between four and ten million children suffer from sensory processing disorder? This little-known disorder has been likened to a "neurological traffic jam."

Some of these children can feel like Alice after she traveled down the rabbit hole, their senses over- or undermagnifying the sights, sounds, and other sensations around them. Colors overwhelming, sounds too loud, textures of food too obnoxious, movement too unsure. A typical classroom can seem like Grand Central Station. A windy day can cause high anxiety. The Fourth of July can feel like the Invasion of Normandy.

Navigating their way from classroom to classroom can be akin to finding their way through a giant maze. Jungle gyms and other typical playground equipment may inspire panic or significant fear. Coloring within the lines or handwriting may seem like an impossible feat.

The sensory child may throw aggressive temper tantrums at the store, park, or other public places over apparently inconsequential things—or, for teachers, the child who will not transition easily between activities, such as going from recess to class or entering school in the morning. They may be the children who still are not sleeping through the night, even into their teenage years.

Sensory children baffle and upset the most seasoned parents and teachers. Their meltdowns and defiant, stubborn behavior can leave parents—and teachers, grandparents, and other caretakers—feeling vulnerable, exhausted, and helpless.

Despite the advice from well-meaning friends, relatives, and doctors, this behavior cannot be resolved with time-outs, rational talking, or simply waiting for the children to grow out of it. In fact, these tactics may only exacerbate the behavior. So what can parents do about this?

They can read this book! *The Sensory Processing Anthology: A Comprehensive Guide for Parents and Caregivers of Sensational Kids* is the most comprehensive resource yet written on sensory processing disorder. This is the first book to provide in-depth information for parents and others who interact with sensory children. Ultimately, this book provides clarity to those trying to understand this bewildering disorder.

The book provides concrete, practical advice for all those living and working with sensory children and illuminates the whys behind the behaviors. This one-of-a-kind resource lends the helpful hand so desperately needed to support adults and children alike in their sensational journey. In short, *The Sensory Processing Anthology* will change lives.

Take the first step toward changing your family's life and read on for valuable information!

One

Overview of Sensory Processing Disorder

What does it mean when your child receives a diagnosis of sensory processing disorder? "Sensory processing is a term that refers to the way the nervous system receives messages from the senses and turns them into appropriate motor and behavioral responses....Whether you are biting into a hamburger, riding a bicycle, or reading a book, your successful completion of the activity requires processing sensation or "sensory integration"[1] Sensory processing disorder (SPD) is the newest term for, and is used synonymously with, Sensory Integration Disorder or Sensory Integration Dysfunction.

Sensory processing disorder gives a name to the adverse behaviors and developmental concerns that have baffled parents, pediatricians and teachers for years. The origin of these problem behaviors and developmental delays lies within the brain. The central nervous system is composed of the brain and spinal cord. The nervous system is the body's primary communication network. Communication originates in the brain—the control center of the nervous system—and has five primary functions.[2]

1) Sensory integration
2) Thinking, learning, language, and perception
3) Fine and gross motor function, non-verbal communication

4) Emotional and behavioral control
5) Autonomic functions (e.g., breathing, heart rate, hunger, digestion)

Inadequate sensory integration can profoundly influence all the other functions in the brain! Sensory integration is a critical aspect of brain function, enabling us to organize, assimilate, and make sense of all the information that comes in through the body's eight senses simultaneously. Integration of all the senses is required to produce appropriate language, motor, cognitive (thinking) and internal body processes (bladder and bowel).

For example, when a child runs up to the line and grabs a dodgeball, the child receives proprioceptive information from his body moving through space, and his arm reaching for the ball. Additional proprioceptive information comes from his fingers as they close around the ball, measuring its weight to judge the resistance needed to pick up the ball, and force to use when throwing it. Tactile information such as its texture, surface, and shape comes from manipulating the ball. He also receives vestibular information such as which direction he is facing, how fast he is moving, and information about whether he is right side up (gravity). Good visual-motor coordination (the ability of the body to coordinate vision with motor movements) and visual-spatial abilities (the ability to manipulate 2-D and 3-D images in the mind) are required to find his target.

It is the *combination* or integration of the senses that allows the child to perform this activity. Sensory information is vital, as we learn everything through our senses. When some of this information is missing, or not transmitted appropriately within the brain, the resulting condition is sensory processing disorder (SPD). Dr. Lucy Jane Miller provides the following formal definition: SPD is a neurophysiological disorder in which sensations from the environment or one's own body, are poorly detected (registered), modulated, or interpreted resulting in atypical behavioral responses.[3]

Researchers theorize the following as the root cause of SPD:

- Sensory information *not getting into the neurological system*
- Sensory information getting in, but *not being transmitted appropriately* within the brain

The study and treatment of SPD originates from occupational therapists (OT). Dr. A. Jean Ayres, an occupational therapist and developmental psychologist, first described "sensory integration dysfunction" in 1972. Dr. Ayres likened sensory integration dysfunction to a neurological "traffic jam" that prevents certain parts of the brain from receiving the information needed to interpret sensory information correctly.[4] The concept of SPD has evolved over the years, but the fundamental idea is that social, emotional, behavioral, academic or motor problems reflect a child's inability to integrate stimuli (sensations) properly. In response, the child may experience challenges during the course of typical childhood activities because processes that should be automatic or accurate, are not.[5]

There is no consensus among mental health professionals whether SPD is a stand-alone diagnosis because some of the symptoms and behaviors are present in other disorders. Because the symptoms of SPD are quite similar to those seen in autism spectrum disorders, attention-deficit hyperactivity disorder (ADHD) and mood disorders, it is not clear to the medical establishment that a distinct new label is necessary. However, it is obvious to occupational therapists that a new diagnostic classification is required because decades of research have shown that some individuals experience SPD without these other diagnoses, and SPD requires a novel treatment approach. Dr. Lucy Jane Miller is spearheading the research and drive for inclusion in the *Diagnostic and Statistical Manual of Mental Disorders* (DSM). The *Diagnostic and Statistical Manual of Mental Disorders*, Fifth Edition (DSM-V), does not list criteria for SPD. Toward this end, Dr. Miller established The Sensory Processing Disorder Foundation. This foundation is committed to enhancing the quality of life for children and their families, as well as adults, with sensory processing disorder (SPD), and collaborating in rigorous research into the causes, diagnosis, and treatment of SPD. The Sensory Processing Disorder Foundation has mobilized the SPD Scientific Work Group and the Sensory Integration Research Collaborative to collaborate on finding research-based answers to questions about SPD.[6] Peer-reviewed research abstracts, articles, and materials are available by topic in the SPD foundation library at http://spdfoundation.net/resources/library/librarybytopic/

Sensory Processing Disorder can affect anyone, and preliminary studies suggest that 5% to 16% of children demonstrate symptoms of SPD.[7] Current research suggests the disorder is frequently inherited, but a definitive cause has yet to be established. Studies have also implicated prenatal, birth complications, and certain environmental factors as playing a role as well.[8]

Sensory dysfunction initiates with the transmission or reception of information, resulting in difficulty modulating or discriminating stimuli in one or more of the eight senses below.

The Eight Senses

- Vision (sight). Vision is more complex than just eyesight, measured by how clearly a child can see an object from twenty feet away (far vision), and sixteen inches away (near vision). Many children with visual dysfunction will pass eyesight tests with 20/20 vision, but experience problems in other areas of visual skills. These include ocular tracking, binocularity (using the eyes together), visual perception, eye-hand coordination (visual-motor integration), visual attention, and visual modulation. Vision is one of the most critical senses due to its universal role in many everyday tasks.
- Auditory (hearing). Most people think of hearing as the ability to perceive sound, known as peripheral hearing. The majority of sensory children with auditory dysfunction pass a standard hearing screening. In addition to peripheral hearing, the auditory sense

includes the brain's interpretation of sound, or making sense out of what we hear. The interpretation of sound is where the crux of the problem is for sensory children with auditory dysfunction.

- Olfaction (smell). Numerous nerve endings on tiny hair-like cilia in the nostrils detect smell. These nerve endings belong to the olfactory nerve that transmits the information to the brain, where interpreted.

- Gustation (taste). Perception of taste is through sensory receptors called taste buds. The taste buds transmit sensory information via neurons to the brain. Taste helps humans detect the difference between safe and harmful food, and is a relatively limited sense; the taste buds detect only the sensations of salty, sour, bitter, sweet, and umami (savory). The broader concept of flavor derives from the integration of several senses. Taste integrates with smell, touch (texture), temperature and pain information in the brain to form flavor.

- Tactile (touch). Tactile sensations register through stimulation of the skin.[9] Millions of nerve endings located in the skin and mouth transmit sensations to the brain. Five separate tactile nerve receptors are present in the skin that register temperature (hot & cold), pain, light touch (surface), and pressure (deep touch). The tactile system is the largest sensory system, and its influence is pervasive. Functionally, the tactile system discriminates between surfaces, shapes, and textures, provides precise, distinct information necessary for fine motor control (use of the small muscles in our hands and fingers), and sensory feedback necessary for gross motor control (use of the large muscles for running, walking, etc.). The skin receptors transmit temperature and pain information to the brain for interpretation. Once the message is deciphered, it is the interoceptive system noted below that regulates temperature and pain through the cardiovascular system within the body.

- Vestibular (movement). The vestibular system located in the inner ear senses changes in head positions, or movement with reference to gravity that enables a child to respond.[10] Movement with reference to gravity includes information to where "down" is, and the direction the body is facing. Information on head movements comes from organs called the otoliths and semicircular canals. The otoliths register acceleration/deceleration of linear motion, and the semicircular canals register acceleration/deceleration of rotary motion. Thus, the vestibular system would sense what direction you are swinging and how fast.

Physiologically, the vestibular system connects to the digestive tract, language center of the brain, the limbic system, and to the muscles of the eyes. A well-functioning vestibular system will thus contribute to healthy digestion, the emergence of receptive (understanding words spoken) and expressive (speech) communication, emotional bonding, and visual focus.[11] In addition the vestibular system integrates sensations, facilitates the development of posture, balance, and muscle tone, and coordinates the two sides of the body. In a larger developmental context, the vestibular system provides physical and emotional security.

- Proprioceptive (position). The proprioceptive system perceives sensations from movement (i.e., speed, rate, sequencing, timing, and force) and joint position.[12] Proprioception senses the force used when a muscle stretches, and how fast. This system discerns where our body parts are without having to monitor them visually, and consists of sensory feedback mechanisms for motor control and posture.
- Interoceptive (internal). Interoception is the sense of the physiological condition of the body.[13] The interoceptive sense operates unconsciously, and regulates vital functions such as heart rate, respiration, thirst, hunger, digestion, state of arousal, sleep cycle, mood, body temperature, pain and bowel/bladder elimination. This sense runs on autopilot until we become conscious of our need to use the bathroom, go to sleep, or

put on a coat. The tactile system transmits body temperature and pain information to the brain, but it is the interoceptive system that regulates these functions within the human body through the cardiovascular system (vasodilation, sweating, and constriction of blood vessels).

Specialized sensory receptors cells in the peripheral nervous system transmit sensory information from the eight senses to the central nervous system (brain). The peripheral nervous system is composed of two parts: the somatic nervous system and the autonomic nervous system.

The somatic nervous system consists of peripheral nerve fibers that send sensory information to the central nervous system, and motor nerve fibers that carry information from the brain to skeletal muscles for muscle and motor control.

The autonomic nervous system is composed of three parts: the sympathetic nervous system, the parasympathetic nervous system, and the enteric nervous system. The autonomic nervous system (ANS) regulates the functions of our internal organs (heart, stomach, intestines), and controls some of the muscles within the body. The ANS functions involuntary, e.g., we do not notice when blood vessels constrict, or when our heart beats faster. The ANS is most important in two situations: in situations that cause stress and require us to "fight" or take "flight," or in non-stressful situations that allow us to "rest" and "digest." The sympathetic nervous system swings into action during stress, and uses energy by increasing your blood pressure, heart rate, and slowing your digestion down. When the body is at "rest," the parasympathetic nervous system works to save energy by decreasing blood pressure, slowing heart rate, allowing digestion. The autonomic nervous system is always working at a baseline level, and not just active during "fight or flight" or "rest and digest" situations. Rather, the autonomic nervous system acts to maintain normal internal functions and equilibrium within the body at all times.

The little-known enteric nervous system is a third division of the autonomic nervous system. The enteric nervous system is a meshwork of nerve fibers that innervate the viscera (gastrointestinal tract, pancreas, and gall bladder).

The central nervous system and the peripheral nervous system work in tandem to transmit, process, and integrate sensations. Sensory integration includes the synchronized processing of information from multiple systems interconnected with every system influencing another, which is why dysfunction may permeate several senses simultaneously in SPD.

Types of Sensory Processing Disorder

Presently, researchers have proposed a classification scheme categorized into three types: sensory modulation disorder, sensory-based motor disorders, and sensory discrimination disorder. Sensory modulation disorder has three subtypes: sensory overresponsivity, sensory underresponsivity, and sensory-craving. The sensory craving subtype is also known as sensory-seeking. Dr. Lucy J. Miller and other researchers have proposed the classification scheme renaming sensory-seeking as sensory craving. Based on this classification, the term sensory craving replaces sensory-seeking in this book. The next type, sensory discrimination disorder, may affect one sense or all eight senses. Lastly, sensory-based motor disorder has two subtypes: dyspraxia and postural disorder.[14] The information in this book reflects current theory. As research continues and additional knowledge unfolds on these disorders, this information may evolve over time. The chart below is the classification scheme proposed by researchers.

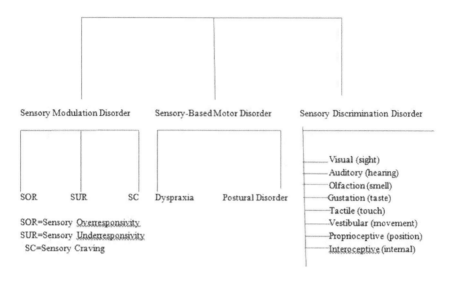

A discussion of the types and subtypes of SPD resides in subsequent chapters of this book. As you read the symptoms of these disorders, keep in mind that the presence of one symptom does not indicate the child has the disorder, and a child is unlikely to experience every symptom. Typically, a collection of these symptoms warrants a screening by an occupational therapist with advanced training in SPD.

The Impact of Sensory Processing Disorder

All parents may see their children within the pages of this book, but the distinguishing factor of sensory children is greater frequency, intensity, and duration of the behaviors. Sensory processing disorder and related behaviors can have a profound influence on development because the disorder interferes with the ability to learn, interact with others, perform tasks, and participate in activities. The result may be a child with delayed development who does not demonstrate abilities and behaviors that are typical of peers. Children with SPD vary significantly in their developmental path, and exhibit a distinctive blend of sensory difficulties. Therefore, you may find that some chapters or sections speak to your family's experiences, and others do not. However, all forms of the disorder affect social interactions, learning, sports participation, and emotional well-being to varying degrees and intensity. Sensory children will not outgrow their disabilities. Therefore, it is important that families seek a professional assessment when problems warrant, and make treatment a priority.

Sensory processing disorder not only affects the child, but also disrupts the family dynamic. Siblings may feel the attention diverts to the sensory sibling, and marriages may become strained due to a chaotic and stressful household. Parents should not hesitate to reach out to mental health professionals should they find their family overly stressed, chronically anxious, and struggling to deal with their sensational child. In addition, each chapter contains parental strategies and advice in order to provide support for families.

Children with SPD require a calm, loving, and empathic environment in order to develop self-regulation (self-calming) skills. *The Sensory Processing Anthology* provides parents and caregivers with a practical understanding of these sensational kids, and comprehensive strategies to nurture a positive family dynamic. The strategies contributed by professionals in this book are those most effective with the largest number of children. Each child with sensory processing disorder has a unique profile, so not all strategies will work for all children. As a result, parents will need to try several strategies, and choose those that work best for their child and the child's family.

Two

Sensory Modulation Disorder

An import aspect of sensory integration is modulation. Modulation is the brain's internal thermostat that automatically adjusts and balances arousal level based on the stimulation experienced by a person. For instance, a person who feels sluggish may exercise, chew gum, or listen to music to increase his arousal level. A child with sensory integrative problems does not have this internal capacity to modulate their level of arousal.[1]

Children with sensory modulation disorder have processing difficulties that interfere with daily functioning at home, at school, or in interactions with peers and adults. In other words, a child with sensory modulation disorder has trouble translating sensory messages into regulated behavior.

According to *Webster's Dictionary*, to modulate is to "regulate by or adjust to a certain measure of proportion." A modulation disorder is one in which the brain cannot adjust or regulate the degree, intensity, and nature of sensory stimuli so that the body can produce appropriate physiological and behavioral adaptive responses. An adaptive response is a successful, goal-directed action on the environment.[2] An inability to produce an appropriate adaptive response may result in the following:

- Aggression, meltdowns, and defiant behavior
- Inability to tolerate transitions
- Sleep problems

- Eating problems
- Attention and memory problems
- Hyper- or hyposensitivity to noises, visual stimulation, touch, or movement
- Motor planning problems
- Communication difficulties

Sensory modulation occurs in three phases:

- Sensory registration is the detection and recognition of sensory input. Children with sensory processing disorder can register low or high sensory information. In order to store information about a current experience, a child must be able to register adequate sensory information. Once information is registered, the child filters through previous situations similar to the one he is registering, to determine the stimulus. If there is no match made, a typical child will orient to the stimulus and store the information for future use. In some sensory children, low registration prevents this storing of information, affecting the child's motor planning and other functions. Low registration refers to a pattern of sensory processing in which children notice sensory stimuli much less than other children. Children with low sensory registration appear unengaged, self-preoccupied and may be flat in affect. They often seem unaware of their surroundings, and miss environmental cues that would direct their actions.[3] High registration patterns refer to a child's inability to filter out irrelevant sensory information, subsequently overregistering the input. High registration may result in distractibility, hyperactivity, inattentiveness, disorganization, shutdown, or fight, flight, freeze behaviors.[4]
- Orientation is the process of taking a registered sensory stimulus and deciding what action to take.
- Arousal is the reaction to a stimulus.

Modulation of sensory input is critical to our engagement in daily living. Modulation enables us to filter sensations, maintain an optimal level of arousal and attention, and respond appropriately to sensory input. When modulation is inadequate: behaviors may appear exaggerated in comparison to the sensory input, the child may have trouble adapting to changes in the environment, and attention levels may be either too low or too high. Children whose attention levels are too high cannot filter out irrelevant information, as their attention perpetually diverts to every change in the environment, resulting in a constantly distracted child. Conversely, children's attention levels may be too low if they do not register enough sensations that would generate notice of things in their environment. Either way, they are no longer in the calm-alert state, the optimal arousal state where maximum learning and teachable moments occur.[5] Additional cognitive functions may also be impacted such as short-term memory, motor planning, and language. Deficits may appear when the child is out of the calm-alert state; these deficits may come and go fluctuating with the child's regulation level.

The majority of children with SPD do not present with one type of modulation disorder, but rather of combination of two or three subtypes. The three identified states include the overresponsive child, the underresponder, and the sensory craving underresponder. Dr. Lucy Miller's preliminary research indicated that of the 25 percent of children who present with one subtype of modulation disorder: 10 percent will be pure overresponders, 5 percent will be pure passive underresponders, and 10 percent will be pure sensory cravers.[6] Data came from only one treatment center, so it may not be representative of all children with SPD. Additional data will be necessary to be confident in these numbers.

The remaining 75 percent of children with either two or three subtypes will present with a combination of regulatory states, and fluctuate from day to day or even hour to hour. These children may stand lethargically in the middle of the preschool classroom at 9:00 a.m. (passive underresponder), and crash, bang, and shout at the top of their lungs by

10:00 a.m. (sensory craver). At the end of preschool, these same children may become overresponsive and meltdown, or become aggressive as the result of a seemingly innocuous stimulus. In other words, most of these children experience several regulatory states every day or hour, and will exhibit characteristics of more than one of the overresponsive and underresponsive subtypes below.

Sensory Overresponsivity

"Imagine if something as harmless as a song on the radio, the smell of pizza wafting from the oven, or somebody accidentally brushing against you readied you for a fight, and you could not flee or calm down.... Imagine what a struggle it would be to stay composed and get through a day!"[7] This can be a typical day for a child with sensory overresponsivity.

Children with sensory overresponsivity (SOR) cannot filter out the irrelevant sensory stimuli resulting in a surplus of sensory stimulation within their neurological system. As a result, children with SOR respond quickly with too much intensity, are extremely sensitive to their environments, and get overloaded easily. Subsequently, these children often experience behavioral and emotional issues including severe anxiety, fear, aggression, distractibility, emotional distress, problems with social interactions, and withdrawal.[8]

The extreme registration of sensory input can result in great distress in the child's daily living. One of the most common sensory modulation problems observed is tactile overresponsiveness (defensiveness). Children with tactile defensiveness experience irritation or discomfort from tactile sensations that are not bothersome for peers.[9] The discomfort may be comparable to the experience of trimming your fingernails too close. The raw sensation experienced by the nerves no longer protected by the fingernail can be irritating or painful. This is similar to the way that a person with extreme touch sensitivity may experience sensations except for two important differences. First, in the case of the person who just clipped their nails, the discomfort comes because previously sheltered nerves now exposed, making the person acutely aware of sensations not ordinarily felt. In this case, the nerve function is normal, but the experience is abnormal. For a child who is overly sensitive to touch, the experiences are normal, and the nerve function is abnormal. Secondly, the child who has clipped his nails will soon become accustomed to the sensation (called habituation), while the child with the overresponsive system does not habituate to the sensations no matter how much exposure.

Dr. Lucy Jane Miller's research supports the notion that an overresponsive child cannot habituate to a stimulus the way typical children do. Her electrocardiogram (EEG) research showed a big spike in their brains' electrical activity with an initial stimulus and, even after the stimulus was removed, observed repetitive spikes.[10] The repetitive spikes indicate the child does not acclimate to the sensation, i.e. habituate. Habituation is what enables a child to tune out the sounds of other children rustling their papers, or the fan running in the classroom in order to focus on the teacher's instructions.

Due to the lack of habituation, the child may feel bombarded by dozens of unpleasant sensory experiences on a daily basis. The child may be acutely aware of the clothes on his body to the point of distraction, as he cannot habituate to the sensation. The child may be distressed or feel pain from light touch, such as "itchy" tags or seams in their clothes. The child may demand to dress from head to toe in soft sweat clothes, even in hot weather, as this prevents his skin from exposure to tactile stimulation, and decreases the sensory invasion of his nervous system.

School may be challenging because the child's filtering system is not screening out the feel of the hard chair, the bumps on the pencil, the sharp edges of the paper, or the air current blowing through the room. The child may dread art projects that include finger-painting, glue, and clay due to the heightened discomfort he feels when touching these substances. He may dislike group games like tag, dodge ball or soccer due to the fear of touch by another child. Typical preschool games such as Ring around the Rosie require holding hands, agonizing for the child with sensory overresponsivity. Standing apart from other children to prevent touch is common for the SOR child, and often inhibits her social interactions. The slightest accidental bump from another child may feel threatening, and he may lash out aggressively. Behaviors of the SOR child may appear impulsive and spontaneous when she becomes aggressive, but, in reality, she is defending the perceived raid of her space as interpreted by her brain. The sympathetic nervous system generates aggression, known as the fight, flight, fright, or freeze response. The sympathetic nervous system (SNS) and the parasympathetic nervous system (PNS) together compose the autonomic nervous system, and these two systems work in tandem to balance the autonomic nervous system. The SNS is responsible for firing up the nervous system, and the PNS "calms down" the nervous system.

Another common sensory overresponsivity problem is gravitational insecurity. Gravitational insecurity is overresponsiveness to vestibular sensations involving linear movement. These children often exhibit fear during everyday activities, especially those characterized by changes in head movements (e.g., tipping the head backwards when getting hair washed) or movements upward through space (heights). Stairs, escalators, elevators, ferris wheels, playground equipment, balance beams, or uneven surfaces (stepping off a curb) may inspire fear, anxiety or avoidance behaviors.

Typical childhood activities may be challenging such as bicycle riding, skating or skateboarding. Therefore, adversely affected social interactions leave some of these children isolated with a lack of self-confidence and low self-esteem.

Another form of vestibular defensiveness is intolerance to movement. This type of modulation challenge results in fear of movement on playground equipment, moving walkways, riding in a car, or being moved by other people (e.g., a teacher pushes a child's chair in toward their desk). Some children with vestibular defensiveness may react with fight, flight, fright, or freeze responses when forced into situations that they would typically avoid.

Fight, flight, fright, or freeze responses are common in children with SOR and exhibited when the child feels assaulted by sensory input that typical people would consider harmless or nonirritating, or when they cannot avoid the aversive stimulus. For example, a baby may cry at the sound of a sneeze. SOR babies are often fussy and irritable due to misinterpretation of sensory signals.[11] These babies may either cry excessively with difficulty self-calming, or sleep most of the time in an effort to avoid or "shut down" the level of stimulation. Toddlers may display discomfort by fleeing from the stimulus, retreating to a safe haven, or lashing out at the person or object that imposed the aversive stimulus. For instance, a toddler may run away at the sound of tearing paper, or slap a parent in the face when overstimulated. Hitting, biting, and throwing are behaviors that often relate to overresponsiveness.[12]Some children with SOR will tolerate sensation if they can initiate and control the interaction. For example, the child may refuse hugs, but agree to give one if she can feel a sense of power and predictability over the situation.[13]

Children with SOR will avoid or attempt to escape sensory input when possible. However, the child may develop inappropriate behaviors in an attempt to escape sensory input and decrease arousal levels. For example, a child may carry an object with him such as a stick to poke other children that come too close. One child would put his hands around the neck of another child that came too close to keep the other child at bay, prompting the nickname "strangler."[14]

Behavioral reactions may relate to a single event, or cumulative sensation throughout the entire day. In the case of a cumulative reaction, the child's response may seem to appear unrelated to the current context, or out of the blue. Often, these children cannot process all the sensory information as it accumulates, and when their sensory buckets overflow, behavioral outbursts manifest. These same children tend to have temper tantrums, meltdowns and aggressive behavior when they are required to process alot of sensory stimuli during a single event, such as at a party or a mall. The threshold will vary from child to child, from day to day, and throughout the day depending on context. Most overresponsive sensory children work hard to control their responses to sensory stimuli throughout the day, especially at school, which is why the after-school transition is so fraught with drama. This accumulation may manifest after school or during the evening as an intense meltdown or other "fight, flight, fright or freeze" response to an otherwise innocuous stimulus because they feel safe at home, safe enough to let out the stress of the day.

Sensory defensiveness refers to overresponsivity to sensory stimuli in multiple sensory systems. Rather than being sensitive to all stimuli in a particular domain, children are overresponsive to specific types of stimuli within that domain (e.g., in the tactile domain, they respond defensively to light touch, but not deep pressure). SOR can occur in one or multiple sensory systems; children are typically overresponsive to more than one sensory channel. Here are examples of how children may be overresponsive to stimuli in each sensory system:

- Vision (sight): Distressed or feels pain by bright, flashing, or fluorescent lights
- Auditory (hearing): Trouble tolerating loud noises that are painful to the child
- Olfaction (smell): Has excessive negative reactions to certain odors
- Gustation (taste): Distressed or feels pain by certain tastes and textures of food
- Tactile (touch): Distressed or feels pain by light touch such as an itchy tag
- Vestibular (movement): Fears heights; distressed by moving walkways, elevators, or cars (resulting in car sickness)
- Proprioceptive: (position): Rigid posture as muscles and joints are overregistering proprioceptive input.
- Interoceptive (internal): Constantly feels the need to urinate; easily overheated

Reactions to sensory stimuli in overresponsive children occur along a spectrum, with some children managing their responses most of the time (usually through either socially inappropriate or sensory-avoiding behaviors), and other children in a continuous state of alert with elevated blood pressure and heart rate twenty-four hours a day. This continuous overalert state leaves the child overwhelmed and anxious around the clock. Parents are often exasperated when their words and instructions are unheeded by the child with SOR. The escalated state of alert takes priority over all other brain signals, and the resulting anxiety snatches their attention away from other important information, such as when a parent or teacher are delivering instructions.[15] Therefore, the SOR child's anxiety will interfere with learning and their grades may suffer.

SOR children are generally irritable, moody, and have difficulty with transitions, unexpected change, and social interactions.[16] Specific behaviors related to children with SOR are listed below.

Behavioral Indicators of the Overresponsive Child

- Can be visually distracted by too much on the walls or by activity outside a window. May cover her eyes or hide under a desk, table, or chair. Prefers low light to bright light, and may squint or get headaches when in the presence of fluorescent or bright light. If the child does not overrespond to tactile sensations, she will prefer to wear caps, hats, or sunglasses to protect her eyes from the sun, and may avoid eye contact with others because it is threatening.
- Fears noisy environments such as movies, concerts, fireworks, a sudden siren, or competitive sports games. Fears certain environmental sounds such as the vacuum cleaner, flushing toilets, slamming doors, sneezes, or cell phones. May hold his hands over his ears to protect himself from loud sounds. May not be able to do homework in the presence of background noise.
- Responds unfavorably to certain smells (e.g., he may not like certain people because of the smell of their deodorant, perfume, or cologne). Has an adverse reaction to smells unnoticed by others,

such as lotion, soap, shampoo, or cooking smells in restaurants and home.

- Avoids certain tastes and textures that are part of a typical child's diet. Can be a very fussy eater and will refuse new foods. Cannot tolerate extremes in temperatures of foods, and may have an overactive gag reflex. Often, the issues of SOR show up first in feeding, when the child is very young, due to the extreme level of touch required in that activity, and the tendency of the suck, swallow, breathe pattern to get out of order.[17]
- Reacts negatively toward certain mediums, such as glue, dirt, shaving cream, or finger paint, because of the heightened tactile stimulation he experiences. This results in a range of behavior anywhere from signs of discomfort to screaming and tantrums.
- Reacts negatively toward tags in her clothes, hats, headbands, seams in her socks or pants, or anything around the neck such as a shirt collar or jewelry. May complain about or refuse to wear certain textures/fabrics of clothing and avoids going barefoot due to the tactile stimulation. Reacts negatively toward brushing her teeth or hair, getting nails clipped, taking baths or showers, or being gently touched. May refuse to wash with a washcloth or use soap.
- May try to rub, wipe, scratch or squeeze the place where she has been kissed or touched.[18]
- Fear of being hit by a ball or touched by another child may result in avoidance of group sports or games, such as dodge ball or tag. As a result, the child may always prefer isolation due to the fear of being bumped, or touched by other children. This will prevent the child from interacting with peers in a typical way.
- Becomes distressed when her feet leave the ground or her head changes position. This condition is called gravitational insecurity, and theorized to stem from difficulty processing sensory information received by the otolith organs in the inner ear. As a result, she may avoid climbing, jumping, and taking

escalators and elevators. May have a significant fear of going up and down stairs and fear of heights. May avoid having her head tipped back when washing her hair. She may avoid sleeping in her bed and demand to sleep on the floor. Many of these children have poor eye convergence, thought to be responsible for their fear of having objects thrown toward them, such as a ball. Postural problems, low muscle tone, and poor body awareness may also be present with this condition.

- Avoids playground equipment that requires movement, such as merry-go-rounds, slides, or swings. Intolerance to movement is the term utilized for this condition. May hate riding in a car and scream throughout the duration of the ride. May refuse to get on moving walkways. May become anxious if she is physically moved by someone else (e.g., if the teacher pushes her chair closer to her desk).

- May refuse to jump, hop or skip and may not like the feeling of pressure on legs or feet. Therefore, these children may avoid sports or activities that require a lot of running, jumping or crashing. They may have rigid or tense posture since they are getting too many proprioceptive signals. The child may have difficulty tolerating other people moving their body, hugging, or stretching limbs or other body parts.

- Elimination challenges such as potty training problems, wetting the bed, or constant trips to the bathroom, due to overresponsivity to sensations in the bladder and bowel are common in the child with SOR.

- Temperature modulation difficulties—too hot or too cold—for situational context, are often present in the child with SOR. The overresponsive child may be oversensitive to pain, and react to a scraped knee as if it were a deep, excruciating gash.

- Has trouble falling asleep, which requires calm and relaxation. Children with SOR have internal engines that are constantly running too high. Sensations for the SOR child are overly magnified, resulting in night awakenings when she hears sounds from another room, or typical home noise such as the dishwasher or air conditioning kicking on.[19]

- Has fight, flight, fright, or freeze responses. For example:
  - May develop pinching, hitting, slapping, biting, or kicking behaviors designed to keep peers from coming too close. May carry a stick or other object to poke other children who enter his personal space. She may kick or hit another child who gets too close to her in line at school.
  - May get overwhelmed easily in busy environments, such as a sports arena, birthday party, mall, or state fair, and scream, tantrum, run away, or become aggressive through biting, hitting, and kicking.
- Falls apart during transitions. There are certain parts of the day when SOR children will predictably fall apart: getting ready for school, leaving the house for school, coming home from school, eating dinner, and transitioning to bed. See "Chapter 9: Transitions" for information and strategies on how to manage transitions.
- Insists on organization of food, toys, or other things. These behaviors may border on ritualistic or compulsive. Children with SOR are unable to filter out sensory information from their environment, and lining up their toy cars along a wall may help relieve the anxiety in an otherwise chaotic and unpredictable world.[20]
- Experiences stress and anxiety physically more than other children. May have frequent headaches, stomachaches, and muscle aches. Children with SOR may visit the nurse's office at school frequently with complaints of discomfort, as they are overly aware of sensations from the alimentary tract (tubular passage that extends from the mouth to the anus that functions in digestion and elimination) such as nausea, hunger, fullness, and thirst.
- Can become overstimulated in play with another child and be aggressive. This translates into an unpredictable child, and other

children are often reluctant to play with them. As a result, the child with SOR may become isolated, which may affect his self-esteem and self-confidence.

- Experiences motor-planning deficits only when dysregulated, whereas the child with a sensory-based motor disorder (see chapter three) will suffer from these deficits continuously. Significant anxiety activates the sympathetic nervous system, and this anxiety propels the child into the overresponsive window, interfering with motor planning.
- Has compromised communication skills when experiencing emotions such as anxiety. The level of speech loss varies depending on whether the situation elicits the fight, flight, fright, or freeze response. In the case of the maximum stress response, the child will be unable to speak at all. In less severe cases, he will lose partial communication skills, and have difficulty organizing thoughts and speech, i.e., the child may have trouble getting sentences out.
- Exhibits attention and/or short-term memory problems when she gets out of the calm-alert (optimal arousal) state. The child's attention constantly diverts to the ongoing environment when out of the calm-alert state, sacrificing short-term memory.
- Exhibits behaviors associated with high anxiety, such as high-pitched squeals, talking rapidly, or chewing on clothing, shirts, or sleeves.

Sensory Underresponsivity

Jenny is sitting in the family room playing a video game. Her mother calls from the kitchen, "Jenny, it's time for your soccer game." Jenny does not respond and continues playing her game. Her mother calls two more times without any response from Jenny. Finally, her mother touches Jenny on the shoulder and looks her in the eyes, "did you hear me?" "Oh, no I didn't hear you, what did you say?" "It's time for your soccer game." Jenny goes to her room to change clothes and takes an excessive amount of time. Finally, Jenny comes out complaining that she does not want to go. Once there, she engages in the game for a few minutes, and then stops running up and down the field. Jenny "runs out of gas" during the game. Afterwards, Jenny and her mother are walking to their car when Jenny trips, falls and skins her knee. She shows no reaction as her mother scurries to find her first aid kit in the car. After attending to Jenny's knee, her mother drives home. Once home, Jenny's mother suggests she go outside and play with the neighborhood kids. Jenny refuses and heads to her room to read a fantasy book.

The above is a typical example of a passive underresponder. These children are very slow to respond to sensory information in their environment. As a result, they look listless, withdrawn and lethargic typically not engaging with people or children around them. SUR children underrespond to sensory information and, therefore, situations. These children require relatively intense or extended duration of sensory messages before moved to action.[21]

Due to poor registration of sensory input, children with SUR do not adequately respond to environmental stimuli at the level of typically functioning children. For example, they may not notice someone calling their name, or touching them on the shoulder. As a result, it may take longer for them to react even as their parents repeat themselves. They may not notice if they are bleeding due to a limited ability to register tactile information from their touch and pain receptors. Passive underresponders often do not seek out the sensory input they need to become actively engaged in the environment, task, or interaction. Therefore, most of these children register some sensory information, but the information is inappropriate, irrelevant, or too minimal for suitable arousal.

Intervention for low sensory registration revolves around increasing the intensity of sensory input to expand the opportunity for noticing and reacting to environmental demands.[22] For example, getting your child out of bed in the morning may require some intense sensory input, such as loud music, hand clapping, bright lights, and significant animation and emotion on your part. Parents often need to use animated communication in order to attract the attention and engagement of the child.

Researchers hypothesize that children with SUR may be receiving an overabundance of parasympathetic nervous system (PNS) signals and/or too few sympathetic nervous system (SNS) signals that may explain low arousal, an inability to register pain, danger, and other sensory warnings that should register automatically.[23]

There are two different profiles for the passive underresponder identified by The Interdisciplinary Council on Developmental and Learning Disorders. Some children tend to be self-absorbed, unaware, and disengaged, while others are self-absorbed but very creative, and overly focused on their own fantasy lives.

A. Self-Absorbed, Unaware and Difficult to Engage
    These children are often quiet, passive, apathetic, withdrawn, and lethargic. They are difficult to engage and typically are self-preoccupied due to the lack of sensory registration.[24] Children with this profile fail to notice things in their environment such as someone calling their name, or the fact that they got a substitute teacher midway through the day. These children may seem to lack the inner drive that most children have for socialization and motor exploration because they do not notice the potential opportunities around them for interaction and play. These children often cannot keep up with fast-moving children on the playground. By the time they notice opportunities to join in play, the other children have already moved on to other peers or activities.[25] Due to their low registration of sensory input, parents may have to repeat instructions, such as 'it's time to get dressed now,' over and over. It can appear that these children do not hear well, leaving parents with the impression that their child has a hearing deficiency that requires testing.[26]

    Emotional expression in children with SUR is often restricted and very limited.[27] Infants with this pattern are overlooked and the "easy baby" because they are quite and non-demanding. Toddlers may not cry when injured in situations that would elicit emotional distress in typical children. Underresponsive children have a particularly difficult time being aware of their own emotional state because this awareness requires sufficient sensory information. A child must be able to identify her own emotions before she can identify others' emotional states. Therefore, not only do these children have trouble understanding what they are feeling, but often unable to read the emotions of others, such as the disapproval or frustration of their parents. For more information on reading non-verbal cues and understanding others emotions, see "Chapter 10: Emotions."

Due to their inability to engage with peers, these children are often isolated with few friends, which limits their opportunities to develop social skills. School is challenging because the child cannot keep pace with peers, as it takes longer for these children to respond. Their social isolation and academic difficulties may leave the child with low self-esteem and a lack of self-confidence. Below are some specific behaviors related to the self-absorbed, unaware, and disengaged child.

Behavioral Indicators of the Self-Absorbed, Unaware, and Disengaged Child:

- Often appears quiet and withdrawn from people and the environment.
- Labeled the "good baby" simply because the baby fails to make demands.
- Toddlers may skip the "terrible twos" because they have difficulty expressing emotions.[28]
- Lacks interest in exploring objects, new activities, and surroundings; seems unaware of what is going on around him.
- Is apathetic and easily exhausted; may appear to "run out of gas."
- Often accompanied by low muscle tone, poor posture, and low endurance.[29]

- May have difficulty reading others' emotions or understanding his affective (emotional) states.
- May be slow to process emotions, reacting to some situations hours, days, or even weeks later.
- May have slow information processing speed. This symptom most often elicits a red flag in school-age children, as they are often unable to keep up with their schoolwork.
- Lacks social engagement. Due to their inactive and uncommunicative nature, they are uninterested in things and peers around them. They end up ignored by active children who want to run and play.
- May verbally communicate less than peers.
- Does not cry when seriously hurt; has high tolerance to pain.
- Does not notice when someone touches her or tries to get her attention. The child is difficult to engage.
- Prefers sedentary activities to physical ones.
- Appears slow or unmotivated when learning to dress and/ or feed himself.

Parents and caregivers need to provide intense sensory stimulation for the child with SUR in order to help engage the child in activities and relationships with others.

B. Self-Absorbed and Creative
    Behavior patterns of self-absorbed and creative children revolve around a tendency to tune into their own sensations, thoughts, and emotions rather than to communication from other people.[30] Children with this pattern exemplify a lack of interest in reciprocal communication with others due to a preoccupation with their own cognitive processing. These children may turn to a world of cognitive ideas to obtain the stimulation their brains need.[31] Infants may prefer to explore objects alone rather than in play

with another infant or parent. When a preschool craft or competition from peers challenges a preschooler, they may retreat into fantasy. If peers do not join in their imaginative and creative fantasy life, the preschooler prefers to play in isolation.[32]

The behaviors associated with the self-absorbed and creative child include all the behaviors' above for the self-absorbed and difficult-to-engage type. In addition, this child is highly intelligent and so engrossed in his own fantasy world that it is difficult to engage the child.

If left unabated, this preoccupation with the self could result in large impacts socially and emotionally. Socially, collaborative pretend play helps a child to learn negotiation skills, problem solving, decision making, turn taking, and sharing. Collaborative play facilitates motor planning through ideation and sequencing. Ideation is necessary when formulating a concept for play, and sequencing when the child moves through the actions of the concept (see chapter three for more information on motor planning). Development of expressive language develops through collaborative pretend play, since this type of play involves language the child would not otherwise use. Emotionally, collaborative pretend play builds self-esteem and emotional security by allowing them to act out their own fears as they take control in play what they are lacking in the real world.[33] Lastly, pretend play is the basis of creativity. As a result, parents should involve these children in collaborative pretend play rather than allow the child to engage in constant solitary play.

Sensory Craving

Harry wakes up earlier than everyone else wakes and runs through the house, jumping on the sofa, and shrieking with pleasure. Once the rest of the family is up, it is time for Harry to get dressed. Breakfast is ready, and he is still not downstairs. Harry's mother hears earsplitting music coming from his room and goes to check on him. Harry has pulled his mattress off the bed, and is jumping from the top of his dresser onto the mattress below, singing along to the loud music. His mother tells him to get dressed immediately and come down to breakfast. Harry sits down at the breakfast table, but only remains seated for a couple of minutes. Harry pops out of his chair and grabs a nearby ball. He starts bouncing the ball off the wall much to the displeasure of his parents.

This may be a typical start of the day for a school-age sensory craving child. Children with this subtype actively seek or crave sensory stimulation and seem to have an almost insatiable desire for sensory input. They vigorously participate in activities or actions that deliver more intense sensations to satisfy this sensory appetite. The quest for sensation may be contained in one sensory domain or involve two or more sensory areas. For example, a child may seek extreme movement (vestibular), loud noises (auditory), and deep-pressure input in the muscles and joints (proprioceptive) simultaneously. Some sensory cravers actually start the day as passive underresponders but transition at some point during the day to actively seeking information, and others wake up in sensory craving mode and continue the quest for input throughout the day.[34]

"The function of the behaviors in a sensory craving child is to obtain sensory input in an attempt to increase his arousal, attention, postural tone, registration, focus and pleasure."[35] In other words, the sensory craver attempts to acquire the sensory input she needs in an effort to self-regulate her body and mind. "They tend to be constantly moving, crashing, bumping, and jumping, needing to touch everything and have difficulty inhibiting this behavior....They may play music or the TV at loud volumes, may fixate on visually stimulating objects or events, or may seek unusual olfactory (smell) or gustatory (taste) experiences that are more intense and last longer than those of children with typical sensory responsiveness."[36] Sensory cravers engage in these behaviors at a much higher level than typical peers and do not have any cognitive awareness of their behavior; they are driven to do it because it feels good. As they age and are able to observe and verbalize their own patterns, they may describe their need for activity and stimulation as a way to feel alive, vibrant, and powerful.[37]

Sometimes, children engage in repetitive sensory activities, such as spinning on a Sit 'n Spin, swinging, or jumping up and down on the bed, because they need the intensity or repetition of these activities in order to acquire the level of sensory input they need. However, the frantic, unstructured sensory stimulation that sensory craving children seek may increase their overall state of arousal and result in disorganized behavior. What the sensory craving child needs is interrupted sensation instead of disorganized frenzied activity. It would not be advantageous to put the child in a rotary swing and spin them around and around. Beneficial for a sensory craving child is to spin in one direction and stop, then spin in an alternate direction and stop, then throw beanbags into the middle of a hula hoop on the ground.[38] Starting and stopping activates the semicircular canals in the inner ear, enabling the therapist to activate vestibular motion through all planes (linear and rotary). This provides additional input that the sensory craving child seeks without the disorganizing effect of rotary swinging.[39] For example, on a safety-netted trampoline, the child jumps 10 times, then stops and gives you a five, or spells horse, then jumps again for 10 jumps. You can also wrap language goals into this by asking "would you like to do it again?"[40]

While many sensory children benefit from rotary stimulation, such as a tire swing, this is generally discouraged for children who shift into SOR quickly or are pure overresponders unless under the guidance of a therapist. Registration of linear and rotary motion is through the inner ear, which is part of the vestibular system. Linear motion produces calmness, relaxation and lowered tone, and rotary motion produces excitation, arousal and increased tone.[41] Therefore, a child with SOR or a sensory craving child that shifts into SOR quickly would want to limit rotary activities.

Because sensory cravers cannot slow their bodies down, they cannot find the calm-alert state. Some children will move from passive underresponder right through the calm-alert state to overresponder.[42] Children may lose motor planning and language abilities, have meltdowns, and exhibit aggressive and defiant behavior when in the overresponsive window. In addition, any activity or task that requires a sensory craving child to remain motionless is excruciating, and usually elicits a melt-down. For example, sensory craving children may have problems riding in a car seat or sitting quietly at school, movies, church, libraries, or the dinner table.

Due to their hyperactivity and lack of impulse control, these children are often confused with children that have ADHD. Because parents and doctors often misdiagnose sensory craving as ADHD, these children are at a high risk of being unnecessarily medicated. Dr. Lucy Jane Miller's research suggested that ADHD and SPD are distinct diagnoses that could occur together or independently in children.[43] Additional information on her research may be found in *Sensational Kids: Hope and Help for Children with Sensory Processing Disorder.*

Because sensory cravers constantly move whenever they can, they develop great gross motor skills, but have little chance to develop fine motor abilities and discrimination, which would require sitting still. These children may crawl and walk early, but be delayed in developing the fine motor dexterity and precision to put small food objects in their mouths, use crayons, or cut with scissors. Frequently, they may fall out of chairs due to vestibular modulation difficulties.

Modulation difficulties may interfere with motor planning, speech, and social interactions. These difficulties may result in inconsistent performance as the child's regulation levels often fluctuate. One day, your child may be able to dress himself, participate in activities, and move through transitions smoothly. The next day, the reverse may be true. Below is a discussion of sensory craving behaviors by age.

Sensory Craving Behaviors by Age

Sensory craving infants love strong movement, sound, touch, or visual sensation. They are often restless and do not sleep or nap well. They may be irritable babies, crying much of the time, appearing colicky. If all other causes for the irritation are eliminated the likely culprit is misinterpretation of sensory signals. They may have trouble with self-soothing activities like getting fingers in their mouths, or curling up in the fetal position.[44] These babies often put their mouths on everything excessively, as sensory cravers learn through touch and movement.

When the sensory needs of preschool and early elementary children go unmet, they can become demanding and explosive in their attempts to fill their quota for sensation, and will have a difficult time controlling their aggressive or impulsive behaviors. They have a tendency to "stay in trouble," constantly engaging in situations considered reckless or dangerous. These children tend to violate personal bubble space as they come too close to people, constantly touch others, run over other kids, and seek physical contact and stimulation through deep pressure. During circle time or quiet playtime at school, they have trouble sitting still, and may wander or run aimlessly around the classroom until an adult intervenes. Alternatively, they may throw themselves against the floor seeking proprioceptive input.

Extreme seeking or craving of sensory input can also disrupt school-age children's ability to maintain attention for learning. These children may have trouble academically because of their powerful drive to obtain extra sensory stimulation instead of focusing on tasks. Often, these children manifest disorganization; their rooms are a war zone and their backpacks are a disaster. They have a chronic and consistent inability to keep track of their belongings both at home and school.[45] Sensory craving children often exhibit impulsivity. For example, these children may shout out answers in the classroom prior to raising their hand, and get out of their seats frequently.

Unfortunately, sensory craving behavior is misunderstood as aggression rather than excitability. Once a peer reacts aggressively toward the child, his own behavior may become aggressive in response. For example, a sensory craving child may jump on top of another child, pushing against the child and applying pressure as he jumps, satisfying his need for deep pressure into his muscles and joints. However, the other child will likely perceive this as an aggressive act and may become aggressive in return. Due to the reckless behavior of these children, expulsion out of multiple preschools, daycares, and playgroups may be common.

Without intervention, these children are at high risk for social, emotional, and societal consequences of being rejected and labeled not as different—but as dangerous or antisocial—and ultimately of being expelled from schools. Sensory craving children may learn to see themselves in exactly the negative and self-destructive terms that others apply to them, instead of just physiologically different.[46] This self-image may ultimately reinforce their way of coping, which is to play the role of the bad kid, fall in with the wrong crowd, and live the labels applied to them.

Sensory cravers may be hyperactive, aggressive and intense. They may be overly emotional and hard to calm. These children may, at times, be excessively affectionate and crave attention.[47] Specific behavioral descriptions are below.

Behavioral Indicators of the Sensory-Craving Child:

- Craves sensory input in one or more sensory systems; this may look like attention-seeking behavior but is actually a quest for sensation.
- Constantly moves and crashes, bumps, jumps, and roughhouses into objects, people, or other children. May jump on top of other children, parents, or pets and apply pressure in order to get deep pressure into her joints.
- Has difficulty sitting still at movies, school, church, and home and is hyperactive.
- Takes excessive risks during play (e.g., climbs high into trees, jumps off tall furniture, swings too high on a swing, runs across the street without looking, and creates situations that are dangerous). Others often perceive parents of high-risk kids as "helicopter" or overprotective parents hovering over their kids instead of letting them learn through experience. However, as

a parent, you must protect these high-risk children from themselves, as neurologic deficits drive their actions, not logic.

- Constantly touches objects or physically intrudes on people; leans against objects that vibrate, such as stereo speakers, the dryer, etc.
- Seems unable to stop talking, and has trouble taking turns in conversation.
- Plays music or television too loud.
- Often licks, sucks, and chews on nonfood items such as hair, pencils, or clothing.
- Gets angry or explosive when asked to sit still, or cease an activity.
- May not notice when they are dirty or hurt.
- Obsesses on visually stimulating scenarios such as fast-moving and brightly lit television shows, video games, marble runs, and moving water (e.g., toilets flushing, faucets, fountains).
- Seeks olfactory (smell) or gustatory (taste) experiences that are more intense and longer lasting than those sought by children with typical sensory desires. For example, the child may love to eat jalepenos, or may crave an intense smell.
- Engages in repetitive sensory activities like spinning, playing on a Sit 'n Spin, swinging, and jumping up and down on a bed, slamming doors, turning the lights on and off, or lining up toys, objects, and food.
- Often experiences elevated anxiety levels that put him in the overresponsive arousal state. The child may experience motor planning deficits in this state as anxiety interferes with the motor system and compromises performance. For example, the child may be unable to generate ideas for a project or have trouble with transitions.
- Communication difficulties are common when the child is suffering from significant anxiety. The child may be unable to speak or have partial language skills, giving rise to disorganized thoughts and speech. He may have trouble getting his

ideas out in coherent, organized language. Written narratives or stories may have a beginning and ending but the middle of the story may lack content, as the child's anxiety will interfere with the child's ability to sequence through the steps of a story.

- Often struggles with transitions. See "Chapter 9: Transitions" for more information.
- Has trouble keeping personal spaces organized, such as their room at home or desk at school.
- Has trouble falling asleep due to the never-ending quest for sensation. Her love of movement leaves her overaroused, which makes falling and staying asleep difficult. See "Chapter 6: Internal Regulation" for more information on sleep.

When children with modulation disorder are treated, they can grow up to lead healthy, happy, and successful lives. Parents are instrumental in the treatment process, and home strategies can help to develop, regulate, and instill a sense of security and well-being in the child. Below are strategies that parents can employ at home to assist the child with modulation disorder.

Parental Strategies for Sensory Overresponsivity

- Sensory Diet. Start with some linear swinging—such as a playground swing—adding in starts and stops for fifteen minutes twice a day, e.g. once in the morning and once later in the day. For example, have your child swing 10 times, stop at the bottom and throw a beanbag into a container. Follow this with deep-pressure activities to calm these children. Push-ups (floor or wall), animal walks, such as crab, bear, or duck walk; or wheelbarrow walking are great options. Swaddling for very young children is helpful in soothing them. See "Chapter 7: Sensory Diet" for more deep-pressure activity options.

- Environmental Modification. Modify the environment by implementing a clutter-free, quiet environment with low natural lighting.
- Parental Interaction Modification. Modify parental interactions by using a slow, soft, monotonous voice and calm speech. Avoid animation and exaggerated movements.
- Oral Motor Activities. Use oral motor activities that are calming, such as sucking a smoothie through a straw, chewing on gummy candy, taffy, or chewing gum, or sucking on hard candies. Sweet flavors are soothing, and will help to relax your child. You can find organic and natural candy at http://www.naturalcandystore.com. Search "Xylitol Gum" and options will come up for chewing gum sweetened with the natural sweetener xylitol. However, be aware that xylitol is toxic to dogs if ingested, so keep it out of reach of furry household members. Some children with chronic anxiety love to chew. Chewlery (chewable jewelry), chewable pencil toppers or other chewable objects are good options for this child. These items can be located in special needs stores, see Appendix B for a resource list.
- Sensory Retreat. Provide a sensory retreat for the child when she gets overwhelmed, e.g., a box with a top or a tent. Place some pillows, stuffed animals or a beanbag chair for the child to sink into—if space allows—in their sensory retreat to provide proprioceptive (muscles and joints) input. You can purchase a big floor pillow at http://ultimatesack.com/pillow_builder.asp or make your own by taking a duvet cover and filling it with pillows. There are multiple options for creating a sensory retreat. Occupational therapist Angie Voss has a website replete with ideas for sensory retreats. You can find it here http://asensorylife.com/sensory-retreats.html. Placing a weighted blanket over the child while in their safe haven is also helpful. Additionally, provide those things that are the most calming for

your child. For example, music (slow, rhythmic songs), art supplies, books, fidget toys, and oral motor items.

- Hand Activities. Koosh balls, Play-Doh, Silly Putty, clay, bendable figures, rubber cars, or Wikki Stix are examples of fidget toys that provide some deep touch pressure. You can place some of these toys in a box in the child's sensory retreat. Make sure your box is portable as fidget toys are perfect aids for waiting periods during transitions.

- Transition and Emotion Strategies. Lower anxiety by using the strategies in "Chapter 9: Transitions;" "Chapter 8: Aggression, Meltdowns, and Defiant Behavior;" and "Chapter 10: Emotions." Transition strategies will help to build structure and routine into the child's day, alleviating anxiety by reducing the unknown. Processing the child's emotions is also critical to relieving the child's anxiety, and "Chapter 10: Emotions" provides the associated strategies. Handling the child's outbursts, aggression, or defiant behavior in an empathic way is important in building the proper emotional connection with your child, thereby facilitating coregulation. Coregulation is a term denoting that a person, in the context of a relationship, can modify another person's actions. In other words, parents have the power to modify their child's behavior through the emotional relationship with the child.

Parental Strategies for Sensory Underresponsivity

- Sensory Diet. Start with swinging first for at least 15 minutes. Typically, underresponders can participate in linear or rotary swinging. Consult your child's OT if rotary swinging would be appropriate for your child. Subsequently, incorporate a sensory diet of bouncing on a therapy ball, or jumping on a safety-netted trampoline or pogo stick. Any of the other deep-pressure activities listed in "Chapter 7: Sensory Diet" would be great options as well. Because this child loves to spend time on the computer and playing video games, physically active games such as Wii and Xbox Kinect are great choices for these kids.

- Environmental Modification. Modify the child's environment by turning up the lights, using bright colors (wearing a bright color also helps), and playing up-tempo songs at a louder volume.
- Parental Interaction Modification. Modify parental interactions by using a louder voice with changing inflections. Maintain enthusiastic, animated communication with lots of gestures when speaking to the child.
- Oral Motor Foods/Flavors. Use arousing oral motor foods, such as chewing on crunchy foods such as pretzels, chips, or raw carrots. Use arousing flavors, such as sour, bitter, spicy, or hot.
- Transition and Emotion Strategies. Use the strategies in "Chapter 9: Transitions" and "Chapter 10: Emotions." Passive underresponders often need help navigating through transitions, and understanding the emotions of others.

Parental Strategies for Sensory Craving

- Sensory Diet. Incorporate a sensory diet of swinging and deep-pressure activities. Have your child linearly swing for 15 minutes in the morning and evening, followed by deep-pressure activities. Any of the deep-pressure activities listed in "Chapter 7: Sensory Diet" would be great options.
- Many of the strategies delineated above for the overresponder are also appropriate for the sensory craving child. For example, many sensory craving children chew on non-edible objects, and can benefit from chewlrey and chewable pencil toppers.
- Some sensory craving children are underresponsive first thing in the morning or sporadically throughout the day. For the child that has trouble getting up in the morning, use the morning

transition strategies for the underresponder in "Chapter 9: Transitions." The use of deep-pressure activities will help the sensory craving child transition into the calm-alert state regardless of whether they are underresponsive or overresponsive.

- The sensory craving child often demonstrates unacceptable behaviors. Below are common behavioral problems of the sensory craving child with suggested replacement strategies for caregivers to try. Please note that sensory children can demonstrate the same behavior for different underlying reasons when the child has more than one type of sensory processing disorder. For example, the child that leans on furniture may lean on it for the proprioceptive pressure it provides (a symptom of a modulation disorder), fatigue related to low muscle tone (a symptom of sensory-based motor disorder), or both. The strategies mentioned below are limited to the child with modulation disorder.

Replacement Behaviors

Behavior	Home Strategies
Jumping off dressers, chairs, or any high place	Provide safe alternatives to jump. You can make a huge launch pillow by taking a duvet cover and filling it with firm pillows, and placing it next to a surface higher than the pillows, or you can buy one from http://ultimatesack.com/pillow_builder.asp Another alternative is to play Simon says and have the child be a frog. "Let's see how far you can jump!"

Bumping or crashing into people or objects	Provide large inflatable toys (such as football players, dinosaurs, punching bags, etc., available at local or online retailers), cardboard blocks, a launch pillow, or old mattress for bumping or crashing.
Always leaning into furniture, walls, or people	Try using a weighted blanket. You can play games such as hamburger, explained in "Chapter 7: Sensory Diet." Any of the deep-pressure activities listed in the sensory diet chapter would also help to alleviate this behavior.
Throwing things in the house	Have the child throw weighted beanbags into a box or bucket. Alternatively, you can also play beanbag toss using conventional game boards utilizing weighted beanbags.
Always running instead of walking	Invent a skipping game, as this will slow the child down. If the child cannot skip, engage him in marching. Suggest a parade and march toward your destination.

Trying to roll on and squish his siblings or pets. Alternatively, he may slide underneath sofa cushions or mattresses.	Incorporate some "pillow squishies" into the child's sensory diet. Take a pillow and squish the child on the back and legs. You can also use a giant rolling pin, therapy ball, or foam roller on the back and legs to implement the deep pressure the child is craving.
Kicking her heels against the chair, or unable to sit still at the kitchen table. Constantly getting up and running around.	If she is kicking her heels against the chair while eating, a great option for a child of any age is to put a Thera-Band on the bottom of the chair, which she can push her feet into when eating. If the child has enough balance and core strength, you can have the child sit on an exercise ball to eat. Movin'Sit blue seat wedges, or lower back massage mats may help the child to stay seated as well. Activities such as jumping on a trampoline with a safety net, walking along a beam (tape on the floor), or doing figure eights with eyes closed provide these children with the intense vestibular input they require.

Constantly chewing on nonedible objects such as shirt collars, hood strings, pencils, toys, or their own hair (the mouth provides more intense information than hands).	Provide safe alternatives such as chewelry, available from special needs stores. Also helpful for these children are chewable pencil toppers. Chewing gum, gummy candy, taffy, hard candies, dried fruit, or chewy bread also reduces chewing on undesired objects. You can find these items at http://www.naturalcandystore.com. When selecting chewing gum, select naturally sweetened gum. Also, keep a sippy spouted sports water bottle handy to suck on as needed, and always use straws in older children's drinks; smoothies are great for sensory kids! Nuk brushes are also great for oral stimulation. Be aware that some children will chew due to zinc or essential fatty acid deficiencies. Have your child's vitamin levels, essential fatty acids, and complete blood work tested to check for deficiencies. Anemic children who have iron and zinc deficiencies, and chew or eat nonedible materials such as dirt, sand, clay, paper, etc., for over one month are considered to have a condition called pica.

	Your child's pediatrician will recommend treatment for this condition should the need arise.
Engaging in head banging	Children may head bang due to a number of medical conditions: ear infections, teething problems, headaches due to sinus pressure from food allergies/sensitivities, environmental allergies, vision problems, abnormal brain fluid buildup, or seizures. Take your child to a doctor who can perform blood work to test for food allergies/sensitivities that can result in increased mucus, inflammation of sinus cavities, or internal biochemical changes resulting in headaches. Have your child tested for environmental allergens that may be resulting in sinus pressure as well. Comprehensive vision exams with a developmental optometrist will rule out vision problems. A condition called hydrocephalus, which is an abnormal buildup of cerebrospinal fluid (CSF) in the ventricles of the brain, can cause a child to head bang.

In rare instances, head banging can be the only sign of seizure. Talk to your pediatrician about these potential causes.

Some children will head bang for self-stimulation or self-soothing. You can try the following tips for these children:

Regularly massage her head and face with hands or vibrator.

If banging is intense, your pediatrician or OT may suggest using a helmet or weighted hat.

Pull the crib or bed away from the wall and place it on a thick rug.

In concert with your OT's recommendations, provide a daily sensory diet.

Let the child push items with her forehead. For example, encourage your child to push her head into a pillow or beanbag chair.

Try pressing your chin into her forehead, moving your jaw back and forth while you hum.

Speak to your occupational therapist and pediatrician for any additional recommendations concerning head banging.

Assuming upside-down positions, bouncing on furniture, spinning in a swivel chair and pivoting around his head on the floor.	These are all signs of the need for intense vestibular input. Jumping on a trampoline with a safety net or holding hands with them while on an indoor mini-trampoline, walking along a balance beam (made with tape or chalk on the floor), or doing figure eights with eyes closed will provide intense vestibular input (closing the eyes isolates the vestibular system, thereby providing more intensity). Eyes-closed activities are the best source of intense vestibular input, but you can also give your child opportunities to wheel-barrow walk, hang upside down from monkey bars, or do hand-stands. Open eye activities are not as effective as eye-closed activities, but will definitely provide some of the needed input.
Sensory craving children love to get messy. If you do not give them an acceptable way to do it, they will indulge in unacceptable activities.	The child needs lots of messy play, such as finger painting, or playing in goop and shaving cream. Pinterest is a good resource for sensory play. Just type in "messy play" and many options will come up.

Touching and feeling everything in sight. For example, bumping and touching others when unwelcome, or running his hands over furniture and walls). The child may touch things that other children understand are not to be touched. He may walk on certain surfaces and textures that other people would find uncomfortable.	Let him play with different mediums such as finger paint, sand, water, Play-Doh, or clay. The more varied the textures you can present to the child, the better. Collect different textures such as smooth, slimy, dull, pointy, wet, hard, bumpy, rough, soft, etc. Have the child play with or touch all the different textures, and discuss the differences between them. For example, you can use a Q-tip, fork, ice cube, feather, or loofah. You can also play a second round with the child blindfolded. Can he guess what touched him? Sculpt with a sheet of aluminum foil. Try making cups, balls, boxes, waves, etc. Afterward, paint the crinkled surface of the foil, and place on a piece of paper, and make a print of your "texture."
Rubbing, sucking, or biting own skin excessively.	Incorporate deep-pressure activities (see list in "Chapter 7: Sensory Diet") along with the use of a weighted blanket.
Turning lights on and off in the house.	Get the child a disco ball, strobe light, and other toys that light up with a switch that he can turn on/off. Put this toy in an acceptable place in your home so that the child may use it when he desires.

Dumping bins of toys into the floor or pulling DVDs and books from shelves.	Many occupational therapists think visual craving is behind dumping bins of toys or pulling things from shelves. Therefore, some OT's recommend giving the child visual toys such as small waterfalls, marble runs, or disco balls that can fulfill this visual need.
Excessively splashing, jumping, and making waves in the tub.	Lay a warm, wet towel over her shoulders and back. Keep it warm by pouring more warm water on it during the bath. The deep pressure of the weighted towel and the warmth are calming.
Engaging in hand flapping	Hand flapping may occur until the child gains shoulder stabilization, at which point he may start opening and closing his fingers rapidly (called distal cupping).
Engaging in distal cupping	Children who have shoulder stability may not ever engage in hand flapping, but may demonstrate distal cupping. When the child is old enough, video tape the distal cupping, and explain when he is most likely to demonstrate this behavior. Likely times will be when the child is watching a moving object, or visualizing a moving object in his mind.

	Have your child place Koosh balls or other preferred objects in his pockets. When your child starts to engage in distal cupping, have him put his hands in his pockets squeezing the objects.
Opening and shutting doors repetitively	When your child demonstrates this behavior, get on the other side of the door and make a game of it to help give the activity some meaning. For example, pretend you are a mail carrier, knock on the door, have your child open it, and deliver a package. You can also exert pressure on the door, and ask the child to try to move the door. This deep pressure will help to alter her arousal level into the calm-alert state.

Summary

Current understanding of sensory modulation disorder reveals that many challenging behaviors are a result of neurological sensory deficits. Parents should use this knowledge to guide and discipline their sensory children. Love, compassion, and empathy are golden keys to a successful relationship with any child, and these keys will go a long way toward promoting self-regulation.

Sensory-Based Motor Disorder - Dyspraxia Part One

Sensory-based motor disorder is the second type of Sensory Processing Disorder. Children with sensory-based motor problems have trouble balancing, moving and performing unfamiliar tasks or activities, or a combination of these.

There are two types of sensory-based motor disorder: dyspraxia and postural disorder. Dyspraxia is a motor planning disorder, while postural disorder affects the child's muscle tone, posture, and stability. Some children with dyspraxia have postural disorder as well and both disorders can result in motor coordination problems. This chapter will help parents understand motor planning deficiencies and motor coordination problems through an overview of developmental dyspraxia.

Developmental Dyspraxia

Billy is an active 2½-year-old toddler who demonstrates excellent motor planning skills. He began by propelling a big dump truck around the edge of the play space, making truck sounds and loading his truck with smaller trucks, balls, and animals. Once the truck was full, he roared to the city dump (his mother's lap) and unloaded his treasures. After a few minutes of this activity, he proceeded to build a road out of large blocks, and raced his vehicles with glee in his make-believe speedway. Billy then pretended that each vehicle carried a circus animal as he had seen on television. Eventually, Billy pushed the cars and trucks down the pretend sidewalk at crashing speeds.

James, also a 2½-year-old, has dyspraxia. He found little to do with his vehicles. James watched Billy's elaborate play, but did not join him. Instead, he pushed his trucks back and forth in a straight path, spun the wheels with his finger, and lined them up in an orderly row. He did try to "drive" his truck on Billy's road, but he had difficulty keeping his truck on the road, and kept tripping on and misplacing the blocks.

The above comparison of two boys is an adapted illustration of two toddlers at play, one typical and one with motor planning deficits, from *Sensory Integration and Self-Regulation in Infants and Toddlers* by G. Gordon Williamson and Marie E. Anzalone.

Professionals consider developmental dyspraxia when no neurological disease or acquired brain injury is present. The term dyspraxia comes from the Greek word *praxis*, which means "doing or acting," and the Greek prefix *dys* which means "bad," so literally, dyspraxia translates to "bad doing" or "bad acting." Motor planning deficits best characterize the disorder of dyspraxia. Motor planning is the ability to conceptualize, organize, and execute a plan to perform an unfamiliar motor task and to adapt in the moment of action around task demands.[1] Dyspraxia affects what a person plans to do and how to do it, so children with dyspraxia have trouble getting their bodies to do what they want, when they want.

Praxis is a brain-directed process that links cognition (thinking) and motor function essentially connecting your brain to your muscles. Praxis is reliant upon unconscious processes involving sensory discrimination and body awareness.[2] Sensory discrimination is the ability to make sense of sensations that are detected. Good sensory discrimination from the tactile (touch), vestibular (movement) and proprioceptive (position) senses is imperative for sufficient body awareness. Body awareness is an internal sensory map of interlocking body parts, how they work in concert and move through space.[3] Praxis is a vital component of our ability to interact with our environment. "Praxis is to the motor world what language is to the social; it enables interaction."[4]

In the American Psychiatric Association's *Diagnostic and Statistical Manual of Mental Disorders* (DSM-5), dyspraxia falls under "Developmental Coordination Disorder." This category is an umbrella term for all children with motor execution challenges. Some children in the developmental coordination disorder category do not have motor planning problems, but pure motor execution deficits. This chapter focuses on sensory integrative-based dyspraxia, a term referring to motor planning disorders that have their basis in poor sensory processing. Professionals base a diagnosis of sensory-integrative based dyspraxia on deficits in one or more of the tactile, proprioceptive, or vestibular domains. Visual-motor discrepancies are also common in developmental dyspraxia.[5]

The primary symptom of sensory-integrative based dyspraxia is motor planning deficits; motor coordination problems may or may not be present and are a byproduct of poor motor planning. The complex nature of motor planning relies on the efficient integration of sensory information and is different from motor coordination, or the ability to control body movements smoothly. Therefore, treatment for motor planning challenges revolves around occupational therapy with an emphasis on ideation and sequencing, whereas treatment for pure motor execution problems centers on neuro-developmental therapy (NDT).[6]

When children with motor planning deficiencies do not exhibit motor coordination problems, their motor planning deficiencies usually go undetected, as parents write off their poor performance in sports and games as individual differences. In addition, children with normal motor coordination in the presence of motor planning difficulties can show surprising skill in performing motor activities that are familiar and well rehearsed. The children who do have motor coordination problems in tandem with motor planning deficits demonstrate more tangible and concrete representations of their disorder. Pediatricians of concerned parents often advise that children with coordination difficulties will out-grow them, but several studies have shown this not to be the case.[7]

The specific symptoms and severity of the disorder vary widely among affected children. Severely affected children have difficulty with all forms of motor planning and execution (some are unable to speak their entire lives), while other children may have subtle difficulties, or can perform some motor tasks well and others poorly. Thus, it is helpful to think of developmental dyspraxia as a spectrum disorder; a child may fall on the continuum between mild and severe.

While praxis has a learned component, innate biological factors predetermine motor development, which occur across all social, cul-tural, ethnic, and racial boundaries.[8] Therefore, dyspraxia can be an inheritable trait and tends to run in families. The risk factors associ-ated with dyspraxia include premature birth, difficult delivery, prena-tal issues, and a family history of dyspraxia or other developmental conditions.[9]

The highest comorbidity rates exist with dyslexia at 30 to 50 percent and ADHD at 40 to 50 percent.[10] One interesting phenomenon is that these three conditions share a common feature—fatty acid deficiency—which is currently under study by researchers.[11]

Scientists do not know what causes dyspraxia. Some scientists believe that in the majority of cases, dyspraxia may be the result of immature neuron development in the brain. Current theory asserts that the sensations that enter the brain do not have enough intercon-nected neural pathways on which to travel. In other words, sensations start traveling on the railroad tracks but run out of tracks. In a smaller number of cases, the neural pathways are intact, but the sensory infor-mation transmits improperly. In other words, there are railroad tracks upon which the sensory information can travel, but some of the in-formation falls off the tracks. Regardless of cause, the brain's neural deficits result in processing problems in one or more sensory systems, which result in motor planning and/or motor execution challenges discussed below.

Motor Planning

Motor planning requires good body awareness, which is an internal model of the body. In order to have good body awareness, a person must have sufficient sensory information from the tactile, proprioceptive, and vestibular senses and be able to store and draw upon neuronal models. Neuronal models are images stored in the brain based upon movement, objects, or interactions we have had with various objects in our environment. The brain refers to these models—or memories—to help motor plan new, unfamiliar movements or generate new ideas. For instance, it is being able to take the idea of cleaning your room to organize your desk in school.

When a child is learning a new motor plan, such as tying his shoes, he must first have an idea about what he wants to do (ideation), then pay attention to his fingers and sequence the steps to tie his shoes (sequencing), and finally complete the task (execution). Once mastered, a task no longer requires the child's concentration, and he does it automatically. Typical children unconsciously internalize each motor plan in a sequenced manner, and they motor plan without thinking about it. In the absence of typical sensory processing, the child would need to monitor and plan his actions visually or cognitively, an exhausting process for any child.[12]

Motor planning impairments often lead to splinter skills in sensory children. The term "splinter skills" refers to the ability to perform a specific task that does not generalize to other tasks.[13] For example, a child that ties a bow on a birthday present may be unable to tie her shoes. The child memorizes each step in order to tie a bow on a birthday present drawing upon her intellect in order to perform the task. When parents see the child demonstrating a splinter skill, they tend to demand that level of proficiency in other activities. Parents and professionals sometimes gear demands to the child's intellectual abilities rather than to her motor planning abilities because they do not understand that children cannot generalize splinter skills. For example, a child may be great at catching a ball thrown to the same spot each time but unable to play baseball, where the ball's trajectory is constantly changing. It can be difficult to understand that while the child is cognitively capable, she is not able to motor plan the task in all environments.

For a child with motor planning deficits in the absence of motor coordination problems, motor planning difficulties may only challenge the child in a multisensory environment. These children may be able to sequence in an environment that requires the simultaneous use of only two senses. For example, if you read one of these children a story and ask her what happened first, second, and third, she may be able to recount the story in the correct order. In this instance, she is only utilizing auditory and visual senses. However, if you place this same child in a multisensory environment where she must utilize all, or most of her senses simultaneously, this requires integration. For example, a child engaged in a bakeshop pretend play scenario. Imagine she is the bakeshop owner and you are the customer, and you enter the shop and ask for three or four different baked goods in a particular order (auditory). To fulfill your request, she must move around while communicating to deliver them to you (vestibular). She must gauge the amount of force to use when picking up the items and know where her body is relative to the baked goods and the customer (proprioceptive). Understanding her relationship to gravity and which direction she is facing is also necessary (vestibular). She obtains tactile information as she picks up the baked goods and manipulates them in her hand. Throughout the scenario, she is using her visual sense to aid her in each step of the task. She may be unable to sequence the steps in the correct order in this dynamic environment, which requires the use of her visual, auditory, tactile, vestibular and proprioceptive systems simultaneously.

Adequate motor planning is critical for acquiring new motor skills and higher-level cognitive skills, such as sequencing multiple-step tasks or daily activities, organizing an approach to play themes, socially interacting without becoming fragmented and adapting movements according to the specific situation. The process involves conceptualizing the idea (or the performance), organizing the movements (sequencing), executing the plan (execution), analyzing the results of the actions, and making any necessary adjustments (adaptation/problem-solving). One of the primary goals of an occupational therapist is evaluating a child to determine where the motor planning breakdown occurs. The child experiences a breakdown in one or more of the following steps of motor planning:

1. Ideation.
2. Sequencing (organizing the plan).
3. Execution (performing the action).
4. Adaptation (problem-solving).

Ideation is the first step of motor planning, followed by sequencing, execution, and adaptation. The sections below provide information on each of these steps.

1. Ideation
   Before motor planning can actually take place, a child must be able to register sensory stimuli. Sensory registration is a subconscious process within the brain. It allows a child to recognize changes in the environment, and react to the stimuli.[14] Some children with SPD fail to react or register things or changes in their environment. For example, if you put a toy in front of the child, does she notice it? Does he notice the pain of a shot at the doctor?

   Next is developing an idea of the multiple ways that toys, objects, or one's body can play. Ideation is the process of conceptualizing a new plan/action, or detecting an object in the environment, and knowing the object's purpose and what to do with it"[15] For example, a typical child will appreciate that there are a number of ways to play with a toy truck.

Children with ideation problems will have trouble generating ideas for action or problem solving. Academically, this will affect them in their ability to write stories, solve word math problems, and imitate the actions of their teachers in art, music, drama, and physical education. Children with dyspraxia have trouble imitating others, as the child must have an idea of the expectation, and the ability to sequence through the idea. These children often cannot remember games and have restricted pretend play. They tend to be very concrete in their play; they do not like to take on pretend roles because they cannot imagine what being someone else would look or feel like.[16] As a result, they may observe peers creative play without participating, or parallel play when it is no longer age appropriate. Ideation prevents these children from the discovery of a toy's purpose for play. For instance, when these children play with a new toy car, they may simply spin the wheels. This inflexibility and lack of creativity prevents them from keeping up with the ever-changing play of peers. Children with dyspraxia tend to use play equipment in simple, repetitive ways because they cannot conceptualize and plan new and complex actions.[17]

A child who lacks ideation may become stubborn and controlling in play. They may insist upon doing things their way to keep the activity within their competency level. The sensory child may become so frustrated with any game or activity that challenges their motor planning ability that they avoid these tasks, have a global meltdown, or become aggressive. His inability to engage in meaningful play with peers may lead to social isolation. Social isolation can contribute to low self-esteem, low self-confidence, and depression.

2. Sequencing

The next step in motor planning is determining how to accomplish a goal that involves sequential actions. This depends upon good body awareness, derived from sensory feedback obtained from previous movement. Body awareness is an internal sensory map of interlocking body parts, how they work in concert, and move through space.[18] Tactile and proprioceptive input constantly generates through our actions while moving, with assistance from the vestibular and visual senses. That input becomes the foundation for our future actions as we learn neurologically from repeated past actions.

Sequencing manifests itself in the majority of our everyday activities. Almost everything we do requires us to sequence through steps, and typical children do so automatically. However, sequencing is not automatic for children with motor planning deficits. For example, these children may not be able to sequence through the steps required to climb stairs, ride a bike, or play with a toy. Children with dyspraxia tend to have difficulties problem solving because it requires the ability to string several ideas together in sequence. In addition, the child will have trouble imitating others due to their inability to generate an idea of what is expected, and sequence through the actions required. Timing, rhythmicity, and sequencing ability allows typical children to make the automatic, reflexive adjustments required to play any type of sports or clap to a beat (this is called feedforward). Children with dyspraxia often struggle with this skill and may avoid sports.

The child with dyspraxia often does not have the ideation or sequencing skills necessary to engage or participate in creative and flexible pretend play. Therefore, these children tend to stay on the periphery of peers' play engrossed in familiar and comfortable activities.

3. Execution
The third step in motor planning is motor coordination, or the ability to execute body movements smoothly. Successful execution depends upon adequate ideation, sequencing, and timing, as well as successful coordination and motor skill. The child with

dyspraxia may have difficulty with fine motor, gross motor, functional vision, or oral-motor coordination.

Dyspraxia presents its most tangible and concrete effects during execution. Children with dyspraxia may have visible motor coordination and motor planning problems participating in activities such as riding a bike, skipping, puzzles, Legos, pretend playing, or sports, and may look markedly different from peers. These children's differences can have a profound impact socially and emotionally. Because these children perform poorly at so many activities that come naturally to typical children, teasing by peers may be common, leading to social isolation. Hyperactivity and emotional outbursts may be problematic at home and school, and contribute to social sidelining by peers.[19] Social sidelining often affects self-esteem and self-confidence, and may lead to depression.

Children with dyspraxia have trouble executing tasks because they experience a breakdown during ideation, sequencing, or both. The sensory feedback a child receives determines how well the child can internalize a motor plan, and perform the task in the future automatically. To compensate, children with dyspraxia may need to visually or cognitively monitor and plan their movements.

In short, poor execution has a tremendous impact on these children and their families. Intervention is critical to enhance the quality of life for both the child and the family. Improving quality of life, social participation, and self-esteem are among the primary goals of therapy for the child with dyspraxia.

4. Adaptation

Lastly, adaptation is often challenging for children with dyspraxia. When a child has an organized plan in his mind, tries to execute the plan, and encounters a problem, the child must be able to adapt his plan, i.e. problem-solve. Problem solving involves the ability to use feedback to change or alter behavior.[20]

For example, if a child is playing with blocks, decides to build a house with those blocks, and then discovers he does not have enough blocks to execute that plan, he must be able to use this feedback to alter his plan. For instance, instead of building a house, he could build a small speedway instead. This requires cognitive flexibility, ideation, problem solving, and good visual-spatial abilities. Children with visual-spatial challenges have trouble seeing the possibilities because they cannot picture them in their minds.

Dyspraxia Indicators

While dyspraxia has many characteristics (covered below), these are the universal primary indicators of dyspraxia:

- Control issues
- Rigid adherence to routine
- Lack of complexity in play, with little to no pretend play
- Social deficits
- Fine and gross motor deficits
- Oral motor problems (speech and nonspeech)
- Lack of ideation (no idea of what to do)
- Trouble organizing a plan for action (sequencing)

Dyspraxia Symptoms

A wide range of symptoms is associated with dyspraxia because this disorder can vary greatly by child. Some children may experience few symptoms and other children more. Keep in mind that while these symptoms are often present in children with dyspraxia, the presence of a symptom does not mean the child has dyspraxia. A combination of symptoms, professional evaluations, and behavioral observation is required for a diagnosis. Below are possible symptoms that may present in infants, toddlers/preschoolers, and school-age children.

Infants

- Typically achieve developmental milestones toward the end of the average range but may bottom shuffle, skip crawling or rolling over altogether, or scoot (crawl with one leg dragging behind).
- Exhibit signs of postural problems, such as sitting in the W-sit position (when an infant or child sits with both legs bent behind her, her trunk and legs resemble a W).
- Have significant feeding issues, such as problems latching onto a nipple or bottle or trouble swallowing; may be colicky and require a restricted diet.
- Have sleep cycle issues and trouble establishing a routine, requiring constant adult assistance.
- Be very irritable, difficult to comfort, and constantly require adult assurance.
- Have high levels of motor activity, constantly moving their arms and legs.
- Exhibit repetitive behaviors such as head banging or rolling.

Toddlers, Preschoolers and School Age
Motor Coordination Symptoms

- Have difficulty with gross motor skills such as running, jumping, skipping, pedaling a tricycle, playing with a ball appropriately, or playing group sports.
- Are slow to establish left- or right-handedness, have trouble with bilateral coordination (using both sides of the body together), have a tendency to not cross the midline of the body, and have a poor grasp of positional concepts such as up/down, front/back, or over/under. Read more on these challenges in part two of this chapter under "Physical Outcomes" subheading "Body Awareness."

- Experience delays in toilet training. Some children with dyspraxia (especially those with somatodyspraxia) may not be fully toilet trained until age five.
- Have hypotonia (low muscle tone) and associated postural deficits. See "Chapter 4: Sensory-Based Motor Disorder - Postural Disorder" for more information.
- Have trouble with activities that require fine motor skills such as, holding a pencil, drawing, and cutting with scissors, using utensils, buttoning, zipping, or tying. Drawing and copying skills may be immature for their age. Handwriting may present significant trouble, which may be slow, laborious, and immature.
- Have poor coordination, which manifests in sports, games, and physical education classes.
- Seems confused, bumps into things, or has trouble finding their way around due to poor body awareness. These children may be unable to judge their relationships to people, objects, and space.

Ideation

- Have trouble developing ideas for play or producing creative products, such as drawings or paintings.
- Due to the lack of ideation, resort to rigid and inflexible behavior, perseverate (stuck on an idea) and prefer the familiar to the novel. For instance, the child may always insist on playing with one particular toy or game, and refuse to engage in a playmate's ideas for play.

Sequencing

- Need visual cues to help them put on clothes in the correct order, and may have persistent challenges getting dressed. Clothes may be in disarray and/or unfastened.
- Have trouble problem solving new tasks.

- Feel challenged by transitions such as leaving the house, adjusting to a new schedule, going to a new school, etc. The child may be slow moving through transitions.
- Have problems with projected action sequences such as kicking a moving ball, catching a ball while both the child and the ball are moving, or any other motor action that requires timing, rhythm or rapid adjustments in the moment of action.
- Unable to organize verbal speech or written thoughts. For instance, the child may stumble getting a sentence out, and have to start two or three times. A written story may have a good beginning and ending, but lack content in between.
- Difficulty keeping personal spaces organized (e.g., rooms are a disaster).
- Slow to perform activities due to an inability to sequence the steps involved.
- Cannot remember more than one auditory instruction at a time, and need several repetitions of verbal instructions, verbal instructions broken down into steps, or visual cues to overcome sequencing problems.

Oral/Verbal

- Have delayed language development, or trouble with pronouncing words and syllables.
- Have trouble eating and chewing. May be messy eaters, prefer to eat with fingers, and frequently spill.

Vision

- Have trouble moving from place to place; may bump into other children or objects, trip or fall down.
- Avoid toys such as Legos, building blocks, puzzles, or shape-sorting games that require visual-spatial awareness.

- Have difficulties copying text displayed in the classroom.
- Demonstrate hand flapping or distal cupping when visually excited.

Social/Emotional

- Have high levels of excitability and a loud/shrill voice.
- Experiences elevated anxiety, compulsive tendencies (with an extreme need for routine and repetition), irrational fears, including night awakenings and night terrors.
- Have low self-esteem, low frustration tolerance, and lack of self-confidence.
- Difficulty interpreting ambiguous social nuances and nonverbal cues; non-verbal communication is accomplished through body language, posture and facial expressions. For instance, if a typical child grabs an unused toy that is sitting in between him and another special needs child, the special needs child may interpret this as a hostile move. This ability to interpret non-verbal communication emerges toward the latter stage of preschool for typical children.
- Have trouble following back-and-forth social interactions with peers.
- Have limited complexity of play. Play may be lacking in creativity with minimal or no pretend play. This makes them incapable of keeping up with the creative and flexible play of peers.
- Tend to think in black and white with few shades of gray.
- Follow rules and get visibly upset when peers break rules.
- Prefer adult company and appear isolated from peers.
- Tend to become easily distressed and emotional, resulting in tantrums, emotional outbursts, or aggressive behavior.
- Avoid social interactions and exhibit an inability to form relationships with other children, and are socially awkward.

Other

- Experience very high levels of motor activity, including feet swinging and tapping when seated, hand clapping, or twisting. The child may be unable to sit still for more than five minutes at a time.
- Use "crash" solutions to terminate demanding activities (e.g., knocking down or throwing).
- Avoid new situations, group activities, and peer play.
- Have short-term memory problems.
- Have slow processing speed (e.g., may have to read material multiple times in order to comprehend the material, or perform slowly in tasks such as dressing).
- Have limited concentration and a very short attention span of only one to three minutes; easily distracted. Often leave tasks unfinished.
- Due to developmental delays, appear immature compared to peers.
- Demonstrate controlling and manipulative behaviors.
- Try to mask dyspraxia by taking the role of "class clown."
- The child may struggle with math, spelling, reading and writing due to visual-spatial, sequencing, or fine motor deficits. Dyslexia and dyscalculia are common co-morbid conditions with dyspraxia. Dyscalculia is a learning disability in math, and dyslexia is a developmental disability that affects the way the brain processes written material.
- Cannot "think and do" at the same time appearing to have an auditory problem. Some of these children have to concentrate so hard on a task that they cannot process auditory information simultaneously. For example, if a child is busy playing and you ask him a question, you may not receive an answer even if you ask multiple times.
- Have a sloppy appearance.

Children with dyspraxia are often misunderstood and receive many negative labels, as parents and teachers do not recognize behaviors listed above as sensory-based instead of behavioral based.

Original Dyspraxia Classification

Jean Ayres identified four types of practic dysfunction.[21]

- Praxis on verbal command, which is believed to be a dysfunction of the left hemisphere, unrelated to SPD, and therefore not within the scope of this book.
- Somatodyspraxia, the first recognized primary type.
- Visuodyspraxia experts now believe may be the end-result of somatodyspraxia and is included in the discussion below.
- Bilateral integrative and sequencing (BIS), the second recognized primary type.

Dr. Jean Ayres pioneered the identification of dyspraxia types many years ago. At this time, most experts refine the sensory-based list to include two types: somatodyspraxia and BIS. Bundy, Lane, Murray theorize that these two types reflect a spectrum of practic deficits, somatodyspraxia being the more severe type, and BIS a milder version.[22] While further research is necessary to be confident in these types, the work done by Ayres helps therapists to target intervention effectively. To grasp fully the types of dyspraxia, we need a working understanding of body awareness, feedback, and feedforward.

Body Awareness

Body awareness is an unconscious process that enables a child to know where his body parts are and how they fit together, an internal map that grounds the body. Without this knowledge, the child does not know where his body is in space without visually monitoring his limbs. For instance, he may be unable to run without looking at his feet. These children may be clumsy, bump into things, and trip and fall. Without adequate sensory information from the child's extremities, the child may slide off a classroom chair, be unable to judge the amount of resistance needed to pick up an object, or coordinate the two sides of their body.

The foundational sensory systems for body awareness are the tactile, proprioceptive, and vestibular systems. The visual system confirms the spatial information, and the auditory system gives us temporal (timing) information such as when clapping to a beat.[23] The inextricable relationship between the three foundational systems often cannot be separated.

For example, when a child runs across a field and reaches down to obtain a ball the child receives proprioceptive information from his body moving through space, and his arm reaching for the ball. He receives tactile information, as he touches and manipulates the ball, learning about its texture, surface, and shape. He also receives proprioceptive information as his fingers close around the ball, and he measures its weight in order to judge the amount of resistance needed to pick the ball up. He also receives vestibular information such as which direction he is facing, how fast he is moving, and information about whether he is right side up (gravity). All of this sensory information contributes to the formation of body awareness. Body awareness is responsible for the following:

- Forming the basis for good motor planning
- Navigating and planning body movements with ease, coordination, precision, and well-regulated, smooth, and accurate movements
- Grading the pressure, force, and speed of arm and leg movements
- Developing gross motor movements in a coordinated, accurate fashion
- Providing information about where the body is in space and how it is moving
- Judging relative distance from other people or objects
- Developing visual perception
- Facilitating postural development

- Developing oral motor control necessary for speech and eating
- Developing fine motor skills

Feedback and Feedforward

Feedback is required for skill acquisition, and this information derives from the body's response to a motor movement or a stimulus. For example, when a child who is standing still throws a ball toward a stationary target, she gets immediate tactile, proprioceptive, and visual feedback, giving her information on how hard and far she threw it, and enabling her to make future adjustments based on this feedback. A typically developing child will learn from everyday sensory experiences as she receives appropriate feedback from her senses. Children with praxis problems, on the other hand, do not receive the necessary feedback from their senses that would help them form the appropriate adaptive response to guide their movements and behaviors. The feedback they receive may be more confusing than helpful, and it can be very uncomfortable.

Feedforward actions are always anticipatory in nature. Feedforward is not dependent upon sensory feedback. Feedforward requires the child to plan a sequence of actions in the future, and is referred to as projected action sequences.[24] For instance, a running child must anticipate where to place his foot to intercept a moving ball in soccer. This movement requires the child to predict the exact point at which his foot will intercept the moving ball, and move his foot to that point before the ball arrives. Feedforward actions require a child to perceive, conceptualize, and integrate multiple dimensions of both time and space.[25]

For instance, when a child playing soccer is advancing toward the goal and preparing to accept the ball from another player, she must have a good spatial understanding of where she is relative to the goal and to the other players on the field. She must be able to place her foot, and intercept the ball at exactly the precise point and time, judge the proper amount of distance to the goal, and time it perfectly to score. In this situation, timing and visual-spatial abilities are key elements to success.

Other examples of projected action sequences are jumping into a series of defined spaces (as in hopscotch), or clapping to a beat.

Problems with feedforward may be present in cognitive activities such as strategy games. For example, a child has to be able to think ahead, anticipate his opponent's move, and imagine his next move in the game of chess.

Types of Dyspraxia

Below is a detailed discussion of the two types of dyspraxia. The key distinction between the types is the presence of tactile discrimination disorder in children with somatodyspraxia. While children with bilateral integrative and sequencing (BIS) are spared this disorder, it significantly restricts the ability of the child with somatodyspraxia to obtain reliable feedback from the tactile receptors in their bodies. The two types have other differences, but this is the most critical one.

A. Bilateral Integrative and Sequencing Dyspraxia
    Bilateral integrative and sequencing dyspraxia involves two primary symptoms: problems with bilateral coordination and difficulty with feedforward-dependent actions.

    Bilateral coordination is the use of two sides of the body like riding a bike, or using two hands together such as using one hand to stabilize a jar while using the other to open it. Other types of bilateral coordination difficulties include avoidance of crossing the midline (e.g., reaching across the body to pick up something on the other side), failure to develop a hand preference, and lack of right-left awareness. Read more on these challenges in part two of this chapter under "Physical/Sensory Outcomes," subheading "Body Awareness." Feedforward problems make it difficult for the child to anticipate the movement of an object in space when the child is also moving, or to anticipate future movements cognitively, as in the game of chess. Examples of feedforward movements include catching a softball or playing hopscotch, where the child has to anticipate where the ball is going to be or where to place her feet, or to anticipate future movements cognitively, as in the game of chess.

Some children with the BIS type will display the SPD sensory craving subtype of modulation disorder. Children with this combination may be unable to modulate touch sensations. These children may seek out all sorts of tactile experiences and want to touch everything they see, but the child will not exhibit tactile discrimination disorder. Read more about the difference between tactile discrimination disorder and modulation disorder under somatodyspraxia below. Children with BIS learn new motor planning tasks more easily as opposed to the child with somatodyspraxia due to better tactile and proprioceptive feedback. Often, children with BIS have low muscle tone and balance issues.

B. Somatodyspraxia

Unlike the child with bilateral integrative and sequencing deficit dyspraxia, children with somatodyspraxia will have tactile discrimination disorder. This is the primary difference between the two types. A child with discrimination disorder is underresponsive to the sensory system as opposed to arousal, in modulation disorder. In other words, children with modulation disorder can detect and make sense of the stimuli; they just need more or less of it to get in the calm-alert zone. Children who are underresponsive to the sensory system cannot make sense of the stimuli (i.e., they can't make sense of what is touching their body, such as fabrics, tags, or seams, and it feels "itchy"). The tactile receptors are located within the skin and inside the mouth. Since the tactile system is so pervasive, the resulting impact manifests in oral motor, fine motor, gross motor, motor planning, and body awareness challenges. Many of these children also have postural problems and low muscle tone.

Another major difference between BIS and somatodyspraxia is that children with the latter will have trouble with feedback. These children do not get reliable sensory feedback from their tactile, vestibular and proprioceptive senses. As a result, they cannot build upon their actions easily. Each time the child tries to climb stairs it may be as if they are attempting the task for the first time. As a result, the child requires significant repetition to learn new tasks. The child with BIS however, can perform a rehearsed task well.

Below are symptoms specific to the child with tactile discrimination disorder:

- The child may not be able to identify objects by feel; for example, if you put a shape into her hand while blocking her vision, and subsequently ask her to identify the shape in her hand, she may be unsuccessful; this is called stereognosis. She may be unable to recognize a letter written on the back of her hand (graphesthesia) with vision blocked.
- The child may be unable to tell where she has been touched on her body without looking.
- The child's overreliance on visual input to compensate for the lack of tactile input may result in slower processing speed, translating to additional required time to complete tasks comparable to typical children.
- The inability to discriminate tactile sensations will result in adverse reactions to tags, seams, certain textures and fabrics of clothing, hats and shoes. The child cannot discriminate (make sense of) what is touching his skin, and experiences his clothing as irritable and itchy.
- The child may have an inability to discriminate a change in surface beneath his feet from carpet to tile or from grass to pavement, and may trip and fall. Because many children with dyspraxia also have modulation disorder, the intensity of the child's sensory defensiveness may fluctuate along with his regulation level.
- The child may have significantly delayed speech or trouble with speech articulation.

- The child may have trouble making oral movements with her mouth, such as sticking her tongue out or smacking her lips. Her tongue may hang out of her mouth, and she may drool beyond when it is age appropriate. She may be unable to feel the food in her mouth and overfill her mouth. She may have difficulty coordinating, chewing, and swallowing her food.

- Lacking internal body awareness is often a significant problem for the child with tactile discrimination disorder/somatodyspraxia. This may result in delayed toilet training, nighttime enuresis, inability to detect hunger and thirst sensations, high tolerance to pain, and obliviousness to temperature extremes. See "Chapter 6: Internal Regulation" for more information.

- Visual spatial deficits are common by-products of body awareness problems. Body awareness deficits render this child unsure of his relative position to others. Because of this, he may stand too close to other children or move in awkward and clumsy ways.

- He may not be able to feel his own body parts, as his extremities can make it difficult for him to move his limbs, affecting his balance and all forms of movement. For example, a child with somatodyspraxia may have trouble putting his shoe on his foot not only because the act of putting the shoe on challenges him (a motor planning problem), but also because he cannot feel his foot is attached to his body (a tactile discrimination problem).

Children with somatodyspraxia often suffer from what A. Jean Ayres called visuodyspraxia, which experts now believe to be the end result of somatodyspraxia.[26] A child with visuodyspraxia will have difficulty with poor form and space perception, visual-motor coordination, and visual construction (such as dot-to-dot designs). See "Chapter 11: Visual Dysfunction" for more information on these visual skills.

Prognosis and Treatment

Prognosis is heavily dependent upon the age of detection and the severity of the disorder. For children with mild to moderate cases, early detection (from infancy through preschool) can make a significant difference in treatment success. Therefore, if parents see any cause for developmental concerns in their children, immediate action is necessary. Treatment can help the child to learn, achieve, and become happy and satisfied adults.

When mild or moderate dyspraxia is not treated or identified until a child reaches school age, dyspraxia's impact on his development may affect his learning and adjustment in mainstream society. The problems the child with dyspraxia may have in motor coordination, planning, and organizing information will have direct and indirect influences on his reading, arithmetic, math, spelling, art, music, physical education, and social and emotional development. However, treatment can greatly help the child develop motor planning abilities, and adjust emotionally if detected during school-age years. For children with severe cases of dyspraxia, their disabilities can present a lifelong challenge. Intensive treatment can mitigate their challenges and help improve their daily lives.

Occupational therapy anchors treatment for children with dyspraxia. The goal of occupational therapy is to help children with dyspraxia make neural connections within the brain. Fun goal-directed activities help them register sensations, and make new neural connections. Therapists provide the "just right" challenge, meaning the new activity will be achievable by the child, while simultaneously challenging the child. The therapist will also provide support in the form of prompts and cues (scaffolding) in order to assist the child in completing a task that the child would not be able to complete by himself. Eventually, the goal is for the child to be able to complete the challenge independently, at which point the child's brain has made new neural connections. In addition, children with somatodyspraxia may require fine motor and speech therapy, and placed on an oral motor and graded feeding program, if eating and feeding are problematic.

Often, parents are under the impression that children with sensory processing disorder will improve with age. Untreated motor planning deficits *never* improve with age, unlike modulation disorder, which does improve somewhat as the child ages.

Sensory-Based Motor Disorder: Dyspraxia
Part Two

Dyspraxia has many potential physical/sensory and cognitive/language outcomes. Each child may exhibit a diverse combination of outcomes, and may fall somewhere on a continuum of deficits, some children exhibiting more severe symptoms and others milder. Physical and sensory outcomes include deficits in fine and gross motor skills, body awareness, posture, and vision. Cognitive and language outcomes include motor planning challenges, oral motor deficits, and speech and language difficulties. There are also social and emotional outcomes, discussed in "Chapter 10: Emotions."

Physical/Sensory Outcomes

Fine motor control is the ability to use the small muscles of the hands and fingers with precision for skilled activity. Fine motor skills depend upon the development of gross motor skills in the early years. For example, the proprioceptive pressure a child experiences while crawling helps develop the arches of the hands, which are crucial for balance, stability, and mobility.[27] In turn, those abilities allow us to write, use appropriate force to grip an object, and lift an object. Children must have body awareness, postural stability, adequate tactile sensations, and discrimination (ability to make sense of the tactile sensations detected) to control and use various objects. Therefore, children with proprioceptive and tactile dysfunction may experience fine motor problems. Some of the fine motor movements that may be difficult for children with dyspraxia include:

- Getting dressed: Buttons, small fasteners, zippers, and shoelaces. He may be able to dress himself one day, but not the next, due to variations in his clothing (e.g., the shirt he wore yesterday was one that he could pull over his head, but today's shirt has buttons that require good fine motor skills).
- Self-care: Brushing teeth, combing hair, or washing his face and hands.
- Precision toys: Completing puzzles, manipulating small objects, and playing with manipulative toys (blocks, Legos, etc.).
- Eating and drinking: Using cutlery, such as a knife and fork, and drinking from a cup.
- Toilet training: Controlling their sphincter muscles often makes toilet training challenging.
- Writing and Drawing: Preschoolers may have trouble coloring within the lines, or using pencils or scissors. In elementary school, handwriting may be nearly impossible to read, and drawings may be immature when compared to peers' work.
- Generalization: Trouble generalizing previously learned motor tasks to a new situation and context. For example, the fact that she learns to tie the sash on the back of a dress does not mean she can tie a ribbon on a birthday present, as every situation requires novel motor planning.

Gross motor skills involve the utilization of the big muscles of the body. Children with dyspraxia may have the following difficulties with gross motor skills:

- Milestones: As infants and toddlers, they may skip crawling or rolling. Many children with dyspraxia achieve developmental milestones at the very end of the average range.[28]

- Big muscle movements: The child may have difficulty riding a bike, climbing stairs, roller skating, skateboarding, catching and throwing a ball, running and playing on playground equipment, skipping, or jumping rope.
- Sports and games: Learning to catch a ball thrown to the same place each time is achievable, as this involves the same motor planning. However, when a child is playing a game such as soccer or baseball where the ball's trajectory is constantly changing, he may struggle because of the heavy motor planning requirements. Sports require a lot of action sequencing with immediate adjustments in time and space (feedforward).
- Group play: Reluctance to participate in new group activities and prefer sedentary activities such as watching TV, playing video games, or reading a book. When young children play, rules constantly change and the child with dyspraxia cannot keep up with the ever-changing, flexible motor planning of peers.
- Endurance and fatigue: Constant visual monitoring of actions result in decreased endurance and fatigue due to poor body awareness, low muscle tone, or postural problems. As a result, these children may constantly lean against furniture, walls, etc.
- Generalization: Trouble generalizing previously learned motor tasks to a new situation and context. For example, a child who learns to climb one set of stairs may have trouble climbing other stairs that are a slightly different height.

Body awareness involves the concepts of laterality, bilateral coordination, crossing the midline, gradation, visual-spatial awareness and interoceptive awareness.

- Laterality. Laterality refers to the preference most humans show for one side of the body over the other. This concept is multisensory and is a combination of visual, auditory, vestibular, tactile, and proprioceptive senses and, to a lesser degree, the other senses. If these senses do not work together properly, the child may experience challenges in right/left discrimination or developing a hand preference.

- Bilateral coordination. Bilateral coordination is the coordinating of both sides of the body. Problems with bilateral coordination may manifest in a poor ability to skip, jump, stride jump, throw or catch a ball, or ride a bike. In addition, sports that require coordinating both sides of the body, such as swimming, are often difficult for the child with dyspraxia.

- Crossing the Midline. "Crossing the midline is the ability to move one hand, foot, or eye into the space of the other hand, foot or eye. We cross midline when we scratch an elbow, cross our ankles, and read left to right. Crossing the midline of your body helps build pathways in the brain, and is an important prerequisite skill required for the appropriate development of various motor and cognitive skills."[29] A child with dyspraxia may move his body to avoid crossing his midline.

- Gradation. Gradation is the ability to discern the appropriate amount of muscle force to use, which is dependent upon adequate proprioceptive discrimination. These children may use too little or too much force when conducting everyday tasks. The child may have trouble attaching clothing snaps, pop beads, and Legos, as they do not have the strength to perform these actions. Conversely, they may hold others' hands with too much grip, shut doors too forcefully, or break toys frequently due to excessive force.

- Visual-Spatial Awareness. Visual-spatial awareness is the ability to determine the positions of objects in space and their relative positions to other objects. Children with dyspraxia may have trouble with positional concepts (up/down, over/under, etc), playing Legos or shape sorters, and finding their way around buildings. The child may appear awkward and clumsy as he trips, falls, and bumps into things or may stand too close to other people. He may be unsure where his body parts are unless he visually monitors them (for example, watching his feet when walking or running). The child may have difficulty discerning the proper orientation of objects in relation to her body causing the child to confuse *b* and *d*, *3* and *E*, *p* and *q*, *on* and *no*, and *was* and *saw*, making it difficult to learn to read, write, spell, and do arithmetic. This problem differs from dyslexia, which affects the way the brain processes written material. The problem in dyslexia is a linguistic one, not a visual one. Mathematics may be challenging due to the abstract concepts of shapes, areas, volume, and space and he may have problems reproducing patterns, sequences, and shapes. Projected action sequences require visual-spatial skills and timing, which are often deficient in children with poor body awareness.

- Interoceptive body awareness. Children with poor body awareness often have interoceptive problems affecting their potty training, temperature, respiratory regulation, and diet. See "Chapter 6: Internal Regulation" for more information.

Postural problems. Children with dyspraxia often suffer from low muscle tone, also known as hypotonia. Hypotonia results in poor endurance, and may lead to the child slumping over his desk like a limp noodle while doing homework, or saying he is "too tired" to play outside with other children. See "Chapter 4: Postural Disorder" for more information.

Vision. Children with dyspraxia and/or postural disorder can suffer from focusing and eye teaming problems, eye movement and tracking disorders, visual perception, and visual-motor coordination problems. See "Chapter 11: Visual Dysfunction" for more information.

Cognitive/Language Outcomes

Motor planning. Motor planning involves ideation, sequencing, execution, and adaptation. Below is information on the behaviors associated with these steps:

- Ideation: The child may have an inability to formulate ideas for action and play. The child may pick up a toy and drop it because he cannot determine what to do with the toy. He may move from toy to toy due to his lack of ideas for play. His play will lack creativity, and his behavior may be rigid and inflexible. He will often prefer solitary play, and parallel play (two children playing alongside one another) when it is no longer age-appropriate.
- Sequencing: Everything a child does requires some level of sequencing. For typical children, the component steps to each task are automatic. In contrast, children with motor planning deficits cannot sequence through steps automatically. This will manifest in some of the following ways:
  - Transitions: Sequencing through the steps of a transition is challenging, and these children may be slow to transition and unable to "switch gears." As a result, plenty of extra time during transitions is often required.
  - Playing with toys: The child may have trouble playing with manipulatives, such as building blocks, constructional toys, puzzles, and shape sorters.
  - Multistep instructions: Multistep instructions require sequencing. For example, most instructions will contain at least three steps. Difficulty sequencing auditory input could leave them with gaps in information; they may only hear the first part of an instruction as processing information is a slower process due to inefficient brain circuitry.
  - Imitation: Imitation, a foundation skill for learning, requires a child to have a good working knowledge of his body—how it is put together and the relationship between the parts. For the child to imitate the actions of another person, he must have the idea of what is expected, organize and sequence the information, and motorically be able to coordinate the movements. Lastly, imitation requires integration between motor movement and vision, called visual-motor integration.

- Organization: Organization is a form of motor planning and sensory children have difficulty organizing not only body movements, but also thoughts, language, time, personal spaces, and possessions. Cleaning up toys is often problematic for young children when they must put them away in different containers or spaces. Older children may have a hard time keeping their personal spaces, such as a school desk, backpack, or bedroom organized due to sequencing problems. In addition, organizing thoughts orally, or in writing, is often challenging. When speaking, the child may have trouble "getting a sentence out," struggling to organize it.
- Making choices and problem solving: Trouble making choices or problem solving is common, as both of these require sequencing by stringing thoughts together.
- Speech: Sequencing deficits influence language production affecting the child's ability to arrange letters correctly in words (spell), string words together to form connected speech, or tell a story.
- Dressing: In addition to the fine motor control problems children with dyspraxia may have when dressing, they may also have trouble putting on their clothes in the correct order, which requires sequencing.
- Self-grooming: Brushing teeth/hair and washing face/hands can be problematic for children with sequencing problems, as they cannot sequence through the steps required to accomplish these tasks.
- Projected action sequences (feedforward): Projected action sequences are those that are anticipatory. For example, anticipating where to move your foot to intercept a ball in soccer, and playing hopscotch are projected action sequences. These sequences are challenging for the child with dyspraxia.
- Social Sequencing Deficits: Social interaction requires constant, rapid adjustments, and reactions to peers' actions. Children with dyspraxia will have trouble adjusting to their

peers' actions in a timely fashion, and will have trouble with ever-changing, fast-moving play, as sequencing is required to adjust constantly. Bossy behavior, difficulty interpreting non-verbal cues and social nuances, inability to hold onto emotional ideas, avoidance behaviors, immaturity, low self-esteem and low self-confidence, hyperactivity, and lack of self-regulation will all contribute to difficulty with social interactions.

- Execution. Execution is the performance of the task (gross and fine motor actions), and is based upon ideation and sequencing. For example, the child who is assembling Lincoln Logs to build a house must first develop the concept of the house, and subsequently sequence the steps to put it together. It is the combination of ideation and sequencing that results in the execution of the task.

- Adaptation. When a child initiates an idea and organizes a plan for action, she may encounter a problem when executing the plan. Good motor planning involves the ability to problem solve around that task and generate a new plan of action. For instance, if a child decides to build a Lego castle and realizes halfway through the task that he lacks enough Legos to build a castle, he must be able to adapt and modify his plan. Adaptation requires flexibility around motor planning, which can be difficult for some children with dyspraxia.

Oral Motor/Speech Problems. Children with oral dyspraxia typically have childhood apraxia of speech (CAS), but CAS may occasionally occur without oral dyspraxia. Problems with CAS and oral dyspraxia can range from mild to very severe, and require evaluation by a speech language pathologist. Below is more information on these conditions.

- Oral Dyspraxia: Children with oral-motor coordination problems have difficulty with nonspeech movements. This may result in excessive drooling, choking or avoidance of textured food because swallowing requires the coordination of muscles. Infants who have oral-motor dyspraxia often have trouble sucking, swallowing or breathing deeply, resulting in feeding difficulties. When the child grows older, they will have trouble chewing, eating, sticking out their tongues, or smacking their lips. Their jaws may hang open, causing them to drool or spill food when they are eating.

- Childhood Apraxia of Speech (verbal dyspraxia): As opposed to oral-motor dyspraxia, in which a child has difficulty purposefully controlling non-speech movement, CAS impedes a child's ability to speak on command. In situations where the child is not consciously trying to speak, such as while playing, children with dyspraxia may make a sound like "ma," but cannot respond to a request to say "mama." When children with dyspraxia speak for one day only, adults without sensory integration knowledge will attribute the child's inability to speak to laziness. Instead, it is the result of neurological connections made in the child's brain that day.[30] The child may have difficulty imitating sounds, whistling, or blowing up balloons. Dyspraxia can also affect rate, rhythm, fluency, and inflection of speech.

There are also emotional and social outcomes associated with sensory processing disorder. You can read about these outcomes under the "Anxiety" section in chapter ten.

Parental Strategies for Dyspraxia

In addition to the strategies below, check Pinterest boards for great activities related to fine and gross motor control, bilateral coordination, and crossing midline. Check with your child's occupational therapist to ensure that any home strategies are appropriate for your child's profile.

Home Strategies for Motor Planning

- Supply deep-pressure input: Prior to participating in any fine or gross motor task, engage your child in deep-pressure activities for at least thirty minutes. This will help alter the child's arousal level to the calm-alert state.

- Talk the child through a task: Tell her how many steps are involved in the task. Then tag each step with *first,* then *next,* and *last.* Talk her through individual movements within each step, if necessary. This helps improve feedforward, the ability to think into the future.
- Practice ideation daily: Engage your child in pretend play as much as possible. When brainstorming for ideas, initially use choices instead of supplying an idea. For instance, "Should we find the dragon, or get some other astronauts to join us?" Eventually progress to prompts such as "Here is some Play-Doh, "What can we make?" or "What can we make out of this big empty box?" "What is your idea?"
- Use backward chaining. Backward chaining is the opposite of forward chaining in that a parent or professional teaches a child the last step first, moving in reverse order through the steps, until reaching the first step. "Backward chaining allows a child to experience instant success. As more steps are added, a child completes the newly taught step immediately, followed by the steps she has already mastered. This can minimize anxiety and provide a child with a sense of accomplishment.... In essence, completion of the steps operates as a natural reinforcer for a child.[31]
- When teaching your child a new motor task, always break the task down into smaller steps. For example, multi-step directions delivered one at a time. A good strategy to use if the child fails a task is to stay calm, acknowledge the failure, and help the child determine a different way to approach the task. State, "Let me see that again—I wonder if it would work better if you tried it this way."
- Teaching self-care skills. A helpful resource in teaching self-care skills is located at http://www.therapro.com. Therapro has a manual that comes with a CD called *Self-Care with Flair!* This manual utilizes fun rhymes and activities to teach self-care skills, and reinforce skills needed. In addition, Therapro has a double-sided dressing vest (one side for boys and the other for girls) where

your child can practice zipping, snapping, buttoning, overall clips, buckle, lacing, tying and Velcro skills.

- Participate in activities or games that promote sequencing. Obstacle courses, games, cooking from instructions and Twister are some activities that promote sequencing in children. For information on setting up a backyard obstacle course, see "Chapter 7: Sensory Diet."
- Delivering instructions. When delivering multistep instructions to your child, alert your child to the total number of steps you are going to give (e.g., "I want you to do three things"), and then "tag" items with words such as *first, last, before, after,* etc., and insert brief (one-to-two-second) pauses between items to enhance processing. Make sure your child comprehends the instructions by asking the child to repeat them back to you.
- Clean-Up. Putting toys away in various places requires sequencing, and may prove challenging for the dyspraxic child. One way around this is to keep all the toys in one bin, if possible. If your child gets overwhelmed with cleaning up, the best way to involve her is to assign her two or three toys to pick up, and put in the bin; you will need to pick up the rest. Very young children may be able to take on only one or two toys, and may need hand-over-hand assistance to put her two toys in the bin.
- Decisions. Decisions require sequencing through strings of thought. Therefore, you can help these children make decisions by offering them a choice between two items: "Do you want to wear the green pajamas or the red ones?" Choice also helps to give them a sense of mastery over their environment.
- Dressing. Dressing requires sequencing. When the child struggles, parents may step in to get the child dressed quickly, but this can be counterproductive, and result in elevated anxiety and behavioral problems. The child will start her school day already stressed by the morning's activities. Providing visual cues, satisfying clothing choices, and emotional support will serve to wrap the child in the support he needs. See "Chapter

9: Transitions" for additional information on helping your child dress.

- Feedforward. Occupational therapist Carrie Murray-Slutsky, OTR/L recommends having your child tell you what he is going to do, like, "I am going to go over there and get that toy."[32]And subsequently to make sure he follows through, and gets the toy. This will help your child to start thinking into the future, and will help with feedforward problems.

- Practice Floortime. A psychiatrist named Dr. Stanley Greenspan developed the Floortime approach. The Floortime Approach helps move a child's development forward, both intellectually and emotionally, through a particular way of interacting with the child. Parents can obtain additional information on Floortime or take a parental course on the Floortime Approach by visiting www.stanleygreenspan.com.

Home Strategies for Visual Spatial Development

- Castle Logix and Block Buddies. In Castle Logix, the child copies castle designs from the included puzzle booklet. In Block Buddies, kids replicate 76 designs in four levels of difficulty. Recommended for children 3 and over.

- Snap Circuits. Snap Circuits Jr comes with over 30 components to create 101 different electronic projects. The components combine to create working circuit boards. Recommended for children 8 and over.

- Connect Four. Connect Four is a vertical tic-tac-toe, except you must get four in a row horizontally, vertically, or diagonally. This game assists in visual-spatial development, as the child must visualize the checkers in space in order to get four in a row. Recommended for children 7-14 years of age.

- Supply reading aids. A teacher supply store at http://www.really-goodstuff.com offers reading strips that highlight text to aid children in visual processing. In addition, many children with visual spatial

problems have trouble keeping letters and math numbers spaced appropriately on a page. Therapro.com offers raised line paper that can assist the child with visual challenges.
- Positional Concepts. A couple of great games for learning positional concepts are Twister and Simon Says.

Home Strategies for Bilateral Coordination Development

- Playing catch: Play catch using Velcro balls with Velcro catch mitts, baseball glove and ball, or Koosh Balls with various textures.
- Opening packages: Open bags of candy and favorite foods, which is very motivational for the child!
- Playing with two-handed baby toys: Play popping beads, Duplos/Legos, My Ice Cream Parlor game from Lakeshore Learning (www.lakeshorelearning.com), or any other two-handed toy.
- Dressing Barbies: Dress dolls. This requires bilateral coordination, as the child must hold the doll with one hand, and put the clothes on with the other. If Barbies are too challenging initially, start with larger dolls.
- Swinging on a trapeze bar: Swing on a trapeze bar, as this requires the use of both sides of the body.
- Stringing beads: String various types of beads made of macaroni, buttons, wood, clay, Cheerios, or Froot Loops on pipe cleaners, shoelaces, string, or licorice.
- Cutting/Drawing: Hold paper down with one hand, and draw or cut with the other.

Home Strategies for Crossing Midline and Directionality Skill Development

- Wash big objects: Wash windows. Have the child wipe with both hands, back and forth in large motions, so that she is crossing her midline frequently.

- Play with ribbon wands: Make (tie a scarf to a stick) or buy ribbon wands and model the dance of figure eights, and big rainbow arcs that incorporate crossing the midline. Dance to music!
- Windmills: Have your child stand straight with feet spread apart, then bend over at the waist and touch the left foot with the right hand. Then stand back up, bend over at the waist, and touch the right foot with the left hand.
- Cross feet: Have the child cross one foot over the other when walking sideways.
- Playing with sand: Have the child scoop sand from the left side of the body, and put it in a bucket on the right side of the body using the same hand.
- Soldier walks: Have your child imitate the soldier walk to a metronome beat of 60–90 beats per minute. A child executes the soldier walk by raising the leg up to the opposite hand, alternating with each step. Query soldier walk exercise online and there are many video demonstrations.
- Arrow charts: Place arrows on index cards in left-to-right order, and have the child step in the arrow direction. Forward is up arrow, backward is down arrow, left arrow, and right arrow. You can make this game progressively harder by placing an entire sheet of arrows in front of the child, which involves the visual skill of eye tracking and body movement simultaneously. Next, you can add a metronome beat of 60–90 beats per minutes.
- Bdpq charts: Many children with dyspraxia struggle with directionality and laterality. If your child has trouble with the commonly reversed letters of *bdpq*, you can teach him to learn it internally within his own body. Teach him that the stick part of each of these letters is the center of his body, and each *c* represents an arm or leg— e.g., *b* = kick out your right leg; *d* = kick out your left leg; *p* = right arm out; and *q* = left arm out. Do this on index cards to start, and then progress to a half page of codes, then a full page. Eventually, add in a beat as well.

- Air mattress fun: Have your child get on all fours on an air mattress or air pillow, and rock on all fours to a beat. Challenge the child by asking her to lift up and balance on three points when you say *b*, *d*, *p*, or *q*. Use the arrow cards to have her "rock in the direction" forward, backward, left, or right.
- Play right and left games: Have the child jump on a mini-trampoline and tell him to turn right or left, and jump in a circle. Throw a small weighted ball and have him hold it up with the arm you call out—right versus left. Also, call out right or left when he throws the beanbag or plays other eye-hand coordination games.
- Whole body games: Animal crawls are great games for children with dyspraxia. Games such as "Simon Says" and "Hokey Pokey" are also good, as you can build in actions that require crossing the midline within these games. See "Chapter 7: Sensory Diet," for information on how to play these games.

Home Strategies for Fine Motor Skill Development

- Jewelry making: String various types of beads made of wood, clay, macaroni, buttons, Cheerios, or Froot Loops on pipe cleaners, shoelaces, string, or licorice.
- Resistive Materials: Play-doh kits, clay, or theraputty are great materials to provide resistance that helps to improve fine motor skills. Spraying water with a spray bottle provides resistance that helps improve fine motor abilities as well.
- Coloring and cutting: Use triangle crayons, Crayola Write Start Colored Pencils, or markers to color predrawn pictures. Cut Play-Doh, cardboard, putty (Silly Putty or Theraputty), straw, or paper.
- Writing and Drawing: Use shaving cream, sand in a box top, vibrating pens, scented crayons/markers, or chalk on a sidewalk or driveway, to write and play. You can also have your child form letters, numbers, or words in the air, or on your back, with you

guessing what she wrote. Dot to dot designs, mazes, coloring books, or card creating are also great incentives for children to practice writing skills. Magna Doodle, Alex Draw Like a Pro, and Squiggle Wiggle Writer are great products to help motivate your child to write or draw. Weights slipped around a pencil or weighted wristbands are useful in helping your child "feel" his hand while writing, increasing success. See Appendix C for writing resources.

- Engaging in arts and crafts: For preschoolers: Make paper-bag puppets, paper-plate fish, or any foam project where the child must glue on small pieces for eyes, scales, or decorations. Sticker book play is also great for preschoolers. For older children: Origami, model cars/boats, yarn projects that utilize needles or a loom, woodworking, and braiding. Wikki Stix forms easily into anything in your child's imagination.

- Picking up objects: Have the child pick up small objects such as pennies, marbles, or beans with either his hands or tongs, and then place them in a bottle or box with a small opening, or a piggy bank. Games such as The Hungry Monkey Motor Skills Game build fine motor skills, and improve eye-hand coordination. In the Hungry Monkey game, the child uses tweezers to pick up a banana and feed the monkey.

- Cooking: Pouring, stirring, shaking, kneading, cutting, pressing, or measuring is great for fine motor development. One motivational task is to have the child take small pieces of chocolate or sprinkles and put them on top of cupcakes.

- Pinching: Play clothespin games, or play with clay, clips, snaps, or Velcro. Have your child find money or small objects buried in Theraputty.

- Playing games or puzzles: Play board games that require moving pieces around the board (e.g., Chutes and Ladders). Other games that are great for building fine motor skills are Lauri Toys Stringing Pegs and Pegboard Set, Geoboards, Lite Brite,

Operation, Perfection, Super Safe Hammering Kit (Lakeshore Learning), Edushape Tricky Fingers (good for ages 4-5), and Kerplunk.

- Constructional games: Build or copy designs using Legos, Knex, Tinker Toys, or Elenco Snap Circuits Junior.
- Dressing. When teaching your child how to dress, Therapro also has a "dressing vest" which makes working on dressing skills fun. The dressing vest is a double-sided vest (one for boys and one for girls) and provides zipping, snapping, buttoning, overall clips, buckle, lacing, tying and Velcro skill practice.

Home Strategies for Gross Motor Development

- Dancing: Get your child moving, either freestyle or through songs, with movements such as "I'm a Little Teapot," "Head, Shoulders, Knees, and Toes," "Freeze Dance," or "Popcorn."
- Participating in sports: Engage in gymnastics, ice-skating, swimming, horseback riding, soccer, tennis, etc.
- Balancing: Have your child walk on a piece of string or tape, a low beam or plank at the playground, or a homemade balance beam.
- Riding equipment: Encourage your child to ride tricycles, or other ride-on toys and to pull or push wagons, large trucks, doll strollers, or shopping carts.
- Building and navigating obstacle courses: Make an obstacle course indoors with furniture, pillows, boxes, and blankets; outdoors with rocks, logs, playground equipment, or an old tire.
- Throwing, catching, and rolling: Use large, lightweight, or soft balls to throw, catch, or roll.
- Playing gross motor games: Play games such as Hullabaloo, Elefun, Dr. Suess I can do that! and Hyperdash. These games are great for developing gross motor skills!

- Engaging in classic backyard games and playground fun: Play games such as tag, follow the leader, or Simon says. Have your child swing, slide, and climb at a playground or indoor play space.

Four

Sensory-Based Motor Disorder: Postural Disorder

Julie is a first grader sitting at her desk, and has just dropped her pencil. Instead of leaning over to pick up the pencil, she cautiously gets up out of her chair, squats down, retrieves the pencil, and sits down. Once in her chair, the teacher tells the class to copy the day's assignments from the front of the classroom. Julie is using her hand to hold her head up, while she is trying to copy the assignments from the front of the classroom. She does not get all of the information copied because she cannot visually keep her place on the lines of information. She then slides out of her chair and lands on the floor. The bell rings and it is time for recess. Julie slowly gets up off the floor, and heads for the door. Once outside, Julie starts running for a bench along the periphery of the playground, but she trips and falls. She cannot play on playground equipment, or participate in typical playground games, such as crossing the monkey bars, climbing jungle gyms, playing four-square or tag because she lacks the balance and strength. As a result, Julie is isolated with few friends, has low self-esteem, and a lack of self-confidence.

In this example, Julie is demonstrating many signs of postural disorder. When Julie got up to retrieve her pencil, she was demonstrating poor core strength. When she used her hand to prop her head up, she was exhibiting poor neck control. When having trouble keeping her place in copying the assignment, Julie is exhibiting an ocular-motor deficit. When Julie falls out of her chair and trips and falls on the playground, she is displaying poor balance reactions. Her inability to play on playground equipment or typical playground games at recess is a combination of poor balance reactions, poor core strength, and poor muscle tone. Lastly, Julie is experiencing emotional insecurity due to her postural challenges.

For children like Julie, physical activity is tiring and difficult due to their balance and postural challenges. They are weak, lack endurance, and may lean against walls or furniture for support when standing. When seated, they may prop their head up with their hand or lean their head on their arm. These children may be clumsy, tripping and falling frequently. Often they have trouble sitting or standing in one position for any length of time. They may have trouble writing or drawing. When reading, they may lose their place frequently because they cannot move their eyes smoothly across a line of print.

Current posture theory asserts that posture is the expression of vestibular and proprioceptive processing.[1] Vestibular and proprioceptive dysfunction can result in postural disorder. Children with postural disorder have trouble controlling their bodies in order to perform many motor tasks.[2] Poor postural control typically involves difficulties with standing posture, inability to sustain postures, and balance reactions.[3] Specific postural and balance challenges are described below.

Postural Challenges

Proximal Stability

The child with postural disorder will have poor strength and stability of the core.[4] Therefore, the child will fatigue easily, have poor endurance, and demonstrate difficulty sustaining standing or sitting positions. As a result, they may lean against furniture or walls as props. Poor core strength may result in a toddler increasing their base of support by sitting in the

"W-Sit" position, where legs bent behind and splayed to either side resemble a W. When seated, children with poor proximal stability may also get up and bend down to retrieve a dropped item, instead of remaining seated. Picking up an item from the seated position often requires too much muscle tone, and core strength, to rotate the trunk for the child with postural disorder. When standing, the child's shoulders may tip forward, and reveal a potbelly appearance. These children may have difficulty in everyday childhood activities, such as roller blading or skateboarding, due to poor core strength. Many of these children evidence a fear of movement due to their underlying postural problems, and may be cautious and slow moving.

Prone Extension

Prone extension is a position where the child is lying face down on the floor with arms, neck, and legs all extended off the floor. A. Jean Ayres stated that the ability to assume and maintain prone extension is a strong indicator of vestibular and proprioceptive processing.[5] If vestibular and proprioceptive dysfunction is present, then the child may have trouble assuming prone anti-gravity positions due to their weak muscles. Such anti-gravity positions as "superman" are challenging for the child. The child lies prone on the floor with arms and legs extended, and lifted off the floor. These children often have trouble with sports and playground games due to their poor endurance, and inability to sustain the positions required to play these games.

Neck Flexion

Children with postural disorder often cannot hold their necks in a sustained position against gravity for long. Often, these children have trouble holding their heads up while sitting.[6] For instance, when writing at their school desk, they may extend far over their paper, or rest their head on their arm when writing. They may have problems copying from the front of the classroom, when looking back and forth, due to difficulty positioning and repositioning their head and neck.[7]

Balance Reactions

In addition to being unable to sustain body positions due to poor muscle stability, children with postural disorder may exhibit any one of three equilibrium responses: postural background movements, protective extension, or co-contraction.

- Postural background movements, also known as equilibrium reactions, are small, rapid and subtle compensatory adjustments made by the head, trunk, or limbs in response to changes in position.[8] Children with equilibrium challenges may lose their balance when shifting weight to sit or stand. For example, when we reach for something, our trunk and legs make automatic adjustments, so the arms can follow through with the task while maintaining balance. The child may have difficulty standing on one foot, or stepping over obstacles.[9] Moving between uneven surfaces is often difficult for the child with postural disorder. Maintaining stable positions requires intense concentration even when performing simple actions, such as stepping onto an escalator or on/off a curb.[10] When accidentally bumped by another child, a child with postural disorder often cannot make the adjustment needed to stabilize afterward. Frequently, the child lethargically chooses not to move, but if forced to move may result in an aggressive reaction.[11]

- Protective extension. When they lose their balance, these children often do not attempt to catch themselves when they fall. An automatic extension of the arms, called protective extension, protects typical children from harm. Protective extension is generated by vestibular and proprioceptive sensations communicated to the brain.[12] When dysfunction is present, protective messages may not generate, and the child may make no attempt to catch himself when he begins to fall out of a chair.[13]

- Co-contraction is a balance response that refers to opposing muscles that produce a simultaneous contraction of equal force.[14] For example, in typical children the following muscles would fire together: quadriceps with hamstrings, abdominals with back muscles, and biceps with triceps. Children with postural disorder often feel unstable, insecure, and unsafe because their opposing muscles do not engage with equal force.[15]

Muscle Tone
Children with postural disorder will also suffer from poor muscle tone. Muscle tone refers to the ability of the muscle to sustain a contraction—as opposed to muscle strength, which is the power of the muscles.[16] Children with low muscle tone will have difficulties contracting muscles against resistance such as reaching, pushing, and pulling appropriately. Consequently, the child may use too little force when picking up an item, and drop it. These children will fatigue rapidly during physical play, have poor endurance, and their muscles may feel soft, mushy, or limp. Low muscle tone is also apparent when chewing, swallowing, or closing the mouth often resulting in drooling. Some children with postural disorder may have difficulty with articulating speech sounds. Low muscle tone can also affect potty training, as it interferes with the child's ability to balance on the toilet, and control their sphincter muscles. Not all children with postural disorder experience developmental delays, but some may have delays in raising the head, sitting, rolling over, and crawling. The lack of core strength to stabilize their shoulders and arms may affect fine motor skills, using scissors, holding on to a pencil or dressing. Children with low muscle tone may also exhibit excessive flexibility of the joints, what the general population thinks of as "double-jointedness." This is easiest to observe in the elbows and finger joints. These children tend to hold a pencil or other tools inefficiently, either dropping them or using excessive force.

Postural-Ocular
Children with postural disorder often exhibit ocular-motor control deficits. The vestibular system triggers the core postural muscles around the

central and vertical alignment of the body.[17] In turn, the core stabilizes the body so that we can use our eyes appropriately. When either the head or body is moving, the capacity to keep the eyes on a steady target (fixation) maintains stable visual images on the retina. When vestibular dysfunction is present, it cannot function properly to guide postural control, or during ocular-motor tasks, such as copying from the blackboard, reading, writing, tying shoelaces, or catching or kicking a ball.[18] Read more about ocular-motor deficits in "Chapter 11: Visual Dysfunction."

Other Challenges

Bilateral Coordination

A well-functioning vestibular system is necessary in order to cross the midline, and participate in bilateral coordination activities. Crossing the midline is when one arm, leg, or eye crosses the plane of the opposite arm, leg, or eye of the body.[19] For example, reaching across with the right arm and picking up something on the left side of the body. Children with sensory-based motor disorders have a tendency to avoid crossing the midline of their body, when observed playing in their natural environment.[20] Crossing the midline is required in bilateral coordination, which is the ability to use both sides of the body simultaneously.[21] Crossing the midline is difficult for children with postural challenges because it requires rotation of the trunk, and low muscle tone prevents adequate trunk rotation.[22] Examples of bilateral challenges may include difficulty riding a bike, hitting a baseball, catching a ball, pumping a swing, stabilizing a jar with one hand and unscrewing it with another, or holding a buttonhole while pushing the button through with the other hand. As babies, they may bang on the floor with only one hand, or avoid reaching across their body to pick up a toy. Rhythmic activities such as bouncing a ball or clapping on the beat also require bilateral coordination.

Emotional Security

Children with postural disorder cannot move and use their bodies effectively, and may become easily frustrated, give up, and lose self-confidence.

They tend to prefer solitary play because they cannot keep up physically with their peers.[23] Children's problems compound when they experience a growth spurt, as they must relearn to balance and move their bodies after these developmental periods.

These children do not develop a sense of security and control over their bodies, and often suffer from emotional insecurity. Children with postural disorder can benefit from mental health counseling to help them deal with feelings of insecurity, low self-esteem, and low self-confidence. Because of the difficulties the child with postural disorder faces, some of the following signs may be evident:

Postural Disorder Symptoms

Infant and Toddler

- Feels floppy, like a sack of potatoes, when held.
- Muscles feel unusually mushy or soft.
- Has a weak suck, has trouble latching to feed, takes longer than average to feed, or fatigues easily during feeding, and needs to rest.
- Often leaves mouth open with the tongue hanging out and drools excessively.
- May exhibit delays in developmental milestones (sitting, crawling, or standing), but not always.
- Sits in the W-sit position due to weak muscle stability in the core, trunk, and back.
- Displays unusually passive environmental exploration compared to typical peers.
- May be aggressive when forced to move. For example, if a peer bumps into a child forcing him to move out of the way, he may respond by hitting or kicking the peer.

Older Child

- Slow, cautious movement or an unwillingness to move.
- Is very sedentary and demonstrates no motivation to run, jump, and play.
- Appears to have poor attention span or concentration; may give up easily.
- Has trouble rotating the body, which requires core strength. For example, it requires rotation of the trunk for a child to pick something up off the floor behind him.
- Avoids climbing and experiences discomfort on uneven surfaces. May be terrified of moving walkways or jungle gyms. Often cannot hang onto monkey bars.
- Often cannot shift weight to sit or stand without falling over.
- May be unable to assume antigravity positions, such as prone extension ("superman").
- Has poor posture when sitting or standing; slumps at the dinner table, or desk. Will tend to sit with back rounded and may lean head on hand or arm for support when writing or drawing.
- Has poor balance and is unable to stand on one foot.
- May appear limp and lethargic much of the time. May tire easily during physical play, dislike long walks, and have trouble going up stairs.
- Due to poor endurance and fatigue, the child may lean on walls and furniture for support when standing. When sitting, the child may lean their head on their hand or arm.
- Avoids or has discomfort crossing the midline of the body, and trouble with bilateral coordination (e.g., scratching an elbow, catching a ball or hitting a baseball).
- Has poor ocular control, such as ocular tracking, visual shifting (localization from near distance to far distance) and visual distractibility. Ocular tracking is required when we read, and

to follow people or objects in the environment. The child may be challenged to isolate head and eye movements (e.g., cannot move only the eyes to look at something to the right or left; instead must move the whole head to look to the side) when following their caregiver across the room. Visual shifting may be problematic for the child with postural challenges. For instance, copying from the front of the classroom would require shifting from far distance to near distance. The child may experience visual distractibility due to problems maintaining visual focus in busy environments or during movement.

- Has a loose grasp on objects resulting in difficulty writing, drawing, turning door knobs, etc.
- Is excessively flexible in some joints (especially elbows and fingers); bends them back easily.
- Eats with mouth open; drools or loses food from mouth.
- May have poor articulation (trouble with speech sounds).
- May become aggressive when forced to move by another child's actions.

Prognosis and Treatment

Current theory contends sensory-based postural problems to be a result of vestibular and proprioceptive dysfunction. Therefore, occupational therapy and/or physical therapy treat postural disorder. Below is information on each of these therapies.

Occupational Therapy

The occupational therapist will create numerous play-based activities that will assist the child to maintain stable positions, move in and out of various positions without losing her balance, and build trunk and core strength to allow sufficient limb movement. Specifically, the therapist may work on extension against gravity, muscle tone, postural stability, weight shifting, or balance.

Physical Therapy

Physical therapists assist children in developing and enhancing mobility, and incorporate various intervention techniques that assist children in realizing their full range of motion and maximizing their quality of life. There is overlap between occupational and physical therapists when it comes to treating sensory-based vestibular and proprioceptive dysfunction. Either of these therapists can treat many of the symptoms of postural disorder.

Physical therapists treat low muscle tone (hypotonia), neck issues, torticollis (asymmetrical head or neck position), scoliosis (abnormal curvature of the spine), trunk difficulties, lag in gross motor skills, motor transitions (trouble going from all fours to standing or from sitting to standing), vestibular and balance problems, delay in creeping or walking, toe walking, and other gait (manner of walking) issues.

Physical therapists may use treatment methods integrating stretching, massage, mobilization, and strength and endurance training. A few popular techniques often utilized include neurodevelopmental therapy (NDT), myofascial release, and total motion release (TMR).

The physical therapist will evaluate what treatment method best fits the postural and motor challenges of the child. Children can achieve tremendous gains in posture from intervention therapy, even to the point of functioning typically. Therefore, intervention is necessary as soon as possible after diagnosis.

Parental Strategies for Postural Disorder

Below are general exercises that address deficits in specific areas. Always check with your physical or occupational therapist for recommendations on home activities, as each child presents with a distinctive blend of sensory and postural challenges. Most importantly, all activities should be fun for your child. If your child does not like a particular activity, try a different one.

1. Prone extension. Good exercises to develop extension against gravity are Superman (child lies on tummy and extends both arms and legs out, with head up, to fly like Superman), monkey bars, or the zip line at your local park.

2. Muscle Tone. Treatment for low muscle tone centers on developing muscle strength. The best sports for children with low muscle tone are swimming, horseback riding, yoga, gymnastics, tennis and skating. Yoga poses, that work on balance and core strength, such as down dog and plank are helpful. Other beneficial activities include jumping on a safety-netted trampoline or hippity hop ball. Use the spider web or other climbing equipment on playgrounds, and work up to coming down the fireman's pole. Have your child lie on their tummy, and pull themselves up the playground slide with only their hands. Check with your child's physical or occupational therapist as to which of these sports or activities best fits your child's needs and skill level.

3. Postural stability. There are three areas to target in postural stability: trunk, shoulder, and wrist. Following are games/exercises to develop stability in each of these areas:
   - Trunk stability exercises. The following will help advance trunk stability: Playing catch in the kneeling position; having the child lie prone (face-down) over a stability ball picking up small objects, such as beanbags, and putting them on a table; having the child lie prone on a scooter board and use his hands to navigate around, or pulling another child on the scooter board. Playing rotation games, such as throwing a ball to one side, and then quickly to the opposite side. Sit-ups, crab walks, and plank are also great for facilitating core strength.
   - Shoulder Stability exercises: Walks such as crab walks, bear crawls, and wheelbarrow walking help acquisition of shoulder stability. See "Chapter 7: Sensory Diet" for information on how to perform these activities. These activities are also beneficial: crawling through and over an obstacle course of

tunnels, barrels and swings; pulling another child on a scooter board or solo on their tummy picking objects up off the ground; playing tug-of-war; and pouring water from a pitcher or sand from a bucket.

- Wrist stability: Here are some simple games to help cultivate wrist stability: Race while holding a tennis ball on a spoon; play with a yo-yo, Lite-Brite or basketball; and My Ice Cream Parlor game from Lakeshore Learning (available from http://www.lakeshorelearning.com). My Ice Cream Parlor encourages the child to hold the ice cream cone in one hand while placing a scoop of ice cream on the cone with the other hand. Not only is this great for wrist stability, but it also facilitates bilateral coordination.

4. Weight shifting. Animal walks such as crab walks and bear crawls over uneven ground are good weight-shifting activities. See "Chapter 7: Sensory Diet" for information on how to perform these animal walks. Games and exercises such as wheelbarrow walking, push-ups, and hula-hooping are great for facilitating weight shifting.

5. Balance. Balance games such as Twister, Sturdy Birdy, and Level Headed will help to develop balance skills. In addition, the tightrope game and penguin walk are fun alternatives to improve balance. To facilitate the tightrope game, place a strip of duct tape on the floor about ten by three (length by width), and have your child walk along the tape without falling off. Over time, add increasingly complex variations such as walking with a book or beanbag on her head, walking backward, or hopping on one foot. The penguin walk consists of the child balancing a beanbag on top of her head and walking like a penguin.

Some occupational therapists recommend warming up the muscles with fun activities prior to a non-preferred activity for the child with low muscle tone. For example, bouncing on a trampoline for several minutes prior to sitting at a desk, or playing with clay before writing can improve grip and fine motor skills while holding a pencil. Ask your child's occupational therapist for suggestions tailored for your child.

Summary

Postural disorder can have a negative impact on academics, social interactions, and self-image in the absence of intervention. Consequently, if you feel something just isn't quite right with your child, don't hesitate to schedule a screening. With appropriate help, children with postural disorder can live happy and successful lives!

Five

Sensory Discrimination
Disorder

Envision someone half-pipe snowboarding (a half-pipe is a circular structure that is 8 to 22 feet tall that snowboarders use to perform tricks with various levels of difficulty). In addition to the modulation of the direct sensations of vision, touch, sound, smell, vestibular, and proprioception, the person needs to know where he is in space relative to his own body and the half-pipe. The snowboarder has to consider the precise timing when moving his body through space, such as how fast he needs to be moving to accomplish a particular trick. He must gauge how much resistance is required to stay upright given the pressure of gravity, and how much force is required to jump off the top of the half-pipe when going into certain tricks to gain the altitude he needs. Understanding what direction he is facing and whether he is upright or upside down, is also vital. Half-pipe snowboarding requires simultaneous consideration of the ability to process the spatial aspects, temporal (timing) aspects, and amplitude of a sensation. In other words, it requires great discrimination.

Discrimination is the third type of sensory processing disorder (SDD). Discriminate means understanding accurately what is seen, heard, felt, tasted, smelled, or detected by the child's muscles and joints, movement, or the body's organs.[1] Good sensory discrimination provides spatial understanding, timing information, and knowledge about the magnitude of a sensation relative to both our body and the environment. Children with this type of SPD cannot perceive, organize and understand the sensory information picked up by their sensory receptors, such as a child not recognizing the fabric touching his skin resulting in an "itchy" feel. The child may not distinguish similarities and differences among stimuli, such as the disparity between hearing wreath and reef, whether the child sees a "P" or a "Q", or whether they are falling to the side or backwards.[2]

While sensory modulation disorder involves underresponsiveness to arousal, sensory discrimination disorder is underresponsiveness to the sensory system. For example, a child with tactile discrimination problems will determine that someone has touched him somewhere on his body, but cannot discriminate where he has been touched. Thus, the child with discrimination disorder will not be able to perceive the stimuli properly. The child with modulation disorder will be able to perceive where someone touched her on her body, but will need more or less touch to remain in the calm-alert state. Although sensory modulation and sensory discrimination are two different disorders, they often coexist together.

Humans store information we learn through our senses; if sensory information is inadequate, then learning is faulty resulting in discrimination deficits.[3] Discrimination may be impaired in any or all of the eight senses (auditory, visual, tactile, taste, smell, proprioceptive, vestibular, interoceptive), resulting in difficulty discerning the characteristics of sensory stimuli. For example, the child with tactile discrimination problems may have trouble telling the difference between a penny and a nickel without looking, or perceiving that he has food on his face, a runny nose, or messy hands. A child with an interoceptive discrimination problem often has difficulty interpreting her internal body signals. She may feel a slight need to use the restroom, when in reality, it is urgent! The child with proprioceptive discrimination difficulties may have trouble judging the amount of distance, force and timing required when jumping into a big pile of leaves. Other children may have trouble reading because they cannot visually discriminate between letters, or identify who is speaking to them because they cannot locate the source of sounds.

Children with sensory discrimination disorder may appear slow and clumsy in both fine and gross motor tasks. Emotionally, they may experience significant frustration and anxiety when attempting tasks that prove unsuccessful. As a result, these children may become aggressive, exhibit temper tantrums, low self-esteem, and a lack of self-confidence.

Sensory discrimination disorder can be a stand-alone disorder, when present in the auditory, visual, olfactory, gustatory, or interoceptive senses, or it can coexist with motor or modulation disorders. When sensory discrimination disorder is present in the vestibular, proprioceptive, and tactile domains, it can underlie dyspraxia, as discrimination is an important component of praxis (motor planning). Children with modulation disorder often experience discrimination problems as well because the basis for perceptual discrimination is sensory modulation and higher cognitive processes.

Occurrence with Modulation and Motor Disorders

In children with a co-occurrence of sensory modulation disorder and sensory discrimination disorder, it is the modulation disorder that interferes with discrimination because inadequate arousal interferes with the discriminatory system.[4] Discrimination challenges are experienced in both children who are underresponsive and those who are overresponsive. When sensory-based motor disorder and sensory discrimination disorder coexist, on the other hand, the discrimination disorder underlies the sensory-based motor disorder.[5]

Sensory Discrimination in the Child with Modulation Disorder

For overresponsive children, the primitive, constantly activated "fight or flight" system can override the detailed (discriminative) system. Therefore, overresponsive children may be unable to discriminate because the discriminative system is unable to engage when the "fight or flight" system activates. As a result, these children do not gain the necessary experience to develop the ability to discriminate things or objects in their environment.

Sensory discrimination disorder frequently co-occurs with both types of sensory underresponsiveness. Passive underresponders may not register toys or objects put in front of them, and may exhibit a general lack of exploration of things in their environment. Their lethargy and low arousal level leave them uninterested, and they have difficulty engaging with people, resulting in a lack of social overtures. Over time, the loss of sensory experiences caused by these children's underresponsiveness may inhibit their discriminative systems.

Underresponsive sensory cravers who are busy crashing and banging often have discrimination issues because they cannot slow their bodies down enough to learn the discriminatory components of sensory stimuli. For example, they may sometimes lag behind in fine motor tasks dependent upon the discriminative system because they cannot sit still long enough to participate in detailed tasks. However, these same children are usually great at gross motor tasks that require large muscle movement, because they are constantly utilizing these muscles.

Sensory Discrimination in the Child with Sensory-Based Motor Disorder

While modulation disorder precipitates discrimination disorder, the reverse is true when sensory-based motor disorder co-exists with sensory discrimination disorder. Underresponsiveness to tactile, proprioceptive and the vestibular systems may result in problems related to poorly developed body awareness, clumsiness, balance problems, motor planning deficits, low muscle tone, and postural problems.

Body awareness is the internal map that tells you where body parts are located in space, in which direction you are moving, and what stimulus is touching you, all without visual assistance. In addition, body awareness provides information about how much resistance to use on an object, such as picking up a pencil or closing a door, and how much or little your muscles are stretching. Information about body awareness travels through the spinal cord and into parts of the brain that are not conscious, which is why we are only cognizant of our own body awareness if we actively think about it. Body awareness contributes to both motor planning and posture. If a child has significant body awareness issues, the child may suffer from postural disorder as well as dyspraxia.

Treatment is critical in order to alleviate the challenges of this disorder because unlike sensory modulation disorder, in which symptoms may fluctuate, sensory discrimination deficits remain relatively stable without intervention.[6]

Signs and Symptoms

Poor discrimination and body awareness can exist in one or multiple systems. Below are the possible behavioral indicators of sensory discrimination challenges by sensory system. While the presence of one or two of these symptoms may not indicate a disorder, several of these symptoms collectively could warrant a professional evaluation.

Visual

Visual discrimination is the ability to determine differences between objects and symbols by sight, to discriminate objects in a background, to detect space and form, to remember visual images, and to sustain and shift attention as needed to function.[7] In other words, visual discrimination disorder is an inability to determine or interpret characteristics of visual stimuli. Occupational therapists report that visual discrimination deficits appear in clusters—if a child has one, they typically have several.[8] Visual discrimination is separate from acuity (the ability to see the big "E" on the wall), and the child's acuity should be tested prior to any visual discrimination testing. Below are symptoms common to children with visual discrimination challenges:

- Form constancy tells us that the form is the same despite changing position or form. Children with this difficulty may struggle to discriminate the spatial characteristics of objects and letters (e.g., *b* and *d*), or the child may have difficulty understanding that the square rotated as a diamond is the same shape.
- Visual closure is the skill that enables a person to identify a symbol or object when the entire object is not fully visible. Children with this difficulty may have trouble identifying dot-to-dot designs prior to completion, or finding a toy that is half-buried under other toys.
- Visual-spatial relationships are those that include the ability to discriminate objects in space relative to other objects.
  - Appear clumsy as they move their whole bodies through space or move body parts for tasks, such as reaching or grasping. They do not have visual maps based on experience to tell them how far an object is from their hand. As a result, they may over or under reach for objects.
  - Constantly bump into things, trip and knock things over.
  - Have trouble playing games requiring discrimination of objects in space such as catching, batting a ball, or throwing to a target.
  - Difficulty navigating the way between rooms in a building.
  - Trouble judging relative distances to other people and objects, and may stand too close to people.
  - Trouble with constructional tasks, such as putting Legos or puzzle pieces together. Difficulty with this skill first manifests in preschool when the child is sorting and matching shapes, letters and designs.
  - Difficulty with reading, as this skill is dependent upon the spatial characteristics of letters.

- Problems with writing, as spatial knowledge is necessary for spacing letters, words, punctuation or math signs and the overall organization and legibility.
- Trouble with math as the spatial arrangement of numbers can dictate the number, and the use of signs can determine how to solve the problem.
- Children with deficits in visual attention often disregard one visual field (usually on the left), and they are less aware of stimuli on that side of the paper or space. In older children, they may start writing a paragraph on the left side of the paper, or in the middle of the page, and then taper off the rest of the page down to a point.[9]
- Visual organization indicates that a person is able to make sense of ambiguous, incomplete, jumbled stimuli, or optical illusions.[10] Some of the challenges in children with visual organization deficits may be:
  - Trouble lining up math columns, or finding words on a page.
  - Figure ground problems. This is the ability to locate an object against a busy background.
  - Constructional tasks require visual organization, such as when the child must arrange the pieces in a certain order.
  - Trouble working with worksheets with a lot of information.
  - Problems with projects that require the child to pull information from multiple sources.

Auditory

Auditory discrimination disorder is the inability to interpret characteristics of auditory stimuli. Hearing acuity is the standard hearing test for evaluation of pure sounds of tone, and is not the same as auditory discrimination. Prior to any auditory discrimination testing, a child should undergo a standard hearing test. Auditory discrimination difficulty can be a symptom of auditory processing disorder. Detail on this disorder is located in "Chapter 12: Auditory Dysfunction." Below are some symptoms of auditory discrimination:

- Unable to identify and distinguish different sounds, such as "t" and "p" in "cat" and "cap" or "g" and "k" in "bag" and "back," or differentiating rhyming words such as "bog" and "log." These children may also have difficulty recognizing sounds in a word (phonemes), or the number of sounds in a word (syllables).
- Inability to reconstruct the order of words in a sound or syllable. For instance, the child may write or say ephelant instead of elephant. The child may mix up the order of words in a sentence such as Over there I went, instead of, I went over there.[11]
- Process auditory information slowly, word by word, and thus may miss content in a sentence.
- Do not recognize you calling their name because they cannot discriminate between your voice and ambient sounds.
- Inability to discriminate emotional tone in a speaker's voice. For example, the child may not discern disapproval in their parent's voice, and fail to adjust their behavior accordingly.
- Appear to stop listening at times or be inattentive.
- Incapable of discriminating which sounds in the environment are relevant. For example, the child may tune into the hum of the air conditioner or the clock ticking, but not notice you calling their name.
- Tune the situation out when overwhelmed by sounds (this may look like inattention).
- Trouble following directions and need directions repeated or broken down into steps, or require associated visual cues.

Gustatory

Gustatory discrimination disorder is an inability to determine or interpret characteristics of sensory stimuli tasted.

- Trouble distinguishing between flavors.
- Unable to determine what they are eating or drinking by taste or texture alone.

- Unable to discriminate when a food or drink is too hot or too cold.
- Cannot detect differences in tastes or textures while eating.

Olfactory

Olfactory discrimination disorder is difficulty determining or interpreting the characteristics of sensory stimuli smelled.

- Trouble identifying the source of odors.
- Unable to discern familiar smells, e.g., mother's perfume.
- Problems distinguishing important smells, such as burning.
- Unable to distinguish between two smells.

Tactile

Tactile discrimination disorder is an inability to determine or interpret characteristics of stimuli touched by feel. There are numerous tactile nerves within the mouth and therefore, the list below contains oral symptoms.

- Incapable of identifying differences between shapes and sizes of objects without looking (called stereognosis). For instance, the ability to discriminate between a triangle block and a rectangle block without looking.
- Trouble identifying and replicating shapes drawn on the back of his hand (called graphesthesia).
- Must visually monitor their body parts and movements in space. For example, they may have to watch their feet while they are running.
- Trouble identifying precisely what is touching them or where they have been touched. For instance, if you ask your child to shut their eyes and you touch them on the arm, can they point to the exact spot you touched?
- Unable to recognize objects in their hands (e.g. pencil or fork) and drop them frequently.

- Do not realize a change in surface such as walking from carpet to tile and consequently trip and fall.
- May be difficult for them to sense their extremities due to their inability to "feel" tactile sensations. In other words, they may not feel their hands or feet attached to their body. An inability to position their arms and legs will lead to balance problems.
- May be unable to discern textures, consistency, or the location of food in their mouths, and have difficulty manipulating the food. These children may rebel against food with mixed textures such as textured soups, chunky peanut butter, lasagna, or certain sauces because they cannot discriminate the sensations from textured foods.
- Leave food all over their mouths and drool.
- Overstuff their mouths.
- Lack the precision to chew properly due to poor tactile discrimination. For example, if a young child puts a small piece of a sandwich in her mouth, she may not chew on the sandwich.
- Eat only particular, familiar types of food because they need to visually discriminate what goes in their mouths. For example, they may eat only certain brands of food familiar to them.
- Language delays or articulation problems are common with tactile discrimination disorder.

Proprioception

Proprioception discrimination disorder is an inability to determine or interpret characteristics of sensory stimuli experienced through use of the muscles and joints.

- Exhibit a deficit in judging force. They may be unable to gauge the amount of force—called gradation—when holding pencils or crayons. They may use too much force, breaking them, or too little force, dropping the crayon. They may use too much force when playing with other children or petting animals, appearing to be aggressive.

- Exhibit a deficit in judging timing and distance. Over shoot or under shoot when reaching for objects, writing or playing sports. May stand too close to other people or objects due to an inability to judge distances.
- Suffer from low muscle tone and exhibit poor endurance.
- Lean against everything.

Vestibular

Vestibular discrimination disorder is an inability to determine or interpret characteristics of sensory stimuli experienced through movement of the body through space or against gravity.

- Struggle to determine the direction their bodies are moving with their eyes closed.
- Unable to sense displacement of their bodies' center of gravity, resulting in poor balance. Unable to determine if they are tipping over and losing their sense of balance, and may fall out of their chair. May know that he is falling, but cannot determine which direction and cannot protect himself.
- Struggle to determine the spatial orientation of their heads (upright from upside down). For instance, they do not like to have their hair washed because their heads tip upside down.
- Cannot distinguish small, rapid movements and, as a result, may lack the equilibrium reactions that occur in response to these movements such as when we are standing and shift our body weight.
- Have diminished post rotary nystagmus. Post rotary nystagmus refers to reflexive movements of the eyes after a quick rotational movement (e.g., spinning). If the nystagmus stops too quickly, is irregular, or non-existent, then the child's eye muscles are not getting enough vestibular input.[12] Testing post rotary nystagmus is a quick and easy method to determine vestibular dysfunction. Your child's occupational therapist may count these reflexive

movements after rotation to see in what range they fall to help determine the extent of vestibular dysfunction.

Interoceptive

Interoceptive discrimination disorder is an inability to interpret characteristics of sensory stimuli experienced through our body organs.

- Poorly understood visceral messages often result in toileting accidents, due to low body awareness. Some sensory children can have nighttime enuresis until ten years of age or older because they are not awakened by visceral messages.
- Overresponsive children will run to the bathroom not when their bladders are full, but every time they have a small amount of urine in their bladders, overresponding to the bladder sensation. They may also overrespond to the feeling of bowel sensations.
- Do not sense hunger or thirst. Their visceral organs will be sending messages to the brain that they are hungry or thirsty, but the brain will not be able to make sense of these messages (i.e., discriminate). This often results in meltdowns.
- Unable to determine that they are satiated, resulting in overeating. May drink glass after glass of water without feeling that their thirst has been quenched.
- Cannot differentiate between nausea and hunger sensations.
- Does not detect pain when appropriate. For instance, the child does not respond to bumps, falls, cuts, or scrapes that can present a danger or contact with objects that are too hot or too cold.
- Unable to differentiate hot or cold temperatures.

Prognosis and Treatment

Intervention is imperative for children with discrimination problems and below is a brief overview of interventions.

Auditory Discrimination

Pediatric audiologists provide intervention for auditory discrimination difficulties, and the audiologist may recommend software that will improve auditory discrimination. See "Chapter 12: Auditory Dysfunction" for more information.

Visual Discrimination

Developmental optometrists treat visual discrimination difficulties, often in conjunction with occupational therapists. See "Chapter 11: Visual Dysfunction for more information on developmental optometrists and vision.

Vestibular Discrimination

Intervention for vestibular discrimination challenges will either be done incorporating linear or rotary activities, depending on where the child has trouble processing information—the otoliths or the semicircular canals—in their inner ears. There are five vestibular receptors located in each inner ear—three semicircular canals and two otolith organs.

The otoliths relate to movement in vertical and horizontal gravity, and linear movement activates the otoliths. The semicircular canals sense acceleration and deceleration and are activated by rotary movement. Children who have trouble processing information in the semicircular canals will have problems differentiating rapid or small movements. This affects equilibrium—the ability to make rapid and small movements when we shift our weight to maintain balance. Intervention for children who have trouble processing information through the semicircular canals will focus on rotary or angular movement. This intervention should occur only under the supervision of an occupational therapist as rotary movement can be disorganizing to some children. Your occupational therapist may incorporate frequent starts and stops, as well as changes in speed and direction, as acceleration and deceleration stimulate the semicircular canals. The child will participate in play-based activities incorporating a variety of different head positions while swinging.

Children who have trouble registering information in the otoliths will have trouble determining the spatial orientation of their head, i.e., upright from upside down. Intervention for children with otolith challenges centers around vertical, horizontal, and upside-down movements within the context of meaningful play-based activities.

Proprioceptive Discrimination

Children who have difficulty discriminating information from the muscle receptors will have trouble discriminating body movements (information about the speed, rate, timing, and sequencing of movements), location of body parts in space (where are my feet in space), and difficulty judging the amount of force needed for a task. Occupational therapy may include active resistance against movement, which involves resistance against gravity, such as hanging from the monkey bars or using a squirt gun.

Tactile Discrimination

Activities that provide rich tactile sensation help to improve tactile discrimination. Deep-pressure activities "wake up" the tactile receptors, and commonly used toward this end. Some examples of intervention for tactile discrimination may include brushing or rubbing the skin with various textures, hiding body parts under big cushions, or having the child search for small objects in various mediums such as macaroni, rice, beans, or corn. The ultimate goal when the child is searching for small objects in different mediums is the ability to identify objects of different shapes, sizes, or textures without looking.

Interoceptive Discrimination

Interoceptive discrimination is a by-product of vestibular, proprioceptive, and tactile discrimination difficulties, and improves when treated with sensory integrative techniques.

Intervention for sensory discrimination disorder can improve motor-planning abilities, fine, gross, and oral motor skills, and speech. These improvements can be substantial with consistent therapy and assist the child socially, emotionally, and academically. Below are some strategies parents can employ to assist a child with discrimination difficulties.

Parental Strategies for Discrimination Disorder

Regulation Strategies

Prior to any discrimination strategy intervention, the child needs to be in the calm-alert zone. Therefore, the first step is to provide twenty to thirty minutes of deep-pressure activities prior to implementing any of the discrimination strategies below.

Deep-pressure activities that involve the whole body, such as going down the fireman's pole or crossing the monkey bars at the playground, are beneficial for regulation. Handstands, chair push-ups, arm push-ups, or walks such as the wheelbarrow walk, bear crawl, or crab walk are also great options. If the child is a preschooler, have the child play tug-of-war with you using a sturdy jump rope. Weighted blankets are great for implementing deep pressure as well.

Auditory Discrimination Strategies

Parents can help their child build auditory discrimination skills by playing the following games:

- Play same and different games. You can say, I am going to say two words, and you tell me if they are the same or different. Then it will be your turn to try, and trick me. Commercial software is also available that has auditory discrimination built into the games (e.g. earobics).
- Have your child listen to sounds of objects around your house with his eyes closed, and guess the name of the object. You can

ring a bell, blow a whistle, shake beans placed in a jar, shut a book, shake a half empty water bottle, bounce a ball, etc.

- Sound Bingo. Listening to sounds and playing BINGO with pictures of sounds. You can find a variety of downloadable sound bingo games at teachers pay teachers website http://www.teacherspayteachers.com/Browse/Search:sound%20bingo
- Sound Walk. Drawing pictures or writing the sounds down heard on a walk.
- Hyperdash. The electronic announcer calls out commands the child must follow.
- Hullabuloo. Another game with an electronic announcer dispensing commands for the child to follow.

Visual Discrimination Strategies

Parents can help their child build visual discrimination skills by utilizing the following home strategies:

- Play the category game. In this game, you select a category that is age-appropriate for your child. Your child then looks around the environment and tries to locate things that fit the category.
- Play I-Spy in the environment for specific objects.
- Use hidden picture books.
- Use Lego Books.
- There are inexpensive commercial products available to help children with visual discrimination skills at http://yourtherapysource. com/visualperceptual.html This website has visual discrimination puzzles, patterns, perceptual games, activities and other options that you can download.

Vestibular Discrimination Strategies

The vestibular system helps you determine where your head is in space relative to gravity, and tells your body how to shift your weight when your center of gravity changes. Vestibular activities stimulate the vestibular organs inside the inner ears, and help the left and right hemispheres communicate. In turn, this promotes body awareness and coordination.

Your occupational therapist will determine whether your child is over- or underregistering movement and subsequently provide a home program based upon your child's unique profile. In addition, here are some home strategies your occupational therapist may recommend:

- If your child has a linear deficit, your child's occupational therapist may recommend your child swing on a linear swing.
- If your child has a rotational deficit, your child's occupational therapist may recommend that your child swing from a single suspended point like a tire swing.
- Start and Stop swing games trigger the hair cells during acceleration and deceleration in the semicircular canals (these canals are also activated by rotary movement).[13] Start and stop swing games are excellent for the child who becomes disorganized by rotary swinging and enables the child to receive vestibular input in all planes by incorporating start and stop games into linear swinging. For example, have the child swing 10 times, stop and throw a stuffed animal or beanbag to you and then swing another 10 times.

Proprioceptive Discrimination Strategies

Proprioceptors give us information about how hard our muscles have to contract to pick up a ball. Proprioceptive discrimination disorder is a condition in which the child cannot determine the appropriate amount of force to use when picking up or putting down objects, shutting doors, holding hands, petting an animal, throwing a ball, or roughhousing with a friend. These children cannot grade the proper amount of force and will use either too little or too much force. In addition, these children have trouble discriminating the spatial orientation of their body parts, (where their body parts are located at any moment), and body movements (information about the speed, rate, timing, and sequencing of movements).

Some home strategies for helping your child develop proprioceptive discrimination are:

- Any whole body movement against resistance such as monkey bars, diving for objects at the bottom of the pool, chair push-ups, wall push-ups, wheelbarrow walks, and animal walks helps the child to register where they are in space.
- Play Wack-a-Mole Tower. A miniature version of the carnival game, your child can grab the mallet and wack the mole that shoots up the tower.
- Marching games at different paces helps the child discriminate movement through space, force required to march at different paces, and timing of the movements.
- Writing on tin-foiled covered foam helps a child who presses too hard on their pencil to use less pressure.
- Target games such as beanbag toss help the child to use feed-back to alter his use of force to hit the target.
- Play Simon Says or Mother May I? performing unusual novel body movements, as this will assist the child to register proprioceptive sensations, resulting in increased discrimination.

Tactile Discrimination Strategies

Prior to having your child participate in tactile discrimination activities, occupational therapists recommend waking up the tactile nerve endings with tactile stimulation and then proceeding with tactile discrimination activities.

- Tactile stimulation (wake up the tactile nerve endings first)
  - Brush or rub the skin with various textures such as bumpy and rough (corduroy, aluminum foil crinkled up, bumpy balls, beaded bracelets, seam of a baseball), smooth (cotton balls, apple, satin, fuzzy hat or blanket, paint or surgical brushes), or grainy (sand, sugar, salt).
  - Tactile Discs is a great game for tactile and visual discrimination. Tactile discs consist of a group of ten discs constructed from soft synthetic rubber with different surface structures

and colors. This game brings the children's senses alive by allowing them to touch the discs with hands and feet. The discs are adjustable to suit age and functionality levels.

- Deep-pressure massages are great for activating the tactile receptors.
- Have the child play in shaving cream, finger paint, and other textures.
- Use a vibrating toothbrush for increasing tactile discrimination within the mouth prior to eating and speech therapy. Nook brushes are great for brushing teeth.

- Tactile discrimination (differentiating between various textures, sizes, shapes, or location of body parts).

  Children with tactile discrimination disorder typically have difficulty determining what they touch by feel (stereognosis); they must see it. This inability to feel what they cannot see extend to their extremities, as in some cases these children may not be able to detect that their arms and legs are attached to their bodies. The child must monitor them visually to understand that they are attached body parts, and to determine their location in space. Below are several things that parents can do with their kids to help improve tactile discrimination. Check with your child's occupational therapist to see which of the strategies would best fit your child's unique profile or to get specific activities customized for your child.

- Bury the child's extremities in the sand; the resistance from the sand helps the child to "feel" his arms and legs. Moving the arms and legs in and out of sight against the resistance of the sand helps the child locate her extremities. If you do not have a sandbox or beach near you, use cushions instead.

- Bury small objects of various shapes and textures such as animals in rice, beans, or corn and have the child search for them. Initially, focus solely on having the child locate the animals; eventually ask the child to find and identify what he has found without looking.

- Write the child's name (or a letter in the alphabet) on his back in shaving cream, and then have the child reproduce what you wrote in shaving cream on the floor. If the child complains, "How am I supposed to do this if I can't see it?" tell him to close his eyes and try to feel it.
- Hide a ball and vibrating toy underneath something. Have the child discriminate between the ball and vibrating toy without the benefit of vision.
- Put several objects in a pillowcase and blindfold your child (or have him close his eyes). Have your child stick his hand in the pillowcase and pick up an object, and try to guess the identity of the object.
- Make some cards with the words smooth, rough, bumpy, sticky, etc. and acquire items that match these descriptions. Have your child sort and match the cards to the experience.
- Get different sizes of balls and have the child discriminate between larger and smaller balls (e.g., tennis balls and Koosh Balls) without looking first. Give meaning to the task by having the child take smaller Koosh balls, squeeze them, and make pretend lemonade.
- Tactile Discs is a great game for tactile and visual discrimination. This game consists of a group of ten discs constructed from soft synthetic rubber with different surface structures and colors.
- The child can be blindfolded and asked to identify or discriminate what texture he is touching

Interoceptive Discrimination Strategies

Some of the things that interoceptive dysfunction may affect in a child are potty training, diet, and sleep. The strategies set forth in "Chapter 6: Internal Regulation" will be helpful in assisting the child with interoceptive dysfunction.

Summary

It is important to understand how sensory discrimination disorder affects children so that you can identify situations in your child's life that are sensory-based and not behavioral based. The more clearly you can identify sensory-based behaviors, the more effective targeted interventions will be to minimize and eradicate your child's challenging behaviors.

Six

Internal Regulation

Five-year-old Riley was building a snowman out in her front yard. It was a cold blustery day, and the snow was coming down heavy. Riley's mother, several yards away, tries to fix the snow blower that had just come to a sudden halt. When Riley's mother repaired the snow blower, she turned to check on Riley. Riley had taken off her gloves, hat, scarf and coat, and was busy placing buttons on her snowman for eyes. "What do you think mommy?"

This is one example of a typical underresponsive child who is unable to "feel" the temperature outdoors. Temperature modulation is but one of several physiological processes, governed by the little-known interoceptive sense, within the human body. The American Heritage Medical Dictionary defines the interoceptive system as the sense that relates to the "sensory nerve cells innervating the viscera (thoracic, abdominal, pelvic organs, and cardiovascular system), their sensory end organs, or the information they convey to the spinal cord and the brain." In other words, interoception is the sense that communicates to the brain what is going on within the body. In the brain, interoception combines with the vestibular (movement), proprioceptive (muscles and joints), tactile (touch), and visual senses to complete the whole picture of the human body. Interoception includes input from the following:

- bowel and bladder
- digestion
- thirst and hunger
- heart rate and respiration
- pain, temperature and itch
- arousal state and mood
- sleep

When sensory integration is adequate and well modulated, these autonomic sensations function largely undetected and unnoticed by most people. In children with SPD, the body's interoceptive sense can be dysfunctional, resulting in internal distress and behavioral disorganization, affecting some, or all, of the autonomic functions of the body. This dysfunction may result in one or more of the three SPD types in the interoceptive sense: modulation difficulties, motor-based problems, and discrimination deficits.

Sensory modulation disorder (SMD) is a problem with turning sensory messages into regulated behaviors that match the nature and intensity of the sensory information. This includes sensory overresponsive and sensory underresponsive behaviors. Children who are underresponsive to interoception may not feel or respond to these sensations appropriately, quickly enough, or at all. Conversely, they may overrespond to internal feelings that are uncomfortable or painful. Children with sensory modulation problems can have difficulty with the following:

- Becoming too hot or too cold relative to peers in the same setting. Difficulty tolerating temperature swings, such as transitioning between winter and summer, going from air conditioning to outdoor heat, or walking from a heated home to cold outdoors. May prefer foods and bath water too cold or unusually hot.
- Difficulty modulating pain responses resulting in a child's inability to register pain until it is extreme or an overregistration of pain to an innocuous bruise or cut.

- Difficulty controlling respiration resulting in respiration that is too fast or too slow relative to the demands imposed upon it.
- Trouble regulating heart rate resulting in an erratic heart rate that increases or decreases too quickly based on the loads imposed upon it.
- Modulating hunger and thirst. The child may always be hungry or thirsty, never hungry and thirsty, or oscillate back and forth.
- Adjusting state of arousal and mood, which may result in unpredictable arousal states that the child cannot control (e.g., shifting from hyperactive to lethargic, or angry to happy in short periods of time, perhaps without visible cause).
- Modulating bladder and bowel sensations. Bladder or bowel sensations in overresponsive children may be painful, causing them to withhold elimination, or they may use the bathroom too frequently, responding to the slightest sensations. Underresponsive children need significant sensation to feel that their bladder or bowel is full, resulting in toileting accidents when the child recognizes sensations too late. In addition, these children may not feel that their diaper is wet or full.

Sensory-based motor disorder (SBMD) is a problem with balancing, moving, performing unfamiliar tasks or a combination of these. Children with sensory-based motor problems can have difficulty with the following:

- Sequencing through the steps to go to the bathroom.
- Sitting on the toilet. Low muscle tone, postural instability and poor balance can result in fear of sitting on the toilet.
- Producing a bowel movement, because it is painful. Children with low muscle tone are especially prone to constipation and a fear of the bathroom because of abnormal colon contractions.

Sensory discrimination disorder (SDD) is a problem with sensing similarities and differences between sensations and making sense of the basic stimuli detected. Children with discrimination disorder will have trouble interpreting their own body signals. People with sensory discrimination problems can have difficulty with the following:

- Recognizing bowel and bladder sensations, resulting in toileting accidents. These children will "feel" the sensations but they cannot make sense of them.
- Determining whether they are hungry or thirsty.
- Understanding when they are feeling warm or cold.

The difficulties delineated above can manifest in bodily functions such as potty training, eating, temperature and respiratory control and sleep. Below is detailed information on each of these functions.

Potty Training

The decision to initiate potty training should not be made until child and parent are both ready. Parents need to understand the psychological and physiological signs of a ready child, as well as consider other factors such as the age of the child, expense of diapers, peer pressure, and preparation for preschool.

In order for a child to cooperate in the potty training process, he must be able to control his sphincter muscles, postpone the urge to defecate, and give a signal he needs to go to the bathroom or get there on his own volition. *Typical* children will exhibit curiosity about potty training between the ages of 18 and 24 months, but some children are not ready until they are 30 months old.[1] However, a child's chronological age is far less important than his developmental age or physiological readiness.

A child's chronological age will often mislead parents into thinking he should be ready, but he will not be successful until his neurological system is mature. Potty training is a variable process, with different ages of completion due to biologic and physiologic reasons in a special needs child. Some sensory children—especially those with somatodyspraxia—do not get reliable feedback from their sensory receptors, resulting in a lack of body awareness. Therefore, these children do not recognize the visceral sensation of their bladder and bowel. Delays will present in those sensory children with the greatest body awareness challenges, not all sensory children.

Well-intentioned family members, friends, day-care providers, or pediatricians often hound parents in respect to potty training their children. These "helpful" people usually do not understand the impacts of SPD, and the resulting neurological reasons that sensory children may not be ready to potty train. They may induce guilt or feelings of parental failure if these children are not potty-trained parallel to peers. These feelings of parental failure may translate into parental pressure on the child, which may result in big behavioral challenges such as meltdowns, defiance, and aggressive behavior. Motivation by peer pressure (whether on you or your child) is an ineffectual method of potty training that can actually delay this developmental milestone even further.

The Impact of Sensory Processing Disorder on Potty Training

In order to understand when a child with SPD is ready for the potty training process, we must first understand the physiological problems these children face from their neurological systems. Often, sensory children have interoceptive (internal) sensory receptors that do not register sensory information or, if registered, the information does not transmit appropriately within the neurological system. The missing sensory information results in overresponsiveness, underresponsiveness, motor, or discrimination problems. Therefore, some sensory children do not receive adequate sensory information from their visceral organs in order to participate in effective potty training. Inefficient sensory processing may affect the sensory child in the following ways:

- The child may have increased awareness of bowel movements and related discomfort due to tactile defensiveness and may fear bowel movements because it is painful. Tactile defensiveness may also contribute to uncomfortable feelings sitting on the toilet seat or rubbing toilet paper on the skin after eliminating. For tactile-defensive children, a padded toilet seat and flushable wipes are usually preferred as they are more comfortable to the child's skin.

- An underresponsive child may not feel or discriminate when his bladder or bowel is full. By the time the child gets a signal from her bladder, and goes running to the bathroom, it may be too late. If the child does not receive any signals at all, her body will perform the task automatically. Some underresponsive children may never feel distressed by a dirty or wet diaper.

- Poor fine motor skills and inadequate body coordination---due to low muscle tone, postural deficits and balance challenges---may manifest in an inability to get their clothes on and off, and coordinate their muscles to climb onto and sit on the toilet. Inadequate trunk muscle stability may render it difficult for the child to sit on a toilet without handrails for assistance. As a result, boys with this problem may have a harder time sitting to pee and prefer to pee standing up. Children who suffer from a form of sensory modulation disorder, called gravitational insecurity, may be resistant to sitting on the potty due to a fear of their feet leaving the ground. If a child suffers from any of these challenges, a potty chair may be a better choice over the use of a regular toilet.

- The child may overrespond to the smell of bowel movements and gag or be hypersensitive to the sound of the flushing toilet, which will lead to avoidance or fear.

- Many children with SPD suffer from transition problems and everyday transitions may result in significant anxiety. Therefore, avoid potty training during major transitions such as separation/divorce, moving, new daycare/school, new relationships, etc.

- Many children with SPD prefer white foods such as potatoes, white rice, white pasta, white bread, and saltine crackers[2]. These binding foods lack fiber, and children who primarily eat them will need a lot of water. Lack of fiber will result in constipation, with hard stools that are painful for the child to eliminate, resulting in a fear of going on the potty. Since many children with SPD will not eat fruits or vegetables, they may need over-the-counter fiber supplements introduced into their diet; please check with your pediatrician for recommendations.

Signs of Child Readiness

Because of the interoceptive challenges that sensory children face, it is critical that parents wait until the psychological and physiological signs of readiness delineated below are evident in their child prior to starting the potty training process. A child has physiological and psychological readiness for potty training if he:

- Stays dry for at least two hours at a time (including nap times).
- Shows awareness that he is eliminating. Often you can recognize signs that your child is eliminating, such as his facial countenance, his designated spot for eliminating, and verbal expressions. When these signs are evident, match this up with his expression of awareness. If he is not yet expressing awareness, label what is happening for your child when you see the signs of elimination.
- Can signal basic toileting needs through either words or gestures.
- Notices or becomes distressed by having a wet or soiled diaper, and asks to have his wet or dirty diaper changed.
- Has enough coordination to walk to the bathroom.
- Can get on the toilet, sit, and get off the toilet independently or with minimal assistance.
- Is able to pull his pants up and down by himself. Sweatpants are great for children with motor problems. You can also purchase soft pants designed to look like jeans or khakis from sites such as http://www.softclothing.net/html.
- Can follow simple instructions or commands.

- Exhibits regular, well-formed, and predictable bowel movements.
- Able to urinate a significant amount at one time as opposed to trickling throughout the day.
- Can imitate behavior.
- Can answer "why" questions (usually by age three for typical children), and can understand why we use the toilet and the positive benefits of being trained.

It is only after a child is exhibiting most or all of these signs *and* you are ready to help your child through this process, that you will start preparing him for the big task of potty training. If your child has an accident, do not respond in a punitive fashion. Realize these children cannot interpret their own internal signals properly due to a neurological disorder; it is literally out of their control.

Some sensory children who have successfully completed potty training may continue to have bed-wetting problems for years afterward. This results from their inability to feel the sensation when they are sleeping. If bed-wetting continues into the school-age years, consult your occupational therapist as to whether an appointment with an urologist could be helpful. Your occupational therapist will be able to determine if your child has enough body awareness to engage in an alarm system successfully. If so, the doctor will rule out any medical source of the problem and recommend an alarm. The alarm will go off at the first dribble of urine, waking your child so that she can go to the bathroom. In severe cases, the urologist may prescribe medication.

Avoid pressuring, forcing, or punishing your child if the potty-training process is not yielding results. In addition, do not chastise, make light of, shame, or instill fear in your child. If the training process is unsuccessful, take a break for a couple of weeks and reintroduce it slowly. Never engage in power struggles over potty training with your child.

Be patient, unflappable, and go the distance. Avoid pressure, power struggles, anxiety about going to the potty, and shame about failure. Let your understanding of the challenges facing special needs children guide you through the training efforts. Most importantly, stick to his timing and pace, not yours.

Nutrition

Nutrition is essential for optimal brain function. Peak brain performance maximizes a child's therapy. Below is a limited discussion of the dietary considerations of SPD.

Modulation Challenges

Children with modulation problems will either overrespond or underrespond to touch, temperature, and texture of food. Some children will fluctuate and experience several over- and underresponsive behaviors as their regulatory states shift over time.

Children who are underresponsive to arousal may demand to eat their food very hot, or very cold. Underresponsive children may insist on eating food frozen, as the extreme temperature helps them to "feel" the food in their mouth. As a result, these children often love frozen treats such as popsicles. Conversely, they may demand to eat their food very hot, which is not feasible due to the risk of burning their mouths. They usually prefer strong flavors such as spicy, salty, or sour because they can only sense flavor when it is extreme. A significant amount of sensation may be required to register it; therefore, hunger and thirst sensations might be ignored until they become overwhelming, resulting in meltdowns. These children may calm immediately when presented with food, or they may need parental help with calming prior to eating.

Overresponsive children experience taste sensations that typical children would find innocuous or pleasant, as distressing or painful. They may eat limited flavors and demand bland foods such as the "white foods" of saltine crackers, white rice, white bread, and plain pasta. Overresponsive children may react to room temperature food and drink as if it were boiling hot. Toothpaste can also be a struggle with SOR children as the taste may burn their mouths. Many sensory defensive children will demand to use the milder training gel even when no longer age appropriate.

Have you ever wondered why you cannot taste food when you have a head cold, or the flu? The senses of taste, smell, touch (texture) and interoception (temperature and pain) are interrelated, and without these senses, a person would be unable to fully experience flavor and enjoy food. Taste is a limited sense on its own, including only the direct tastes of sweet, sour, salty, bitter, and umami (or savory). What most people think of as taste is actually flavor. Flavor is an integration of the taste, smell, touch (texture), and interoceptive (temperature and pain) receptors in the brain. If any of these senses are functioning atypically, then a person's ability to experience flavor is compromised. Therefore, if a child's sense of smell is compromised, this can be a contributing factor to mealtime battles and picky eating.

A poor sense of smell in underresponsive children can make food seem unappealing, since they experience flavor in only one dimension, instead of many. Some children may like strongly scented food, as intense sensation is required to register the smell. These children will not notice noxious or rancid smells that bother other people.

Overresponsive children will be sensitive and offended by smells others do not tend to notice, such as perfumes, bathroom odors, personal hygiene smells, cooking smells, or restaurant smells. Specific smells may result in rejection of certain foods or make the sensory child gag or feel nauseated. Refusal to play with particular children or rejection of certain adults due to their smell is common with the SOR child. School cafeterias can present a significant challenge for sensory children due to the smells of food, garbage, and other kids in the room.

Discrimination Challenges

The somatosensory (tactile and proprioceptive) system in the mouth is responsible for eating (chewing and biting), nonspeech movements (such as smacking the lips, sticking out the tongue or chewing food), sucking through a straw, feeding from a bottle or nipple, and speech. Children with discrimination problems may be unable to detect when their hunger or thirst has been satiated, or conversely, when they are hungry or thirsty.

Unlike children with modulation disorder, who need more or less sensations to feel hunger or thirst, these children cannot make sense (discriminate) of the hunger or thirst sensations felt.

Infants with tactile discrimination disorder often suffer from low muscle tone making it difficult to suck the nipple, resulting in fatigue. Drawing the nipple into the mouth may also make the infant gag. Older children may have an overreactive gag reflex, and become nauseated frequently.

Tactile discrimination disorder may render the child unable to move the muscles of his face or mouth accurately (including the tongue), in order to manipulate food in his mouth. Underresponsiveness to somatosensory input may be comparable to the numb feeling after receiving an injection of local anesthesia at the dentist. Envision eating when your mouth is numb with difficulty moving your tongue. These children often only eat certain textures of food. One possible explanation could be based on human instinct—the fear of obstructed breathing due to a lack of sensory awareness and oral motor control. When textures or other qualities differ, it may leave them feeling defenseless.[3]

When children have trouble manipulating food in their mouth, they will often eat only certain textures and consistencies of foods, and refuse to try anything new or different. Foods may seem unappetizingly bland because they may not taste food in their mouths. They may avoid typical textures such as chewy or dry foods, and always demand food of similar texture. They may avoid, spit out, or gag on food with combined textures, such as chunky peanut butter, stir-fry, lasagna, soup, or foods that transition from one texture to another while eaten (such as oranges). The child may be unable to differentiate between tastes, such as whether something is a little sweet or very sweet. Young children may drool and overstuff their mouths, never perceiving when their mouth is full. These sensory problems preclude these children from monitoring what their tongues are doing. Therefore, children with tactile discrimination disorder can only determine what food they are eating by looking at the food. As a result, the child may often visually inspect food, and only eat foods that are similar in size, texture, or color.[4] Children with tactile discrimination disorder can sometimes manifest eating disorders and, in extreme cases, manifest a condition called failure to thrive. Failure to thrive refers to children whose current weight, or rate of weight gain, is much lower than that of other children of similar age and gender.

Therapeutically, a child with tactile discrimination disorder may participate in an oral-motor and graded feeding program to assist with body awareness and diet. Oral-motor programs are programs that provide sensory input to the mouth in the form of vibration, deep-touch pressure, and proprioceptive input. This input is especially helpful when applied prior to eating or speech-language therapy. An oral-motor program occurs for several weeks prior to the introduction of a graded feeding program. In a graded feeding program, new foods are introduced gradually using various techniques to phase in new tastes and textures.

Other Nutrition Concerns

Food allergies can interfere with brain performance. The most common allergies in children are casein (a protein found in cow's milk), eggs, fish, peanuts, shellfish, soy, tree nuts, and gluten (found in wheat, barley, rye, and triticale). When a food allergy is present, the immune system becomes overly reactive to a protein in the food eaten. As a result, symptoms often include itching, swelling, diarrhea, wheezing or a life-threatening reaction called anaphylaxis.[5]

Many parents confuse food allergy with food intolerance. When a child has food intolerance, they have difficulty digesting a particular food. Food intolerance typically involves the gastrointestinal tract, causing uncomfortable symptoms like abdominal pain, nausea, vomiting and diarrhea, but there is no risk of anaphylaxis, as food intolerance does not elicit the immune system response.[6] If you suspect that your child has a food intolerance, journaling the food eaten, time of day, how much food was eaten, the child's reaction and how long the reaction lasted will be helpful information to take to the doctor. Discuss next steps with your child's doctor.

Test for environmental allergies if your child is symptomatic as they can negatively influence your child's diet and behavior. Chronically congested children will have an inhibited ability to smell and taste their food, restricting what and how much they will eat.

Researchers have found that many children with dyslexia, dyspraxia, ADHD, autism and learning difficulties are deficient in omega-3 fatty acids and/or the nutrients (vitamins and probiotics) needed to utilize them properly.[7abc]   Therefore, it is advisable to get any child with dyspraxia tested for essential fatty acid deficiencies and consult with your child's pediatrician on any supplementation. According to researchers, preliminary studies with omega-3 fatty acids may offer a complementary approach to standard treatments. These studies with omega-3 supplementation (particularly EPA) of deficient children noted improvements in working memory, attention, and learning.[8] However, large-scale studies are required to confirm these results.

If your child's pediatrician recommends supplementation, it is important to note that fish-oil supplements vary widely in both their composition and quality. Fish-oil supplements should be purity certified by the manufacturer to be free of mercury, PCBs, and dioxins. The quality of fish oil supplements is destroyed by exposure to light, heat, and air, so the packaging and storage conditions should minimize any such exposure, and consumers should abide by the expiration dates clearly marked on the container. Vitamins and minerals are necessary to assist in the conversion process of essential fatty acids.[9] Consult your pediatrician and dietician for guidance on how to choose a vitamin for your child.

Temperature and Pain

Some children with modulation disorder are underresponsive to temperatures, and cannot feel excessive heat or cold outdoors. Often, these children may refuse to wear a coat, hat, or gloves in freezing weather. Parents need to ensure that these children dress warmly, as underresponsive children will insist on going out into inclement weather with minimal clothes. Other children may eventually tune into the outdoor weather. For these children, carrying back-up clothing when they register the weather is essential. For example, "Oh, your fingers and hands are getting cold?" Here are some mittens. Provide alerting input for thirty minutes to alter their arousal level prior to going out, as this can help them register the weather. Examples of alerting activities include swinging on a rotary swing, singing up-tempo songs, spinning in a swivel chair, and jumping on a safety-netted trampoline.

Both underresponsive and overresponsive children may have problems with overheating. The underresponsive child may overheat because their interoceptive system does not detect the sensation of overheating. Overresponsive children may easily overheat when not in excessively hot environments, or react to fall weather as if it were arctic cold. These children have a high threshold for sensations, meaning that minimal sensation is required to reach that optimum level, and typical sensations land them in the overresponsive window. Difficulty going from one extreme to another, as when experiencing the change of seasons, going from air conditioning to outside heat, or stepping outside from a heated home to a cold climate is common. Bath water may also be challenging as the child demands water that is too hot or too cold.

Underresponsive sensory children may be unable to register pain appropriately. These children may touch hot surfaces or objects, such as a stove or light bulb, and not register the pain until it is a third-degree burn. Overresponsive children may register slight bruises as life-threatening injuries, screaming and crying as they overrespond to basic bumps, bruises, and cuts.

Heart Rate and Respiration

The sensory child's respiration rate and heart rate may run too fast or too slow, or the child may be unable to switch back and forth easily to meet the situational demands of the activity. The child's respiration and heart rate may take longer than expected to slow down during, or after, exertion or fear.

For children who are hypersensitive to interoceptive input, a pounding heartbeat might be overly painful or inspire fear. Conversely, underresponsive children may rarely feel themselves breathing or their hearts beating.

Sleep

Sensory processing disorder may interrupt a child's sleep cycle. Children with SPD may have trouble falling asleep, staying asleep, waking up in the morning, or getting enough deep sleep. Below are the most common factors that affect a sensory child's sleep. Parental strategies associated with each of the factors are in "Chapter 9: Transitions."

- Get enough sleep. If your child does not get all the sleep he needs, he may seem either drowsy or hyperalert. If either state persists, the result is a moody child with hard-to-control behavior. When babies or children miss the sleep they need, the fatigue causes the release of chemicals in the body. These chemicals directly affect their behavior and interfere with maintaining a calm wakeful state or sleep. Loss of sleep produces central nervous system hyperarousal.
- Sensory defensiveness. Children with hypersensitivities (sensory defensiveness) to touch and sound may experience sleep problems. Sensitivity to the feel of the bed sheet or pajamas on their body interferes with the capability to settle into the contented and relaxed state that is required for sleep. Hypersensitivities to sound can also make falling and staying asleep challenging. The slightest noise may awaken them or reduce sleep quality; this problem compounds in a noisy household. As babies, children with SOR (sensory overresponsivity) will appear colicky, irritable, and fussy, with crying bouts that can last up to several hours. Parents often seek answers from their pediatrician who eliminates acid reflux and food allergies as causal. The doctor may then be at a loss to explain

or identify what is making the child uncomfortable not realizing misinterpretation of sensory signals is to blame.

- Movement regulation. Daytime activities affect a child's ability to sleep. The frenetic, unstructured movement of the sensory craving child often results in a hyperarousal state, making settling down for sleep problematic.

- Low arousal levels. The nervous system of passive underresponders may be in such a state of low arousal in the morning that it is difficult to rouse them. These children may require loud music, clapping, bright lighting, and massage to help get them moving in the morning.

- Separation problems. Some sensory children struggle with falling and staying asleep because of problems related to separation. Problems separating from the caregiver have many potential causes, but in children with SPD, separation problems can exist due to the overwhelming sense of loss that results from unmodulated emotions. The sense of loss when separating from a caregiver magnifies exponentially in these children.

- Nightmares. Unmodulated emotions may give rise to frequent nightmares in sensory children. It is common for a sensory child to wake up during the night, get up, and go into the parent's bedroom. Unmodulated emotions may also lead into irrational fears, such as monsters under the bed or in the closet, insects, or thunderstorms. In sensory children, these fears will persist with greater frequency and extended periods of time when they are no longer age appropriate. Some sensory children will experience panic attacks when these fears arise.

Summary

It is important to understand how SPD affects your child's internal regulation processes. Many parents perceive their children's picky eating, potty training refusals, or unwillingness to go to bed as defiant behavior. Once parents gain an understanding of the impact that inadequate sensory information can have on these internal systems, they can employ strategies to eliminate power struggles. Dealing with these internal problems in an empathic way will maintain a loving emotional connection with your child, and promote coregulation resulting in a positive family dynamic.

Seven

Sensory Diet

"Sensory diet" is a term coined by Patricia Wilbarger, an occupational therapist, clinical psychologist, and leading expert in the area of sensory defensiveness. A sensory diet is an assembly of sensory-related activities made available to a child who exhibits difficulty modulating and discriminating sensory input. Modulation and discrimination challenges often result in emotional and behavioral problems. By providing sensory input needed at regular and appropriate intervals throughout a child's day, he can better register or process information from his environment resulting in improved self-regulation. In turn, this enables the child to eventually participate independently in meaningful everyday activities.

If possible, build in a task while the child is participating in a sensory activity. For example, have them swing high ten times, then stop at the bottom and pick up a stuffed animal or other object, and throw it into a hula-hoop or to you. This will help the child to integrate the sensations as well as improve her self-regulation. Read more about the difference between sensory stimulation and sensory integration in Chapter 13: Diagnosis and Treatment.

A sensory diet program is more reflective of a sensory lifestyle as the family must set up the contexts for the child to regulate their sensory systems within the family's overall lifestyle. Below are some core concepts of sensory diets.

Core Concepts of Sensory Programs

- Sensory activities should be structured and playful.
- Parents are an invaluable part of the success of the sensory diet program. It is always important to use your relationship with your child to engage and soothe him.
- A new activity creates a stronger response because children adapt to familiar ones. Use a good variety of new activities in your child's sensory diet.
- Tailor sensory diets to meet the individual needs of the child.
- Children will have varied reactions to sensory input. Some children may be fearful or withdraw, while others find sensory-stimulating activities enjoyable. Respect your child's response to sensory input, and do not force a child who is fearful or distressed to participate.

Every child with SPD has a unique profile. As a result, not all children require the same type of sensory diet. Some children may require a structured sensory diet implemented every two hours throughout the day, while other children may require a sensory diet designed around the child's most challenging situations. The content of the sensory diet will also depend on your child's sensory characteristics. Some children need alerting activities; others need calming activities. Many other options are available, and your child's occupational therapist will choose those that fit your child's distinct profile. If your child's occupational therapist recommends a sensory diet implemented throughout the day, try incorporating a variety of these into everyday activities. The activities should fit the child's preferences, motivation, reactions, and your family's everyday life routines.

Monitor your child's reaction to each activity, and do not proceed with activities that seem to cause distress or dysregulation. Watch for signs that your child is becoming unsafe, overly silly, or extremely hyperactive. Also, watch for signs of sensation overload such as sudden yawning, hiccoughing, burping, or changes in skin color. Do not confuse these symptoms with those of emotional overload delineated in "Chapter 8: Aggression, Meltdowns, and Defiant Behavior." At the first sign of over-stimulation in your child, drop your voice to a softer, slower tone and explain she is going to have three more turns, jumps, or bounces in the current activity, and play a fun game afterward. Then have her count to ten before each turn, jump, or bounce. Next, implement a deep-pressure game that your child loves, e.g., the hot dog game.

Occupational therapists work with children to raise awareness of their arousal states, with the long-term goal of a self-initiated sensory activity. However, most sensory children require parental cuing for an extended period before they are competent to initiate self-regulation. Two programs utilized to teach children, parents, teachers, and therapists self-intervention strategies are the Alert Program detailed in the book *How Does Your Engine Run? ® A Leader's Guide to the Alert Program® for Self-Regulation* and *The Zones of Regulation: A Curriculum Designed to Foster Self-Regulation and Emotional Control*. Both programs help students to choose appropriate sensory strategies to change or maintain states of alertness. The difference between the two is that *The Zones of Regulation* incorporates cognitive behavioral strategies designed to elicit flexible thinking. Your occupational therapist will recommend the program that best fits your child's needs.

Below is information on each type of activity to help you select those that meet your child's situational needs:

Auditory

Children who are hypersensitive to sounds can benefit from the following accommodations:

- Smaller classroom placement with less noise.
- Quiet, low-stimulation environment to eat lunch during school.
- Preferential seating in front of the classroom near the teacher (away from the back of the room, open window or hallway)

- Noise-reducing headphones. You can locate inexpensive child-sized headphones at local hunting stores or online. Additionally, the deep pressure of the headphones is beneficial in calming the child.
- Try Putty Buddies Floating Silicone Ear Plugs for swimming or bathing. Developed by an ear, nose, and throat physician to prevent swimmer's ear and assist kids with ear tubes, they can also keep water and noise at bay during visits to loud public pools. Putty Buddies' bright colors and floating nature make them easy to find should they pop out in the pool. If your child will tolerate it, pair Putty Buddies with an Ear Band-It swimming headband to keep Putty Buddies in, and filter additional noise. Both are available at http://earbandit.com.

Vestibular

The vestibular receptors are located in the inner ear. Any type of movement will stimulate these receptors, and the effects will last between 4-8 hours with at least fifteen minutes of movement.[1] The type of movement will influence the child's arousal level differently.

- The otolith organs in the inner ear register linear movement, such as a typical swing at a playground. This movement is calming to the nervous system, as stimulation of the otoliths produces calmness, relaxation, and lowered tone.[2] Slow, rhythmic swinging is the strongest of any sensation, and the effect lasts the longest in the brain (between four and eight hours with just fifteen minutes of swinging). Slow, rhythmic swinging from a single suspended point—a cocoon swing—provides the strongest vestibular input. Of course, two suspension swings such as a typical playground or porch swing will also provide effective vestibular input. Your sensory child will benefit greatly from at least two fifteen-minute swinging sessions a day, one first thing in the morning and the second in the afternoon.

- The semicircular canals in the inner ear register rotary movement such as a tire swing. Stimulation of the semicircular canals produces excitation; arousal and increased tone.[3] Rotary movement can be helpful with the passive underresponder, who needs highly alerting activities. However, SOR children, or sensory-craving children who shift into overresponsiveness quickly, should avoid rotary activities unless under the direct supervision of an occupational therapist.
- Flexion, disc swings, gliders, and rocking chairs are great options for sensory children.
- Movement activities such as Wii or Xbox Kinect can be helpful with the sensory underresponder who needs alerting activities to "wake up" their nervous system.[4]
- Jumping combines vestibular and proprioceptive calming inputs, and indoor mini-trampolines and outdoor safety-netted trampolines are wonderful for children with sensory or attention issues.
- If you have a child who constantly inverts into a chair or on the ground (stands on head and is upside down), this is a manifestation of a need for intense vestibular movement. Closed-eye activities would benefit these children, as closing the eyes isolates the vestibular system and will provide more intense input. You can have the child participate in the following activities with eyes closed: jumping on a trampoline with a safety net, walking on a balance beam on the floor, or walking figure eights (use duct tape to create a balance beam or figure eight on the floor).

Tactile

Whether your child suffers from modulation disorder, dyspraxia, or both, always avoid light touch and textures your child has an aversion to, and never force touch or textures on your child. Occupational therapists utilize the tactile activities below to stimulate touch receptors and develop discrimination.

- Food play is a great opportunity to work on those picky eating and texture habits along with tactile stimulation. Let your child help you cook by using utensils to play and scoop; this will help her habituate to food textures. Set up a food town on a large baking pan utilizing different textured foods to create the town, and include cars and people or make letters or shapes in the food. Often, using canned goods can provide a platform for building tolerance for touching veggies and fruits that she finds aversive.

- Cornstarch play is also great for introducing textures, and you can add in some discrimination tasks as well. Put some cornstarch in a bowl and gradually add water. It will feel crunchy and gradually soften. The more water you add, the looser the cornstarch will get. When allowed to sit, the cornstarch will harden on the bottom of the bowl and remain watery on the top. Hide poker chips, coins, small objects, etc., in the mixture. Allow him to dig his fingers in and retrieve the hidden objects. As he pulls the cornstarch up from the bottom of the bowl, it will feel crunchy, and then gradually soften in the child's hands.

- Rice play is a texture that helps to stimulate the child's touch receptors. Hide objects in a tub of rice and ask the child to retrieve them (this develops discrimination). Acquire a large Tupperware tub and help the child tolerate sitting and playing in the rice (for very small children).

- Tactile Discs is a great game for tactile and visual discrimination. This game consists of a group of ten discs constructed from soft synthetic rubber with different surface structures and colors. The game brings tactile senses alive by touching the discs with their hands and feet. The discs are adjustable to suit age and functionality levels.

- Light touch is alerting and therefore, is a treatment option for passive underresponders. The light touch receptors in our skin activate the protective (flight, fight, fright, or freeze) system.[5] Light touch options include touching the child with a feather duster, tickling the child, lightly brushing the skin with a surgical brush, and encouraging the child to play in sticky gooey substances.

- The Wilbarger Brushing Protocol. This distinctive technique for tactile defensiveness occasionally treats other sensory processing difficulties. An occupational therapist professionally trained in this treatment method must teach a parent this technique. If used without proper training, this technique can generate significant dysregulation in the sensory child.

Prioprioceptive

Deep-touch pressure elicits a calming effect because it activates a different system within the human body, the discriminative system.[6] Deep-touch pressure activates both tactile and proprioceptive receptors. The proprioceptive system governs the vestibular (movement) system providing a modulation effect.[7] Occupational therapists have found that deep-touch pressure activities are calibrating—they help both the underresponsive and the overresponsive child transition to the calm-alert state. If the child is hyperactive, deep-touch pressure will provide a calming effect. If the child is too lethargic, it will "wake up" the vestibular system.

Proprioceptive input, which comes from sensations in the muscles and joints, will affect your child's nervous system for up to two hours with intense input.[8] Engage in proprioceptive activities after swinging and the brushing protocol, if you are utilizing this therapy.[9]

A difficult aspect of parenting a child with SPD is recognizing when the child is overresponsive or underresponsive in a given moment, and providing the appropriate sensory diet activity. Proprioceptive activities that provide deep-touch pressure work no matter where the child is on the over/under spectrum. Deep-pressure activities benefit children with sensory processing difficulties by increasing attention, decreasing sensory defensiveness, improving body awareness, increasing muscle tone and muscle coordination, and modulating arousal. These activities are especially helpful for children with modulation disorder.

What are deep-touch pressure activities? They can be exercises, games, or activities that involve heavy resistance and input to the muscles and joints. Deep-touch pressure is essential to help our bodies assimilate and process both movement (vestibular) and touch (tactile) information. Deep-touch pressure actions include whole-body actions that push joints together, such as pushing, pulling, or lifting something heavier, or that pull joints apart, such as hanging from monkey bars. Other types of deep-touch pressure include oral actions such as chewing, sucking, and blowing and hand actions such as squeezing, pinching, or fidgeting.

Some of these activities are suitable for younger children and others for older children; choose those that are age appropriate for your child.

- Hot dog game. Use your child's weighted blanket or other heavy blanket to play this game. Have your child lie on one side of the blanket. Put on the ketchup, mustard, and any other toppings rolling a small therapy ball over the backs of their arms and legs, or use weighted beanbags to place on arms and legs. Then roll the child up in the blanket to make the hot dog.
- Crawling through a tunnel. Set up your home with tunnels, tents, air mattresses, and other things to crawl over, under, and on! Younger children like to imitate bear and crab walks. Do creeping and crawling activities for at least ten minutes each day!
- Crab walks and bear crawls.
- Neck Massagers or lower back massage pad. These can be helpful during seated work such as homework.
- Sensory retreats. A tent or a corner with a massage mat the child can lay on can function as a sensory retreat. You can even use a massage mat within a tent, if space allows. Be sure to get a massage mat with low to high settings, and something to put over

the child to apply deep pressure, such as beanbags or weighted blanket. There are multiple options for creating a sensory retreat. Occupational therapist Angie Voss has a website replete with ideas for sensory retreats. You can find it here http://asensorylife.com/sensory-retreats.html

- Jumping on a trampoline/hippity hop ball. Have your child practice multiplication, spelling, or other memorization needs while taking a jumping break from homework time.
- Using a weighted blanket. Weighted blankets are usually weighted at 10 percent of the child's body weight plus one pound for baseline weight.[10] Other variables are also considered, such as the child's height and personal sensory needs. Children with low muscle tone usually require less weight than other sensory children. Check with your child's occupational therapist for a recommendation on the best weight for your child.
- Using a weighted lap pad. These can be helpful when the child is doing homework, using the computer, or watching TV or videos.
- Tug-of-war. If the child is younger, try sitting on the ground and singing row, row; row your boat pulling the rope back and forth between you and your child.
- Chair or wall push-ups.
- Hanging upside down from a trapeze bar.
- Using resistive exercise bands.
- Jumping through a line of items. Make a line of hula hoops or draw squares with sidewalk chalk and have your child jump from one to another.
- Bike riding. Not only is this a great activity to provide input to the muscles and joints, it also develops bilateral coordination. However, this activity can be challenging for some children with dyspraxia.
- Sports. Sports such as gymnastics, ice skating, swimming, bowling, martial arts, soccer, football, basketball, baseball, bowling,

horseback riding, lacrosse, rowing, cheerleading, Pilates and age-specific yoga will provide proprioceptive.

- Daily household work. Incorporating deep-pressure activities into daily routines can help meet the need for sensory input. Have your child help carry groceries, move books, rake leaves, shovel snow, sweep, vacuum, or wash dishes.

You can also combine many of the vestibular, tactile, and proprioceptive activities above to create an obstacle course. Arrange vestibular activities prior to deep-pressure activities. For example: have the child walk a figure eight pattern (with eyes closed if the child has intense vestibular needs), jump on a hippity hop ball, hop through a line of hula hoops, crawl through a tunnel, do the bear crawl across a sheet, throw weighted beanbags into a bucket, and find objects buried in a tub of rice. Pick activities that match your child's skill level, and let her select the activities and set up the course.

In addition to tactile, vestibular and proprioceptive inputs, there are two remaining inputs—oral and hand inputs. Oral and hand inputs last only for a short time (typically a matter of minutes) and are mood changers. These mood changers can help the child get through a situation, such as completing homework, transitioning from one place to another, or when emotionally escalating. Below describes each of these inputs.

Oral Actions

Occupational therapist Bonnie Hacker, MHS, OTR/L states, "While oral sensory input does not have the long lasting effect on the nervous system that the powerhouse sensory inputs offer (tactile, vestibular, and proprioceptive), the effects are often immediate....These activities tend to encourage deep breathing which is organizing and regulating."[11]

The use of oral input is helpful when a child is escalating or moving through a transition. Below are Ms. Hacker's favorite oral activities that have proven the most effective over the thirty years she has been treating sensory children at her clinic, Emerge–A Child's Place, at http://emergeachildsplace.com/.

The following is reprinted with permission from Special-Ism.com:

- Bubble Volcano: Fill a large bowl or bucket about ½ full of water and add a few squirts of dishwashing detergent. Give the child a long straw, preferably a curly, crazy straw and have them blow into the water. They keep blowing until the bubbles they are creating spill over the top.
- Blower Knockdown: This is a very popular activity, especially with little boys. Set up small figures or animals on blocks or books. Have the child lie on his or her stomach. Then using a party blower, they can pretend to be a lizard, using their long 'tongue' to knock down the figures. Lying on their stomachs helps to minimize excitement translating to improved regulation during the activity.
- Straw Art Pickup: Either you or the child creates a basic picture (e.g., a tree). Precut small apples, about ¾" in diameter to decorate the tree. The child then uses a straw to pick up 'apples', by sucking in and places them on dots of glue to complete the picture. This activity elicits precise control and attention.
- Blow String Pipes: While whistles of various types provide oral input, string pipes are great because they are quiet and require sustained breath to keep the string moving. Blow string pipes are available from www.dysphagiaplus.com.

Read more great sensory solutions from Bonnie Hacker, MHS, OTR/L at http://special-ism.com/author/bonniehacker/.

Hand Actions

Fidget toys, which are toys that employ the use of the hands, are great tools for transitions. They are especially helpful during waiting times, which can be difficult for the sensory child. Some examples are Play-Doh, Silly Putty, clay, Koosh Critters or Balls, bendable figures, rubber cars, or Wikki Stix. If your child's school will allow, Koosh Balls are great items for children to put in their desks (or pockets) to have at the ready during class for some quick proprioceptive input should the need arise.

Oral and hand actions are great tools to pull out when the child is transitioning, or is starting to escalate. They can be just the edge to get your child through that transition or to curb the overstimulation. Put a couple of these into your portable sensory toolkit.

The school day can be excruciating for some sensory children with all the noise, visual stimulation, social and academic demands. Often, the sensory child needs some accommodations to minimize anxiety in order to maximize learning. Below are examples of accommodations to assist the child throughout the school day.

School Sensory Diets

Below are basic tips that can help the sensory child navigate her school experience more easily. However, each child is unique, and your child's occupational therapist may provide a customized accommodation that falls outside of the list below. When working with your child's school, never allow the school to remove recess, gym, or a movement opportunity for your child for any reason.

- Incorporate planned movement breaks during the child's school day. Some teachers elect to include a movement break within the classroom routine for all the children. For teachers who include movement breaks, *Tool Chest for Teachers, Parents, and Students: A Handbook to Facilitate Self-Regulation* by Diane Henry is a good and easy reference. In the absence of teacher-initiated breaks for the entire classroom, other great ideas for indoor sensory breaks include art, resistive bands, jump ropes, or mini-trampolines. It is important for the school to have a special room available for these children to retreat for their sensory breaks. In the absence of an available designated sensory room, teachers can create a massage mat corner, which can be a great option for a sensory break within the classroom.

- Movin' Sit helps active children stay seated using an inflatable dynamic cushion that activates intrinsic trunk muscles to encourage active sitting and support the spine. The Movin' Sit seat wedge is ideal for all ages that require dynamic seated activities. Some children prefer a lower back massage pad slipped on their chair that provides vibration. The vibration provides deep pressure and is very organizing to a child's nervous system helping them sit and attend longer.

- The Time Timer clock can aid a sensory child for "seated time" prior to a sensory break, as she can visualize the time. Visualizing time helps children reduce the unknown, thereby reducing anxiety.

- Resistive bands tied to the front legs of a child's chair or to their desk. The child pushes their feet into the band, which provides good proprioceptive input through resistance.

- Provide non-distracting fidget toys at their desk such as a Koosh ball or other type of squeeze ball.

- Incline or slant boards provide assistance with writing tasks. For more information about these boards, visit http://www.bright-hubeducation.com/special-ed-inclusion-strategies/76678-about-adjustable-writing-slant-boards/ Ask your child's occupational therapist if your child could benefit from this equipment.

- Request that your child's school reserve a playground swing for at least fifteen minutes a day during recess.

Summary

Parents can enhance their children's lives with simple activities that everyone can enjoy. Providing sensory activities does not have to be difficult or expensive and builds a foundation for lifelong skills.

Eight

Aggression, Meltdowns, and Defiant Behavior

No! I won't do it! Does the word 'No' come out of your child's mouth constantly? Does your child consistently throw temper tantrums in restaurants or other crowded places? Do playgroups exclude your child because parents deem him too aggressive?

Expressions of aggression in children are a product of poor self-regulation, which is the critical ability to regulate one's attention, emotions, and behavior.[1] Some children exhibit aggression multiple times a day while others only a few times per week. Many children's outbursts are limited to home, others to school; still others, in both settings.[2] Children with SPD may experience aggression for longer durations and with more intensity and frequency than typical children.

At the center of every aggressive act is a child's attempt to communicate his feelings, usually manifested as anger in response to hurt feelings, frustration, anxiety, disappointment, or jealousy. Even though children behave aggressively for different reasons, they have not yet learned to create the thoughts or feelings in their minds as a way of delaying or pondering their course of action.[3] In other words, the child has not yet developed an emotional idea. For example, a child who can say, "I am mad" can substitute the *idea* of anger for the *action* of anger.

When the sensory child becomes aggressive, it is because he is in a situation that requires a skill set he lacks, and life's demands exceed his capacity to respond adaptively. Children are inherently motivated to do well and their challenging behavior is about delayed development, not poor motivation.[4] As a result, when your child melts down or becomes aggressive, a consistent and nurturing approach will provide the necessary support.

First steps are to understand the underlying reasons and potential sources of aggression in the sensory child. Subsequently, you will be better equipped to help your child identify his feelings, shift out of a reactive response, and use a more appropriate one. Aggression exhibited by children with SPD is multifaceted. They may experience aggression due to modulation disorders, sensory-based motor disorders, sensory discrimination disorder or a combination of these. In addition, there may be behaviors that mimic aggression. Below is information on the sources of aggression as well as the behaviors common to each of them.

Modulation Disorders

Sensory modulation disorder is an inability to regulate responses to everyday sensory stimulation to which most people easily adapt.[5] Sensory modulation is what enables children and adults to maintain self-regulation.

"In many ways, self-regulation is like a thermostat. A thermostat senses and measures temperature and compares its reading to a preset threshold. When the reading passes the threshold, the thermostat turns the heating or cooling system on or off. Similarly, children must learn to evaluate what they see, hear, touch, taste, and smell, and compare it to what they already know—the preset threshold."[6] Children with modulation disorder do not receive accurate feedback from their senses, causing their preset thresholds to be too high or too low. Their inner thermostat either kicks in too soon (the overresponsive child) or not soon enough (the underresponsive child). Many children fluctuate between these states based on situational context. Anxiety, frustration and fear are the by-products of sensory modulation disorder and these big emotions can boost the child into a state of hyperarousal significantly impeding self-regulation. Self-regulation may affect motor, language, and cognitive (thinking) systems. Poor self-regulation can also result in high activity levels, impulsivity, disorganization, meltdowns and aggressive or defiant behavior.

Two types of sensory children over respond to sensations. One is the child who is over responsive the majority of the time and is sensory-defensive twenty-four hours a day. Few children fall into the pure sensory-defensive category; preliminary research indicates that less than ten percent do.[7] More common is the underresponsive sensory-craving child, who can land in the overresponsive window due to situational anger, frustration, excitement, fear or anxiety. Below is additional information on each of these types of children.

Overresponsive Child

The sensory-defensive child, who lives in a perpetually overresponsive state, may develop aggressive behaviors in an attempt to avoid or escape sensory input. This child's nervous system can respond as if getting touched is a life-threatening event. His emotional responses mirror his overregistration of sensations exhibiting strong and powerful emotions. At the root of his emotional response is chronic and significant anxiety.

In an effort to deal with his anxiety, he may start to carry something with him to poke another child if that child comes too close. He may develop pinching, scratching, or slapping behaviors, which are intended to say, "Don't touch me; don't come that close." If the sensory-defensive child is bumped while waiting in line, he is often aggressive in response. He may hit or kick the child who bumped him to send the message, "Get away from me."

The sensory-defensive child's occupational therapist will design situational interventions in partnership with the child's school in order to facilitate successful social interactions and maximize learning and skill acquisition. The occupational therapist also works with the sensory-defensive child to reduce sensitivity to sensations.

Underresponsive Child

In contrast, the underresponsive child is the child whose threshold is set too low. There are two types of underresponders, the passive underresponder and the sensory craving underresponder. Problems with aggression are not typically present in passive underresponders. The sensory child's emotions mirror their registration of sensations. In other words, the passive underresponder does not register enough sensations to notice things in their environment and their emotions are understated. Something that should elicit a strong emotional response does not, such as an injury or the loss of a close relationship. Although their condition can lead to academic, motor planning, and social problems, they do not exhibit aggressive behaviors.

However, sensory craving children often vacillate between low and high thresholds. As a result, they can jump from the underresponsive state to a state of hyperarousal very quickly, resulting in aggressive behavior. For example, a toddler may sit in a parental lap very calm and happy one moment, and slap or bite the parent the next. The toddler's reaction may be a response to overstimulation from direct eye contact or overwhelming sensations when the parent tries to engage him.

Some of the triggers that propel the sensory craving child into a state of hyperarousal are: environmental sources of overstimulation (crowded malls, summer events, state fairs, TV or video game overload, birthday parties, or holiday parties), physiological sources (hunger, fatigue, illness, thirst, heat, or cold), and transitions. In addition, social interactions and the lack of a warm and nurturing adult the child can use to calm when under stress (such as a classroom teacher) will result in hyperarousal.

Sensory-Based Motor Disorders

Developmental dyspraxia and postural disorder were presented in chapters three and four. Following is a discussion of how each of these conditions can contribute to aggressive behavior.

Developmental Dyspraxia

Children with dyspraxia often experience a behavioral pattern of hyperactivity and emotional outbursts. Emotional outbursts in the child with dyspraxia may result from challenges with ideation and sequencing. These triggers activate strong feelings of anxiety, frustration and anger. Children are often unable to stay regulated when experiencing big feelings and respond with a tantrum or aggressive behavior.

For example, a preschooler during free play wandered around the classroom hitting other children until a teacher intervened, and engaged him in an activity. This child suffered from ideation problems and could not develop ideas for play. As a result, she did not know what to do and became frustrated and anxious. Sequencing problems will manifest in all aspects of the child's life: self-care skills, group play, sports, academics, and social interactions. Sequencing will affect gross and fine motor abilities. Language delays or articulation challenges are common.

Language delays may occur in children with dyspraxia and contribute to their challenging behavior. At the root of the problem is a child's failed communication attempt, the genesis of which could be a receptive, expressive, mixed receptive/expressive, or pragmatic language disorder.

Receptive language delays affect children's ability to understand spoken, and sometimes written, language; they have difficulty understanding speech and organizing their thoughts. Expressive language delays affect their ability to communicate in words that a listener will understand. Many children have a combination of receptive and expressive delays, called mixed receptive/expressive language disorder. Pragmatics is the use of language in social contexts, so children with pragmatic difficulties have trouble using language socially in ways that are appropriate or typical of children their age.

Language is the same process as motor planning. In order to form language, you must first conceive of what you want to say, sequence words together to form sentences, and string sentences together to form thoughts. Finally, you must be able to control your oral muscles in order to execute the thought. This is why so many children with motor planning deficits also have language impairments.

Like motor planning, social knowledge—including pragmatic language—relies upon adequate sensory input in order for a child to interpret sensory information, and execute movements based on this information. If sensory feedback is impaired due to SPD, access to social knowledge may also be impaired. Deficits in pragmatic language affect a child's ability to interpret social cues and nuances, appreciate the impact of her behavior on others, engage other children in play, and understand and follow rules in play. For instance, Carmen is admiring her tall tower block creation when Tony came into the room. Tony runs over and knocks the tower down resulting in Carmen's distress. Tony engages in negative attention-seeking behavior because he does not have the pragmatic language ability to say, "May I play?"

Due to an inability to express their own thoughts and feelings in words, the child with a language delay is unable to inhibit impulses, resulting in poor self-regulation. This poor self-regulation manifests behaviorally, often through aggression driven by the child's inability to communicate. For example, Nora is wandering around the classroom until she spots a toy that she would like to play with. Two other children are waiting to play with that toy, and Nora is told she will have to wait her turn. Nora gets mad and starts hitting the two children because she cannot utilize words to express her feelings and contain impulses.

Once these children gain language-processing skills, they will rely less and less on negative behavior and physical aggression. Until then, teach them alternative communication methods such as sign language, gestures, or pictures. Providing an avenue to communicate their thoughts and feelings reduces aggressive behavior significantly. This representation of their thoughts and wishes is a means of regulating affect (emotion) and impulse, which will serve your child well.

Speech-language therapists (SLP) treat speech difficulties. Speech-language therapists assess, diagnose, treat, and help to prevent communication and swallowing disorders in children.[8] An SLP can help your child gain control over her speech to produce controlled sounds at will, plan language, and use language in social contexts. The American Speech-Language-Hearing Association has a speech development chart from birth to age five, delineating the age at which most children accomplish speech milestones, at http://www.asha.org/public/speech/development/chart/

Postural Disorder

Children with postural disorder experience difficulties with posture, muscle tone, and motor control, and these challenges can contribute to aggression. Children with postural disorder often experience hypotonia, which refers to low muscle tone or tension present in a muscle. When feeling stressed and anxious, muscles tense up. Children with low muscle tone cannot hold tension in their muscles appropriately and may lash out aggressively in response.[9]

A lack of balance leaves the child fearful to move, and the fear puts the child into a state of hyperarousal. Therefore, the child with postural disorder may become aggressive when accidentally bumped by another child, forcing him to move.

Sensory Discrimination Disorder

Tactile discrimination disorder contributes to the more severe form of sensory-based dyspraxia called somatodyspraxia. With tactile discrimination disorder, children will have trouble discriminating and feeling tactile sensations. For example, these children may not be able to feel touch on their bodies or that their feet and hands are connected to their bodies. Consequently, these children have tremendous trouble conducting everyday tasks and activities, such as climbing stairs, putting on shoes and clothes, riding a bike, socializing with other children, or writing. This difficulty leads to extreme anxiety and frustration that propels them into the overresponsive window. This can generate the fight-or-flight response, resulting in aggressive behavior.

Children who experience severe olfactory, auditory, visual or interoceptive discrimination disorder can also be aggressive when sensations overwhelm them. For example, when bothered by smells she cannot escape (olfactory); when she cannot make sense of what others are saying (auditory); when struggling to read or perform in math and sports (visual), or feeling overwhelming hunger sensations she cannot unscramble (interoceptive).

Fight, Flight, Fright or Freeze Behaviors

Fight, flight, fright or freeze signals originate in the brain stimulating the sympathetic nervous system, which is responsible for mobilizing the stress response.

Below is a description of the fight, flight, fright, or freeze behaviors.

- Fight behaviors include expressions of rage or aggression toward the self and others, explosiveness, or defiant verbalizations (e.g., "I won't," "No!" "You can't make me!").[10]

- Flight behaviors include "hyperactivity, gaze aversion, moving or pulling away, distractibility, clowning, redirecting others' attention, or dismissive verbalizations such as 'this is babyish,' 'boring,' or 'stupid,' or 'I'm tired and want to leave.'"[11]
- Fright behaviors "include the reluctance to separate, reluctance to try new things, crying, whining, clinging, or dismissive verbalizations (e.g., 'I can't,' 'I don't like this.')."[12]
- Freeze behaviors include shutting down or rejecting support.

In the case of the fight response in a young child, the child will often have no memory of the actual incident (e.g., hitting another child) because there is no organized thought attached to the aggression. Instead, the act is a release of an impulse automatically generated by the sympathetic nervous system. Therefore, it is critical to understand that this reaction is not behavioral but a sensory-based physiological reaction. When the child is older, fight, flight, fright, or freeze behaviors may be more pronounced when the child is in the midst of trying motor planning activities such as games, sports or toys that require heavy sequencing skills; activities that require fine motor skills; learning that requires attention and memory; or challenging social interactions. In addition, these children may have difficulty with transitions or exhibit mood swings.

Recent studies suggest that the sympathetic and parasympathetic nervous systems are not functioning typically in children with SPD.[13] As a result of the faulty autonomic nervous system activity, children with SPD may experience fight, flight, fright or freeze behaviors.

Here are some examples of the fight, flight, fright, or freeze behaviors:

- Fight response: One young boy Aiden was at the Children's Museum, in the grocery store play area. He was in the checkout line and had scanned all his items. Aiden proceeded to lean over and grab an item from Henry's cart in the adjacent lane. Henry walked over and asked Aiden for his item back. Aiden interpreted Henry's movement and verbal demands as a threat, which triggered his sympathetic nervous system resulting in Aiden hitting Henry. A museum employee asked Aiden's mother to leave. At this point, Aiden's mother took her son to a calming spot and said, "I understand why you would be frustrated and angry because you wanted to scan Henry's item, but you can't hit." Aiden responded by stating, "I hit somebody?" This is an example of the "fight" response. He had no conscious awareness of this automatically generated response from his body.

- Fight Response: You take your child to a restaurant for lunch (a transition). You sit down and order lunch. You ask your child to go wash her hands in the restroom. She appears very agitated and starts whining, at which point you insist that she wash her hands. She gets up, kicks her chair, and starts screaming at the top of her lungs, "I won't." Defiant behavior is very common in children with SPD, and is a form of the fight response.

- Flight response: One day, a family went to the local zoo. As they were walking around looking at the animals, their son Jerry turned in the opposite direction and started running. When Jerry stopped running and his mother caught up to him, Jerry looked at his mother and said, "Why did I run away, Mommy?" The family was uncertain of what triggered the flight reaction, but due to Jerry's auditory hypersensitivity, his mother suspected it could have been a loud, unexpected noise.

- Freeze response: Jenny attended a friend's birthday party. She walked in the door, observed her surroundings, and found herself a seat on the periphery of the party. Jenny sat and observed everyone else having a good time without talking to her peers. This is an example of the freeze response. Freezing is a shutdown response in which children will withdraw from people, activities, or tasks in order to block the world out when they are overstimulated.

So, how can fight, flight, fright or freeze reactions be diminished? An immediate short-term solution is to remove the stimulus, if possible (i.e., the object, place, or person precipitating the reaction).[14]

This stimulus may be another child who is challenging your child's regulation, loud noise, crowds, situations that are visually overwhelming, transitions, etc. The long-term or permanent solution to the problem is occupational therapy. Occupational therapy helps the child to integrate their senses enabling them to produce appropriate responses. As the child integrates their senses, fight, flight, fright, or freeze behaviors will diminish. Children integrate at different rates, so the frequency and intensity of the fight, flight, fright or freeze reactions are highly variable among children.

Aggression, Meltdowns and Defiant Behavior

Defiant Behavior

Children with SPD may display defiant behavior with parents and other adults, disobeying rules and refusing to comply with requests. It is easy for parents to interpret this behavior as the child's intentional effort to bait them into the power struggle. However, defiant behavior is common in children with SPD and occurs when the child feels threatened or upset by events. Children with sensory overresponsivity, motor planning/posture deficits or difficulty modulating movements may become defiant due to elevated anxiety. Children with elevated anxiety will use defiance as a form of control due to their feelings of powerlessness. Typical children may exhibit defiant behavior as well, but children with sensory processing disorder can exhibit these behaviors with greater frequency, duration, and intensity.

Children with dyspraxia long for control because they feel powerless over their body and environment. Dr. Lucy J. Miller, in *Sensational Kids*, states, "When his mother says, Jimmy, will you....? The answer *no* is already formulating in his mouth. He becomes contrary as a way to keep some control over something." Sensory children with motor planning problems may become defiant as a defense mechanism. When faced with a problematic transition, task, or activity, these children may respond with an automatic "no!" In a child with sensory overresponsivity, she may become defiant in order to meet her sensory needs. For instance, she may refuse to hug grandma because of heightened tactile sensitivity.

When your sensory child becomes defiant, first reactions should be to help your child return to the calm-alert state prior to continuing with the situation, task or activity that elicited the behavior. For example, engage your child with a deep-pressure activity selected by the child. Another strategy for helping children feel a sense of power is providing choices. Instead of directing Jimmy to get his pajamas on, give him a choice between two pajamas. Involve the child in making the rules, making decisions about playtime, what he is having for dinner, and any other appropriate decisions. The transition strategies in chapter nine, motor skill strategies in chapter three, and modulation strategies in chapter two will also serve to wrap the child in needed support. Once the child with SPD gets support around transitions, motor planning tasks, and modulation challenges, defiant behavior is mitigated—if not completely eradicated.

Temper Tantrums and Meltdowns

Temper tantrums and aggression are common for *typical* children ages eighteen months to three and a half years.[15] During the early part of this period—between eighteen months to 24 months—the toddler has cognitive and language limitations that contribute to his difficulty with self-regulation. Due to these limitations, it makes her world unpredictable. Toddlers have not yet acquired the language they need to express their wishes and thoughts. As a result, they make take a more action-oriented approach, hitting or kicking to express their needs. Between the ages of two and three, cognitive and linguistic skills improve; their budding language skills become a means of organizing feelings and experiences. Around this time, they will begin to form an idea around a feeling, substituting the verbal expression "I am mad" for hitting. However, preschoolers may still be physically and verbally aggressive at times, but with less frequency than toddlerhood. Other factors also contribute to aggressive behavior including temperament, parenting methods, maternal emotional support, and sex (boys are more physically aggressive than girls are). In children with SPD, temper tantrums and aggressive behavior can extend beyond what is age appropriate due to developmental delays and sensory reactivity.

Emotional outbursts and aggressive behavior in sensory children can be sensory or behavioral but which is it?

Emotional outbursts or aggression may be behavioral and revolve around a child's wishes or needs, such as when the child tantrums and hits you when told he cannot have a toy, or when you turn off the television. Sometimes a child's emotional outburst or aggression is purely sensory, with a child reacting to loud noise, crowds, scratchy clothes, hair washing, or touch from another child. Sensory-based behaviors are linked either to a single event or to the result of cumulative sensory sensation. When you try to determine triggers and you cannot identify a single source, such as a task or transition, think about the entire day and what may have contributed to the sensory bucket. Changes in routine often trigger negative behavior. For example, did your child attend a school assembly that day? Did your child have a substitute teacher? Did relatives come to stay with you, interrupting your child's routine? Heightened sensory responses can also relate to global transitions, such as when seasons change, clocks shift for Daylight Saving Time, or the school year winds down; these transitions can create heightened sensory responses.

Alternatively, behavior can stem from prior sensory challenges. For instance, Jack is receiving occupational therapy intervention for sensory processing disorder. Each time Jack becomes reactive, Mom showers Jack with attention whisking him away to his calming sensory retreat (a correct approach). However, the child may learn that meltdowns equate to attention from Mom and when sensory processing issues start to resolve, a child may tantrum on occasion when craving attention from Mom. Another example is the child with an oral sensory sensitivity. The child may experience discomfort and pain from trying to swallow textured foods so the child learns that eating food is very uncomfortable and painful. After occupational therapy, intervention resolves the oral sensitivity, the child tantrums and throws food on the floor when presented with a new texture, as he recalls the past.

Sensory and behavioral outbursts are often intermingled blurring the lines between them. For example, Jack may throw a temper tantrum or become aggressive because he does not want to go to bed. If Jack's parents relent in order to stop the tantrum, the behavior is reinforced. Reinforced behavior, whether inadvertently or purposefully, is more likely to continue. Therefore, because this behavior works for Jack, it is likely to persist. If Jack has sensory processing disorder and experiences distress from scratchy pajamas, fear of the dark, and over-arousal, then his tantrum or aggressive behavior may be a combination of both sensory and behavioral. In order to get the child regulated, parents must first address the underlying sensory problems. For instance, Jack's parents may find soft pajamas free of tags, seams and applique. They may install a night light in his room, and use calming strategies to address his overarousal. After addressing the sensory issues, the parent's behavioral strategy may be taking him by the hand, and leading Jack to bed when he has recovered from the tantrum or aggressive behavior. Jack will then learn that a tantrum will not give him what he wants.

Therefore, parental strategies should revolve around both sensory supports and behavioral plans in order to best deal with a sensory child's emotional outbursts. Consult with your child's therapists on what supports and plans are best for your child. One important note is that when utilizing behavioral strategies, *never* withhold sensory diet activities as a punitive measure. Sensory children need their sensory diet in order to stay regulated.

So how do parents start to tease out sensory related behaviors? Behavioral analysis is helpful in pinpointing the drivers behind behaviors. When there is a problem behavior, the first step is to look at the function of the behavior. If the child is bouncing up and down on a sofa, what purpose is the behavior serving? In this case, the child is doing it for the sensory input their nervous system needs. Behavioral interventions in this instance would not work, such as taking away toys, video games, or other favorite things. When behavioral interventions fail to curb a behavior, this is a hint that the behavior may be sensory. Instead, the child's parents may find an acceptable alternative such as a trampoline or hippity hop ball for the child to use.

One helpful application is the "Tantrum Tracker" available for both Apple and Android operating systems. The tantrum tracker enables adults to gain an understanding of the potential causes of a child's tantrums, and tracks the date, time, severity, location, and precipitating event. You can record or import photos and videos to create a visual record of tantrums in the Apple version. You can also choose to track your child's tantrums by keeping a journal. Be patient, and eventually you will have a clear picture of what elicits meltdowns or aggressive behaviors in your child.

Learn to identify the warning signs of agitation in your child. Warning signs are unique for each child, but some children start whining, getting restless, distracted, and disorganized in their behavior. The child may become defiant, refusing to cooperate or shutting out sensory input. When you see the warning signs in your child, try to redirect your child away from the situation or items causing the agitation and engage in a deep-pressure activity or redirect the child to a favorite activity.

When dealing with a sensory behavior, it is best not to give the child a punitive time-out. Instead, give a nonpunitive time-out and call it a "break." Take the child to his sensory retreat during his break. The nonpunitive time-out removes your child from his environment and gives him time to regain control over his emotions and behaviors. Due to the high degree of variability among children with SPD, managing aggression is not a science. What works for one child does not always work for the next. Below are some strategies to try when you find yourself in a situation trying to deescalate a sensory tantrum or aggressive behavior.

Stage Characteristics and Plans

There are two types of aggressive children: (1) the child who escalates in stages and (2) the explosive child who goes from zero to five hundred in a split second. The explosive child will not escalate in stages, and you will need to utilize the maximum response stage strategies below for this type of child. For the child who escalates in phases, there are three identifiable stages. These stage concepts were originally conceived by occupational therapist Carolyn Murray-Slutsky, OTR/L and physical therapist Betty Paris, PT, M.Ed. C/NDT, for clinical use. These stage concepts have been modified and stage strategy plans added to better address the home environment.

Stage one, the physiological stage, does not raise the fight, flight, fright or freeze response, but is a stage where the child will experience the sympathetic nervous system arousal. Stage two, the heightened arousal stage, may or may not produce the flight or freeze response, but the child will be in a more heightened sympathetic arousal state than the previous stage and exhibit specific, identifiable behavior. Stage three, the maximum response stage, is the full-blown fight response. Often, the child experiences the fight and flight response simultaneously in the maximum response stage.

If you can identify when the child is in the physiological or heightened arousal stage, intervention can be successful. If the child reaches the maximum response stage, intervention is targeted to facilitate the child's safety and recovery. There are times when you can intervene in the maximum response stage successfully, but most times, you cannot.

Stage Characteristics

1. Physiological stage. Physiological signs may include a pounding heart, rapid or irregular breathing, sweating, trembling hands and feet, blood pressure surges, perspiration, bruxing (tooth grinding), flushing (red patches somewhere on the skin, usually on the face, the neck, or on the back of the arm), pallor (paleness of the skin), dry mouth, hairs on the skin standing up, dilated pupils, and increase in blood sugar levels that creates a burst of energy. Digestion stops as blood diverted from the stomach and intestines to the brain and skeletal muscles, sometimes causing the sensations of light-headedness or "butterflies" in the stomach. Vocalization may increase in pitch and rate. Behavioral signs may include whining or restlessness, or your child may become distracted and disorganized. She may become silly and too excited or overaroused to participate in a productive manner or register limit setting.

2. Heightened arousal stage. Your child may resist making eye contact with you or a task, push people away, scream and throw objects. She may run away and demonstrate very high activity levels.[16]

3. Maximum response stage. When pushed to the maximum, the child will have the fight response or both the fight and flight responses simultaneously. This will manifest as defiance and aggression toward others.

Stage Strategy Plans
Physiological and Heightened Arousal Stages
Immediately lower your voice, keep language to a minimum, speak softly, lower lights, and reduce noise. Next steps depend on your child's personality. Here are the options:

1. Go to a sensory retreat. Set up a sensory retreat within your home, such as a box with a top or a tent. There are many options for sensory retreats. Occupational therapist Angie Voss has a website replete with ideas for sensory retreats. You can find it here http://www.asensorylife.com/sensory-retreats.html Sensory retreats can offer proprioceptive input through a bean-bag chair or special pillows available from special needs stores or http://www.ultimatesack.com (or make your own by filling a duvet cover with pillows). Once in the retreat, cover your child with a weighted blanket or provide other weighted objects available from special needs stores, such as stuffed animals. Neck massagers or massage pads are also great options. If your child is old enough, coach him through the calming process by teaching him to use deep breathing, counting slowly, closing his eyes, and trying to reorganize conciously. If your child is not old enough to participate, then have him blow bubbles through a wand, as this forces him to breathe deeply. If you are unsuccessful in drawing your child to his sensory retreat, then implement cognitive redirect immediately (see below).

2. Implement deep pressure. You can immediately implement deep-pressure activities. Choose from the list in "Chapter 7: Sensory Diet" and the activities will provide deep proprioceptive and organizing input. If you are unsuccessful in encouraging your child to participate in deep-pressure activities, implement cognitive redirect immediately.

3. Implement cognitive redirect. You can create a cognitive redirect by using something your child loves most. This may be a favorite toy, game, television show, sensorimotor activity, art, etc. Put a weighted blanket over your child, if possible. This creates the opportunity for you to coregulate your child by remaining with her and providing warm and nurturing hugs (unless the child is sensory-defensive or does not want hugs). Coregulation is the concept that a child's actions can be

modified by the actions of her parent. Therefore, a calm parental disposition is necessary in order to coregulate a stressed child. Keep conversation minimal—at this point, the less language the better. If you are outside the home, cognitive redirect is your best option. Always have portable games or toys with you that your child loves to play. Pull them out when your child starts exhibiting challenging behavior.

4. Self-initiated breaks. When children develop awareness of their own dysregulation (usually older children between ages nine and twelve), they can effectively self-regulate by requesting a break. When a child is escalating, becoming overwhelmed, or spiraling out of control, a self-initiated break can give him the edge he needs to regroup and organize.[17] One of the goals of teaching the child to request a break is to empower him to change his arousal level and behavior. Therefore, part of empowering your child involves encouraging him to initiate requests for self-regulation breaks, as well as allowing him to be involved in choosing the break location.

5. Process Emotions. Regardless of which approach you use, after calming your child, help him process the anxiety that precipitated the reaction by talking it through. For example, "I understand why you would be frustrated that you couldn't get your shoes on." or "I understand why you would be angry you can't go to the movie." Discuss your child's frustrations with him, and utilizing a collaborative problem-solving approach, try to solve the problem by asking the child what better choice he could have made (you may have to provide the answer for young children), teaching him alternative strategies.

The Maximum Response Stage

When a child has reached this maximum stage, he may meltdown and become aggressive, hitting, kicking, or biting you. During the physiological or heightened-arousal stages, intervention can be successful in altering his arousal level. Generally, parents cannot employ a strategy to bring a child down in the maximum response stage. At this point, your job is to facilitate safety and recovery.

Step 1: Realize that your child's meltdown or aggression is not intentional or manipulative. He simply has no other coping strategies to deal with his stress and anxiety.

Step 2: Remain calm. A child's emotions are frequently so intense that adults can become overwhelmed. It can be difficult for parents to manage their reactions when trying to deal with a child who is out of control. However, try not to react verbally or physically because if you escalate, your child's meltdown and aggression will escalate. Adult emotions can be very frightening for a child; it is your job to regulate and soothe your child. Your child needs you to remain in control so he can use you to regulate himself. You are setting a great example by demonstrating the ability to control your emotions, and your child will gain confidence in his ability to do the same with your positive example. A parent needs to identify the child's emotion, help him calm, and provide acceptable strategies on what he can do in the future when he feels the same emotion that precipitated the event. However, should you lose control in the moment; the most important thing is the "repair." You must repair the lost emotional connection by apologizing to your child and letting him know that everyone makes mistakes, including you. It is important that every parent understand that admitting mistakes is not a weakness, but actually teaches your child one of the most important lessons in life: that we will all make mistakes throughout our lives that affect our emotional connection with someone, but re-establishing that connection is what is important.

Step 3: When your child is having a severe meltdown or physically attacking you, lower your voice and speak softly, turn down bright lights, and reduce noise. Then, implement the following:

    a. Take the child to a "Cool-Down" area. This cool-down area cannot contain any sensory items such as a beanbag chair, pillows, etc., as you have to be careful not to reward extreme negative behavior with immediate sensory activities because the child will begin to associate acting out with increased attention and sensory calming, and the negative behaviors will intensify. When your child becomes physically reactive say "You are so mad!" and let him know his response is unacceptable. In this situation, keep language to a minimum. Do not start trying to talk him out of his dysregulation or using logic to tell him why he should not be feeling this way. It is important to note to your child when he is calm that we cannot stop an emotion. Everyone gets angry, frustrated, sad, overwhelmed, jealous, etc. The reaction to these emotions is what produces good or bad choices; therefore, it is the response to an emotion we are trying to control, not the emotion. Once your child is calm enough to listen, go to process emotions below.

    b. Process emotions. After your child is calm, help him process the anxiety that precipitated the reaction by talking it through and discussing alternative strategies utilizing a collaborative approach. For example, for the younger child, "What did you feel that made you mad?" "What did you do wrong with that feeling?" and "What can you do next time when you are angry that is a better choice?" For young children two to four years of age, you may have to provide the answers to those questions. If your child is older and can identify emotions, you can say, "I would be frustrated too if I couldn't get my shoes on," or "I understand why you would feel angry because Jack teased you!" Discuss your child's frustrations with her, and problem-solve by teaching her acceptable alternative strategies.

c. Sensory input. Once the child has calmed and you have talked through the situation, it is acceptable to provide calming sensory input for the child.

Behaviors that Mimic Aggression

Some behaviors that simulate aggression are not emotionally based, but sensory-based. For example, the sensory craving child's behavior patterns will involve high activity, which can lead to unintended intrusions into others' personal space. The child will also have a desire for deep-pressure input. "For example, she will shriek with joy if you sit on her because she seeks contact and stimulation through deep pressure....At times, this desire for contact coupled with poor motor planning and disorganized motor skills can lead to accidental breaking of objects and unprovoked hitting....These actions are often misinterpreted as aggression, so other children may respond with aggression, which may then prompt the sensory-seeking child to develop aggressive behaviors."[18]

Another common behavior that mimics aggression is gradation problems. Adults often perceive gradation problems as aggression, but they do not have roots in emotional regulation. Gradation, or the grading of movements, is exerting the appropriate amount of force or pressure as we flex and extend our muscles enabling us to judge how forcefully we should move. Gradation allows us to gauge the amount of force to use when picking up a cup or grabbing someone's hand. Gradation problems are rooted in somatosensory (tactile and proprioceptive) dysfunction, particularly inaccurate feedback from the muscles and joints. A child with gradation problems may be playing "policeman" and want to take people to jail. When he takes a friend to jail, he may unknowingly squeeze the other child's hand too hard and drag the child along too forcefully.

This is really a manifestation of the child's inaccurate sensory feedback and not an aggressive act.

Children with poor muscle tone and postural problems may also have trouble controlling their body parts. If a child unintentionally hits her mother's nose when she means to touch it lovingly, her mother may misinterpret the gesture as an act of aggression. Her mother may respond with anger inadvertently teaching the child to restrict her actions and feelings.[19] These behaviors are the by-product of poor sensory feedback in one or more systems, and not the result of poor emotional regulation.

Discipline

Be consistent with rules, discipline, and your expectations. Setting rules and then enforcing them intermittently, or not at all, only confuses your child and leads to defiant behavior.[20] One thing that helps children recover control best is consistent, predictable adult responses. Keep your rules broad so they include groups of behaviors.[21] For example, instead of no hitting, set the rule to no hurting other people, which would include all forms of physical aggression. To make limits as effective as possible, parents should involve children in setting the rules, whenever they can. For young children, keep rules to a minimum (no more than five), as they do not have the cognitive ability to track and understand numerous rules. This concept and other information on limit setting can be found in *Setting Limits with your Strong-Willed Child* by Robert J. MacKenzie.

Use positive attention and praise to reinforce positive behaviors. The most powerful reinforcers are relationship based: eye contact, a smile, a hug, a high five, and praise. Be careful how you phrase statements around negative behaviors. For example, if you tell your child that she makes messes everywhere she goes the child will believe it. Instead, say, "You are not like this; you are a much neater person than this," and she may believe the message and carry it out. If you have a child with dyspraxia, do not wait until the child completes all steps to give him positive reinforcement; give reinforcement for the steps the child is able to complete.

Other Strategies

Use stories at home to normalize angry feelings and appropriate ways to deal with them. You can use books or social stories. You can find a wide range of good children's books by searching online.

A child who becomes overstimulated when playing with another child often cannot slow his body down, without the aid of an adult. As a result, he may become aggressive and hit, bite, slap, or kick another child. When a child commits an aggressive act, take him to his "cool-down" area. Once there, say "I see your body isn't feeling good right now, so you can regroup here. When your child is calm, guide both children to a slow-paced activity, such as reading a book or drawing, as this will help the child continue to calm.

An important way for young children to manage their aggression is by playing "good guy, bad guy" games in which they can play the role of the biggest and most powerful superhero or the most talented princess in opposition to an imaginary foe. Each time your child can imagine herself to be bigger, stronger, and faster than the scariest monster in her dreams, she gains more control over her life. Expressing aggression through symbolic play is a healthy opportunity for children to explore assertiveness, as it minimizes their need to act out in real life and gives them an avenue of expression. This symbolic expression of aggression will be a tool available to your child well before she can utilize language to express her aggression.

Feelings of frustration, stress, and exhaustion are perfectly normal when dealing with a sensory child and not signs of bad parenting. The circumstances can lead to a vicious cycle as the child's sensory anxiety gives rise to challenging behavior, and the child's challenging behavior feeds the anxiety in siblings and parents. Siblings often feel significant resentment and anger as they view the sensory child getting a more lenient set of rules and most of the parental attention. As a result, this family pattern creates an atmosphere that serves to keep the family entrenched in anxiety. Parents should not hesitate to get help from a mental health professional, as dealing with a sensory child can be stressful for the entire family.

Summary

Managing aggression requires a multifaceted approach; however, two of the most important aspects of controlling aggression are parental regulation (remaining calm) and helping children process their emotions (see "Chapter 10: Emotions"). Never omit these two tactics from your strategic plan. You cannot implement the strategies above inconsistently and achieve results. However, with consistent application, your child's aggression should become manageable and family events more enjoyable, and that is the goal!

Nine

Transitions

Jack took a swimming lesson every Monday. Jack's mother had to re-schedule his swim lesson to Wednesdays because of a scheduling conflict. As his mother was getting him ready to go to his first Wednesday lesson, Jack started whining that he did not want to go. When pressed by his mother to get his coat and leave, Jack had a meltdown. Changes in routine can be challenging for a sensory child as they represent a big transition.

Sensory children often face transition issues that interfere with daily functioning at home, performing at school, or interacting with adults and peers. These children have trouble with transitions with greater frequency, more intensity, and longer durations than typical children do. According to *Webster's Dictionary*, a transition is a passage from one state, stage, subject, or place to another: change. Why do children with SPD have so much trouble with transitions?

In children with SPD, either sensation from sights, sounds, tastes, smell, touch, proprioception, and movement is not registered by the nervous system, or is registered but the associated neural connections are not made. In order to move smoothly from one state to another, our neurological system must be in balance. In the sensory child, missing sensory information creates an imbalance in the nervous system that affects one or all domains. This neurological imbalance results in transition difficulties for the child with SPD. In addition, a contributing factor to their transition challenges may be the oft-seen inability to picture the future event in their minds, as sensory children often struggle with holding on to thoughts. Both children with modulation disorder and children with sensory-based motor disorder may experience transition problems. For example, they may have a hard time figuring out how to get from one classroom to another (motor planning) or how to feel the feelings that come with saying good-bye to a classmate (modulation).

During transitions, children may become overresponsive to their overwhelming feelings of anxiety (i.e., unable to modulate arousal due to emotions). These big, unmodulated feelings can send children into a state of hyperarousal when they cannot process feelings appropriately. Children with motor planning problems have trouble with transitions primarily due to sequencing deficits and may have trouble determining the right steps in the correct order. With this in mind, consider that everything you do involves sequencing, even mundane things such as leaving home in your car. You complete individual steps, including getting your keys, walking to your car, getting into your car, putting your keys into the ignition, and turning the key. The majority of people can sequence through these steps automatically. Children with motor planning deficits cannot sequence through activities automatically. They may have trouble getting their coats, walking to the car, and getting into the car. When motor planning deficits are less severe, they may be able to get into the car but do so very slowly.

The latest research indicates that many sensory children have elements of motor planning and modulation disorders concurrently.[1] Hence these children will experience transition difficulties from sequencing deficits and arousal problems. While any change in mood, action, thing, place, or topic of conversation can be difficult for a sensory child, the most challenging types of transitions for these children are the following:

- Transitions between activities within a given setting, such as from playtime to dinner, playtime to bedtime, or waking up to getting dressed.
- Transitions between multiple settings on the same day (e.g., preschool to therapy or school to an after-school child-care program).
- Transitions between institutional programs, such as graduating from one school and entering a different one or the beginning and ending of each school year.
- Starting daycare.
- Saying temporary and permanent good-byes (e.g., death of a loved one, moving, or a teacher's maternity leave).
- Entering new relationships, such as with new caregivers or classmates.
- Participating in birthday and holiday parties.
- Starting a new activity (e.g., learning to swim, play the piano, or gymnastics).
- Transitioning between thoughts and ideas.
- Traveling.

Transition stress can manifest in unusual ways, including sleep disturbances, toileting accidents, tantrums, and a low threshold of frustration. Transition stress can have a lag response time in underresponsive children. A stressful transition at the end of one day may not manifest behaviorally until the next morning, as your child gets ready for school. If your child experiences a parental separation due to divorce, the impact may show up weeks or even months later. This lag response time is due to the child's underresponsive nervous system, which has a slower emotional processing speed.

When sensory children move through a transition, it can elicit sympathetic nervous system reactivity. This three-stage reactivity, discussed in detail under the section "Temper Tantrums and Meltdowns" in chapter eight, may escalate to the maximum stage three, or only lead to symptoms in the lower two reactive stages. Alternatively, the child may escalate directly to stage three bypassing the lower stages (especially in the case of the child with significant sensory defensiveness). During the fight, flight, fright, or freeze response, sensory children's autonomic nervous systems can respond in a primitive manner. This results in tantrums, meltdowns, physical attacks, verbal attacks, property destruction, or shutdown. When a child exhibits challenging behavior, he feels frightened and desperately needs a parent or caretaker to provide empathy, love, and guidance during this difficult time.

Perhaps your child is not the child who is melting down and aggressive, but has trouble navigating the course during transitions (which is often the case for passive underresponders). In this case, your child needs you to be the pilot and assist him through the transitional maze.

Below are typical characteristics of children with transition problems. The list is not exhaustive but merely provides a sample.

- The child processes a transition very slowly. In other words, he is extremely slow to dress, leave the house, get in and out of the car, etc.
- You need to tell the child multiple times to get dressed, get his clothes on, get in the car, etc. Even after multiple requests, he still has not complied.
- The child responds with aggression when you try to lend a sense of urgency to the situation. She may react with everything from pouting to slamming doors to a full blown meltdown.
- The child may have trouble transitioning from one idea to another and will keep mentioning the same idea or thought repeatedly. She may be "stuck" on her idea for play and unable to transition to another child's idea for play.
- The child cannot bear to have anything thrown away, even unneeded old pieces of paper, old artwork, broken or unused toys, etc.

- The child becomes highly disorganized. Responses can range from running away, hiding, crying, or screaming, to aggressive behaviors such as hitting and biting. This behavior may escalate as the child moves through multiple transitions throughout the day.

Now that you have a sense of what transition issues may look like, let us look at the root cause of these problems in detail: modulation and motor planning problems.

Modulation Issues

On a cellular level, two types of signals come into the central nervous system. One is called the excitatory signal (the "go" signal), and the other is the inhibitory signal (the "stop" signal). A typical person's nervous system will receive just the right amount of each of these signal inputs and adapt to environmental changes efficiently. In a child with SPD, these signals are out of balance, throwing off the child's adaptive response. On a behavioral level, we refer to modulation as the ability to register, attend to, and interpret sensory input. Children's underresponsive and overresponsive behaviors reflect modulation dysfunction. Children experiencing either extreme often have transition challenges.

The overresponsive child can be overresponsive the majority of the time, or he may be a sensory craver who fluctuates between underresponsive and overresponsive states. Sensory craving children can be in a state of underresponsiveness one moment, standing still in the middle of the preschool classroom looking lethargic, and be running around screaming and laughing, unable to calm, the next. When overresponsive children (including sensory craving children) navigate a transition, their neurological imbalance gives rise to elevated anxiety. This anxiety propels them into the hyperarousal state, and the response could be anything from mild physiological symptoms to a fight, flight, fright, or freeze response.

Passive underresponsive children are very slow to process the sensory signals they need to accomplish everyday tasks. These children generally have difficulty navigating through transitions and central to their success is parental guidance.[2] Sensory activities to "wake up" their bodies and increase arousal level are imperative to help get them moving on time for an impending transition. Passive underresponders generally do not have transition problems as severe as overresponsive children do because they are not as sensitive to changes in their environment.[3]

Motor Planning

Sensory modulation is one important aspect of sensory integration that helps us understand how children register sensory input, attend to it, and interpret it. The concept of praxis helps us understand the difficulties children face in using the sensory input they obtain from their bodies and the environment.

Motor planning is the ability to conceptualize, organize, and direct unfamiliar, purposeful action. It involves the planning and sequencing of novel motor acts and provides a bridge between cognition (thought) and motor abilities.[4] Everything we do requires motor planning in life such as getting out of bed, eating breakfast, completing an arts and crafts project, going to the bathroom, and preparing for bed. Motor planning is the process of figuring out how to accomplish a goal involving sequential actions. The sequencing aspect of motor planning often interferes with the motor-disordered child's ability to make smooth transitions. Transitions require the child to sequence through a series of steps and children with motor planning problems cannot always sequence effectively. Children with motor planning difficulties tend to withdraw from situations that may challenge their motor planning abilities or become more controlling or bossy. Their bossy behavior is an attempt to maintain control of activities or games to ensure the motor planning demands are within their competency level. An impending transition may result in tremendous anxiety that perpetuates the hyperarousal state. When forced to confront the trying transition, her conduct may become chaotic and disorganized and lead to challenging behavior.

Now that you have some background on the source of transition problems, let us look next at how to identify transitions in your child's life.

Identifying Transitions in Your Child's Daily Life

Create four columns on a piece of paper or on your computer, labeling them, from left to right: transition type, time of day, minutes spent during the transition, and level of difficulty. Then start filling in your child's information. If you have trouble identifying transitions in your child's life, first think about the times during the day when your child's behavior becomes challenging. Then, consider what preceded the behavior: Was your child transitioning to a new activity, leaving the house, or getting dressed, for example? Note the type of transition, how much time spent in the transition and its level of difficulty for your child. You will prioritize your intervention based on the level of difficulty so you can tackle the most difficult transitions first, which generate the most anxiety and challenging behavior in your child. When you have identified the transitions in your child's daily routine, you can apply strategies to help you guide your child through these difficult moments.

One word of caution when it comes to transition strategies: when using rewards to incentivize sensory children's behavior, relationship-based rewards are the recommended choice. To use other types of rewards treats their challenges as behaviorally based instead of sensory-based and will undermine your parental efforts. Relationship-based rewards help to bolster the emotional connection between parent and child, which helps to regulate the child and foster a supportive and stable environment.

The transition strategies below provide a general framework. Because each child with SPD has a distinctive profile, you may need to work with your child's therapists to formulate a customized intervention plan for challenges unique to your child.

Transition Strategies

1. Routines and structures. It may sound counterintuitive, but the best way to deal with a child's inflexibility is to create routines. Children with SPD rely on routine to know what will happen next. Routines provide them with a sense of predictability maximizing their sense of safety[5]. Since any abrupt or unexpected change can send the sensory child into a meltdown, it follows that routines minimize these unexpected moments. Here are tips on how to implement routines in your child's life:

   a. Visual cues. Visual cues are more effective than auditory cues because the visual system requires one less neurological processing step than the auditory system, and in children with SPD, one less step makes a significant difference. Therefore, use visual cues as primary communication and auditory cues as reinforcement.[6] Visual cues remain essential even after children begin speaking because sensory children continue to have slow auditory processing speed. The best way to provide visual cues is to create a transition board that contains a picture sequence of the day's events. At the start of each day, go over the day's agenda. There are many options available for visual schedules. See appendix B "Communication Aids" for recommendations. Include actual stop and start times for older children as this helps them stop play and transition to a less preferred activity. For activities that are challenging, e.g., dressing, provide a picture sequence showing each individual step of the activity.

   b. Auditory cues. Constantly communicate transitions verbally even after you have visually gone over the day's events. You should start auditory cues at least twenty minutes before the impending transition.

   c. Home routines. Create consistent and predictable routines within the home for the times when transition challenges are most likely to occur, such as bedtime, getting dressed, bath time, mealtimes, and leaving the house. Establish routines that are identical each day and executed at the same time. Include the sensory diet activities. If your child is a sensory craver or overresponsive then prepare activities that are relaxing and enjoyable for the child, such as reading with weighted lap friend or blanket, art, and deep-touch proprioceptive activities. Conversely, if your child is underresponsive, structure activities that are alerting for the child, such as up-tempo music, deep-touch proprioceptive activities, or rotary swinging.

2. Other Parenting Strategies.

   a. Use positive behavioral momentum. The following information is cited from the book *Is It Sensory or Is It Behavior?* By C. Murray-Slutsky and B. A. Paris 2005 and is reprinted with permission from Hammill Institute on Disabilities. Positive behavioral momentum builds the child's self-esteem and gives the child self-confidence. Because the targeted task is buried within a series of positive rewarding tasks, the child complies without realizing it is a less desirable task. Here is an example:

      • Getting Mireya dressed and ready to go to school in the morning is a strenuous feat resulting in her screaming and running through the house to avoid being caught. The morning usually starts with Mireya having breakfast, watching TV, and then getting ready for school (the fight). The sequence was changed to assure positive behavioral momentum and compliance. In her room, after awaking, she was asked: "Do you want to have breakfast?" "Are you hungry?" "Do you want to watch TV?" Each question received a "yes" answer. Enthusiastically, the next statement was "Let's get your shirt on, pants, then socks." Mireya complied.

b. Use simple language. Children with SPD often have slow auditory processing speed. Therefore, keep your language as simple as possible. Instead of "Suzie, you need to stop screaming and put your coat on because we have to go to preschool," use more concise phrases, such as, "First coat, then go."

c. Visual rules. For younger kids, nonverbal kids, or slow auditory processors, use pictures to show the rules so that the child can understand the cues to process the rules. For older children without processing problems display written rules.

d. Limit transitions. Limit the number of transitions as much as possible by not going home for transitions under one hour. Instead, find a quiet place to spend that time with a transitional activity

e. New Visitor. If possible, buy a new activity or game (or make one if you are crafty) for this occasion that the child can play nearby while you are visiting with the new person. Ensure that the activity or game is one in which the child will not need adult assistance.

f. Develop a sleep and wake schedule. The National Sleep Foundation provides guidelines on children and sleep. Refer to Appendix B for links to the guidelines. These are general guidelines; there is individual variation because not all children require the same amount of sleep. Other concerns factor in as well, such as homework, activities, parent's work schedules, and school start times. Each family must determine what sleep schedule works best for each individual child

g. Attachment relationship availability. If possible, the person with whom the child feels most comfortable should be physically available at times of known challenging transitions (e.g., when the child comes out of school, at bedtime, and at dinner). When children are feeling anxiety from a transition, they often look to attach to a secure adult.

   h. Use positive reinforcement. When the child navigates a transition successfully (or makes maximum effort toward navigating a transition), provide positive feedback. The most powerful reinforcements are relationship-based. This could include praise, a hug, a high five, eye contact, and interacting with the child over her favorite dessert or sensory activity

3. Irrational Fear Strategies.
   a. Nightlights. Use a nightlight to help allay fears. Many different types are available that plug into the wall socket. If you are using My Tot Clock, it comes with a built-in nightlight.
   b. Night Fear. Many children have spontaneous irrational fear of monsters, or other dangerous entities that lurk in their rooms. To help children with these fears, Dr. Jodi Mindell recommends monster spray strategy and a pet (if a pet fits the family lifestyle and budget). Fill a spray bottle full of water and spray the monsters away. Collaborate with your child on solutions whenever possible to help him gain a sense of mastery and control.[7] Dr. Mindell further advises, Play flashlight tag, or hide glow-in-the-dark items and do a treasure hunt in the dark.[8]

4. Coaching and Connectivity.
   a. Playful Parenting. Use Playful Parenting (coined by Dr. Lawrence J. Cohen) with a doll or action hero to "act out" bad behavior during transitions. For instance, if your child has trouble going to bed, incorporate a bedtime scenario into her play such as one doll giving the parent doll a hard time about going to bed. This enables her to express any bedtime separation anxiety through play, which will give her a sense of control and mastery over the situation. Then, hand your child the 'parent' and play out the scenario again, with you being the kid.[9]
   b. Emotionally connect. Spend at least five minutes emotionally connecting with your child during transitions. Focus one

hundred percent of your attention on your child no matter what your child is doing. Conversely, spend at least five minutes reconnecting with your child in the evening, providing a loving incentive for the child to transition into the bedtime routine smoothly. Also, empathize with, label, and validate her emotion. For example,d. when dropping off your child to daycare or preschool, "I understand why you would be feeling scared right now, but Mommy always comes back." Focusing your child beyond the immediate experience emphasizes that you are returning. For instance, "when Mommy picks you up, we will do your favorite activity or go for your favorite snack." When leaving your home and your child is in the middle of an activity or project, allow your child time to finish, if possible. Otherwise, say, "What safe place would you like me to save it until we return?" If your child cannot designate a spot, then choose one and say, "How about we put it here? It will be safe until we get back."

5. Previewing
    a. Preview the day's agenda on your child's transition board. You can say, "You like to know what to expect, so let's go over the plan for today."
    b. You can preview events with your child by using social or sensory stories. Social stories preview an event, such as going on a trip. You would create a story about packing your luggage, getting in the car, going to the airport, etc. A sensory story also previews an event, but includes built-in sensorimotor strategies if your child is overresponsive. If your child is older, then initiate a discussion with him surrounding the details of the event and discuss sensorimotor strategies that your child can utilize during this event, if overresponsive. Information on where to purchase social or sensory stories is in Appendix C, under previewing aids. You can also create

your own storybooks by creating text, adding pictures, laminating and binding the book.

c.   Share important information regarding your child's preferences, strengths, and weaknesses and convey what strategies have worked in the past for new teachers/caregivers. Relaying recent milestones and special events may provide a platform to bond with your child.

d.   For daycare, visit two or three days before childcare starts for children under age seven and a week prior for children seven and older. Talk to children about the types of things they will be doing there and other children who will be a part of the experience. Take your child to preview the daycare and meet the caregivers.

e.   For a new school, visit several times prior to the child's transition and during the summer to play on the school's playground. If your child is transitioning to kindergarten, two weeks prior to the start of school, read books recommended by your local librarian about starting kindergarten.

f.   Request a meeting with your child's new teacher and preview the layout of the school. Familiarizing your child with his new teacher before school starts reduces his anxiety by eliminating one of the unknowns. Ask your child's teacher if she will be displaying the daily schedule in the classroom. If not, explain that your child needs a visual representation of the daily schedule to reduce stress. Ask your child's teacher to alert you of any major changes in your child's day, such as a substitute teacher or school assembly, if possible, and include it on your child's transition board. If necessary, ask school personnel to review skills for lining up, circle time, going to the bathroom, lunch, and indoor recess. If your child takes his lunch to school, then practice packing, and unpacking, lunch and snacks in and out of your child's backpack. Pack food that is easily accessible and simple to eat. Unwrap commercially wrapped food and put it in a plastic bag or container for easy access.

g. Preview visits with family and friends, and new activities by observing the activity once or twice before starting. Learn your child's upcoming physical education agenda. For example, if your child will start jumping rope in gym class in a few weeks, ask your child's therapist to include jumping rope in the child's weekly sessions; this will help him keep up with peers.

h. Preview playdate strategies. Preview strategies with your child for a playdate. Prior to an impending playdate, say to your child, "John is coming over, and he may not always want to play the way you do. How do you think you'll feel when that happens?" Help your child anticipate how he will feel and discuss any strategies that may resolve conflict such as "we will take turns and play your game first, mine next," or teach your child how to flip a coin as a decision-making method.[10] Role play the other child, and rehearse various scenarios and positive responses in advance of the playdate.

i. Preview the location of the party or event. If the party is at a commercial location, visit more than once as needed. Try to arrange a playdate in advance so your child is familiar with the setting, if the party is at a friend's home. Previewing the outside of the house will help if you cannot arrange a playdate in advance! Preview the food and determine whether you need to bring your own. Preview any holiday event location with your child, if possible. Preview party events, menu, and a safe location to take a break from all the people, noise, and bright lights. Preview any religious service and associated rules with your child.

j. Read about and watch videos to give your child a visual representation of a flying experience. A number of good books and videos introduce flying to children; ask your local librarian for references; visit http://www.jetvideos.net. There are also videos of jet crashes on this site, so locate an appropriate video in advance and link directly to it. Preview the airport with your child, if nearby. Spend time watching planes take off and land so that your child can experience the hustle and bustle of a busy airport.

k. The TSA Cares help line is for individuals with special needs, medical conditions or other circumstances who would like to preview the screening process prior to flying. Travelers may call 1-855-787-2227 with questions about screening policies and procedures. Also, check your airport to see if it has a special TSA-operated lane at each security checkpoint allowing individuals unfamiliar with air travel procedures and special needs to go through security at their own pace.

l. When travelling, include chewy snacks, gum, and cold drinks with straws if your child is overresponsive, as each of these has an organizing effect on your child's nervous system.

m. Social and sensory stories can help your child adjust to new situations or situations that provoke a negative reaction. Sensory stories are for sensory-defensive children, and social stories are for all children. Children flourish with predictability, and social stories provide them with a visual representation of what to expect. This eliminates much of the anxiety associated with the situation.

An example of a situation that may require a social story would be the child's first flying experience. You would prepare a story about all the steps, packing, riding to the airport, etc. Also, prepare stories about delays, cancellations, and screening procedures. Read the social story to your child at least once per day for a week prior to the trip. Use any other visuals such as photo albums, maps, and schedules to illustrate where you are going and whom you will see. For older children, talking through and allowing them to rehearse any situation, including social and motor-type activities, is vital. Rehearse how the situation may unfold and discuss possible alternative scenarios.

Sensory stories embed sensorimotor strategies to help an overresponsive child get through a stressful event, whereas social stories preview a new situation and are appropriate for all sensory children. The socially acceptable sensory strategies provide the child with calming sensory input through deep touch pressure, active resistance to movement, and slow linear movement. The strategies should be practiced before the event several times, with the caregiver coaxing and guiding the child. Sensory stories are available in customizable versions, which allow caregivers to alter the stories to fit the needs of the child.

n. When riding in a car, sensory craving children need to stop frequently for movement breaks. In *The Survival Guide For Traveling with a Sensory Kiddo* (2012), occupational therapist Angie Voss suggests stopping every hour for a sensory break.[11] However, due to individual variations, this time may be adjusted to fit your child's needs. Incorporate some mobile deep-pressure activities at each stop. For example, marching in a parade, bunny hop, or jumping like a frog. For school-age children, you can have them jump rope or do animal or wheelbarrow walks.

o. Create an emergency toileting plan in advance. Sensory children can have interoceptive dysregulation that results in an inability to modulate their bowels or bladder. Some children can be either overresponsive—peeing constantly—or underresponsive to internal messages, resulting in an accident.

6. Use of calendars. Calendars can be helpful when used in the following situations:

   a. A calendar can mark the time leading up to the start of school, the end of school, holiday breaks, commencement or termination of relationships or activities, or any other significant event in the life of the child. Use stickers or a marker to have your child track the days leading up to the transition.

b. During transitions between parents in the event of a divorce or separation, a calendar can illustrate the time spent with each parent.

7. Use of picture books. Picture books are helpful in the following situations:

a. Permanent good-byes. If a long-term relationship in your child's life is permanently ending, take pictures of the person who is leaving along with pictures of fun things your child did with that person. Assemble all the pictures in a book and have it laminated. Your child can use this book after the person has left to maintain the sense of connection.

b. If your child is transitioning to a new school, ask your school social worker to make a picture book of the exterior and interior of the school, and include pictures of key personnel your child will be interacting with during the school day. If possible, include pictures of your child's classroom, lunchroom, and the school's playground. If your child is to receive formal school support, the school's social worker or psychologist may provide a book for your child to preview as part of your child's school support plan.

c. If your child is transitioning into daycare, after-school care, or a summer program, make a picture book of the interior and exterior of the facility and include pictures of the caregivers. Also, include pictures of the things your child will do at the facility, if possible. If age appropriate, include a picture of a clock on the last page of the book with the time that you will return. Several days prior to the start of the program, give your child the book. Talk to your child about the daily activities, the caregivers, and the other children who will be a part of the program.

d. If your child has trouble transitioning into preschool or kindergarten, develop social story pictures that will help your child see the sequence of activities during the day. Have the teacher put the social story in an accessible place for your child. Give a spare copy to the teacher in case your child becomes reactive in school. At this point, the social story will help alleviate your child's anxiety by reminding him of what to expect.

e. If your child can transition into school but displays signs of anxious behavior, put together a photo album with pictures of your family, including pets, your child can take to school. This album will help the child to feel connected to the "safe" individuals in her life.

f. Give your child a Haggadah, Bible, or other religious text with many pictures and few words, as opposed to one with just words. Picture books help them follow the story as they make associations between the pictures and the text. This is important because most sensory children are slow auditory processors.

8. Use of visual timers and concrete language.
    The use of a visual timer that marks time as it elapses can be helpful in giving children a concrete, representation of time, thereby reducing uncertainty. A visual timer is helpful to mark time between activities, before a transition, or during an activity. Provide ample time, at least ten minutes, to adjust to the transition. An example of a visual timer is a Time Timer, which also comes in apps for iPhone and iPad. Another helpful clock is My Tot Clock, which changes colors to teach little ones when to sleep (blue light) and when it is OK to get out of bed (yellow light). This clock has numerous other functionalities as well, such

as a night-light, lullabies, etc. Another good way to count down during a transition for young children is to use concrete language. For example, if the child doesn't want to stop playing with a toy train, tell her, "Three more turns! Then we are all done." Draw three trains and cross one train off during each turn.

9. Use of transitional objects. The child may need to have a familiar transitional object (e.g., a teddy bear, toy train, or blanket—let the object or objects be the child's choice) when transitioning from place to place or person to person. Familiar objects help the child feel safer during these transitions. These objects often function as the representation of the attachment relationship (usually a parent). Children will use transitional objects to help them cope with separations from parents, such as at bedtime, and other potentially stressful situations. Children will typically settle on transitional objects themselves.

10. Use of physiological activities. You can help the child diminish his anxiety by teaching him relaxation techniques, including breathing techniques, relaxing imagery, and yoga.

    a. Breathing techniques. When used effectively, breathing techniques can help reduce heart rate, fast breathing, and blood pressure, which can increase in children who are experiencing stress and anxiety. Therefore, deep breathing is calming and helps older children to relax. Young children cannot deep breathe on their own so teach them to take in a relaxed breath and exhale by blowing soap bubbles through a wand.

    b. Guided imagery. Guided imagery is another great tool. This type of relaxation offers your child the opportunity to become deeply relaxed and release tension and stress. The techniques can be exceptionally helpful at bedtime, when your child may be experiencing significant anxiety. Books or audio recordings are available.

    c. Yoga. For children old enough to participate, yoga is a great relaxation technique that provides deep-pressure input to the muscles and joints. Yoga improves motor planning, balance, breathing, strength, and self-regulation. For children who are not old enough to participate in yoga ask them to imitate stretches you perform while imagining they are their favorite animal, playing Simon Says, or following the leader.

d. Sensory diet. "A sensory diet is made up of the right type, amount, frequency, and rhythms of sensory experiences that help a disorganized child become more organized and calm."[12] Every child's needs are unique and your child's occupational therapist will prescribe a sensory diet that is organizing for your child. Follow the diet prescribed by your child's OT when your child is moving through transitions.

11. Use of transitional and oral activities. Waiting is exceptionally difficult for children with sensory dysfunction, as they do not have the internal control to self-organize.[13] Waiting is often unstructured time, which means it is full of the unknown and creates anxiety. Therefore, transitional activities are important to keep the child busy thereby dispersing his anxiety.

a. Prepare a collection of short transitional activities or games. If you have a high-energy child, then puzzles and educational games should definitely be included in your transitional kit. Include a neck massager or weighted lap pad/blanket, if possible. A small collection of oral sensory items should be included as well, such as chewy snacks, gum, sour candies, a CamelBak water bottle, smoothies, and Chewelry. Customize your kit according to your child's ability level. For example, if your child has significant visual-spatial or fine motor deficits, you would not include Legos, puzzles, stacking toys, or art that requires the use of small crayons or markers.

b. The sensory child can become dysregulated quickly due to hunger or thirst, so always travel with food and drink. Snacks can be a mood changer and are great for transitions.

c. When you need to transition the child from play to eating, it is often helpful to call him to the dinner table and play a favorite quick game. This transitional activity is especially helpful when calling the child in from outside play.

d. If you are home with multiple children, and one or two finish an activity prior to others, sing songs, or play games until everyone is done.

e. If you have trouble getting your child into the car seat, give him something to keep his hands busy, such as a transitional object/activity like a book to read or something to eat. You can provide a video (either through the car video system or a portable unit) to serve as a distraction.

f. You can also use movement games that provide deep pressure while you are waiting, such as crab walks, wheelbarrow walks, bear crawls, handstands, etc. This is especially helpful prior to boarding a plane. Deep-pressure activities will help transition your sensory child into the calm-alert state and will have an effect on your child's nervous system for up to two hours.[14]

g. A helpful strategy at the grocery store is getting the child involved in the shopping. Ask her to find specific items and put them in the cart; include a few heavier items such as canned or bottled goods to provide deep-touch pressure. This can keep the child occupied throughout the shopping trip and help to organize her nervous system. If your child is too young to participate, take along a transitional activity kit with some favorite items.

12. Delivering directions. Give clear, concise, simple directions; state them slowly and clearly facing the child. If you are dealing with a toddler, give only one direction at a time. With a preschooler, give only two directions at a time. When delivering multistep instructions to your child, alert your child to the total number of steps you are going to give (e.g., "I want you to do

three things") and then "tag" items with words such as *first, last, before, after,* etc., and insert brief (one-to-two-second) pauses between items to enhance processing. Make sure your child comprehends the instructions by asking the child to re-peat them back to you.

13. Delivering choices. Provide the sensory child choices when pos-sible, as these children often feel little control over their world. Offer the child a choice between two items or activities. "Which activity, A or B, would you like to do first?" If it is time for your child to get dressed in the morning, choose two outfits. Ask him, "Which of these two shirts would you like to wear today?" Let the child make small decisions so that he feels empowered. Avoid open-ended questions such as, "Do you want to ___?" unless you are ready to accept no for an answer.

14. Many children with SPD exhibit reflexive negativity as a defense mechanism. This means that they may automatically say "No!" every time plans change or a new idea is presented. Even if they are interested in the new activity, they may immediately refuse due to their transition and motor planning problems. If the child is at home and finishing an activity, she can transition more eas-ily if she presents an idea that is her own. If you have to present the idea, then giving the child a choice will give her a sense of power: "We could do X or Y when you are ready," and suggest you transition to her selected activity in ten minutes. Then set the Time Timer clock.

15. Music for managing transitions. Songs can be a very effective tool in managing transitions. Young sensory children respond well to songs, as they are calming, rhythmic, and routine. For example, after you give the child visual and auditory notices that a play session is ending you can sing the clean-up song from *Barney & Friends* when it is time to pick up toys. Children are naturally drawn to music, which is why preschool and kindergarten teach-ers often use this strategy.

16. Playdate strategies.
    a. If the playdate is at your home, put your child's favorite toys out of reach prior to the playdate so that sharing will be easier for your child.
    b. Facilitate a playdate based on the developmental level of your child as sensory children often have motor and language delays that affect their social interactions. One way to facilitate a successful playdate is to keep it sensorimotor. Sensorimotor activities are any of those listed in "Chapter 7: Sensory Diet" or on the list given to you by your child's occupational therapist. For instance, you can have the children jump on a safety-netted trampoline or hippity hop balls, play with shaving cream, blow bubbles, crash into pillows, or play tug-of-war. Sensorimotor activities do not require pretend play and only limited negotiation skills, thus are a good choice for sensory children.
    c. The person your child is most comfortable with (usually a parent) should accompany the child when beginning a new relationship in order to reduce stress and maximize your child's sense of safety.
    d. If your child is prone to aggression when overstimulated during a playdate, switch the children to a slow-paced activity when your child approaches that state. Examples of slow-paced activities are reading, listening to calming music, painting, or drawing.
17. Gradual introductions. Introduce new things gradually. The following suggestions may help:
    a. When introducing your child to a new babysitter, build this relationship gradually. The first visit should be no more than thirty minutes. If your child hides when the babysitter comes over, play fun games with the babysitter for thirty minutes and then have the babysitter leave. Continue this until your child comes out during the babysitter's visit. Once the child comes out, start building

the time the babysitter is there with you (i.e., forty-five minutes, and then an hour). Then gradually reduce the time you stay there with the babysitter and child from an hour to forty-five minutes, thirty minutes, and fifteen minutes. You can adjust the frequency of babysitter visits based upon your child's individual needs.

b. When trying to get your child to transition from a preferred activity such as playing outside to a nonpreferred activity such as dinner, it is helpful to call her in for a quick, fun game at the dinner table before eating.

18. Dressing strategies. Dressing is a transition that is especially difficult for children with sensory-based motor disorder or sensory-defensive children. Below are some helpful tips.

Tips for children with sensory-based motor disorder:

a. Provide a visual schedule to show your child the order in which to get dressed.

b. A child with balance difficulties or poor postural stability may benefit from sitting on the floor with her back resting against a wall.

c. Allow your child to choose her clothing, as the child will select those items most comfortable, facilitating the process.

d. Choose loose-fitting or slightly oversized clothing, such as sweatpants and sweatshirts, as these will be easiest for your child to manage.

e. Provide clothing with large-sized buttons. If your child has severe difficulty learning to button, sew Velcro closures on instead.

f. For the child who confuses right and left or front and back, use clothing markers, such as Sharpie fabric markers, to indicate the orientation of clothes.

g. Use backward chaining to teach shoe tying, which can be especially challenging. Try buying two pairs of laces in different colors, cutting each set in half and then retying so each lace has a different color on each side. This helps your child to visualize the steps. A good resource for learning about backward chaining is *Steps to Independence: Teaching Everyday Skills to Children with Special Needs* by Bruce L. Baker and Alan J. Brightman. If shoe tying is too challenging, use Velcro closures or slip-ons.

h. Buy tube socks, which are usually easier for children to put on than those with a well-defined heel are.

i. Therapro has a dressing vest that enables the child to practice zipping, snapping, buttoning, overall clips, buckle, lacing, tying and Velcro skill practice. You can find the "I can dress myself" vest at http://www.therapro.com. Also available from Therapro is a book with accompanying CD that teaches children self-care skills through pictures and rhymes. The self-care skills covered are dressing, eating, grooming and toileting.

Tips for the child with sensory-defensiveness:

a. Whenever possible, incorporate some deep-pressure activities for at least 30 minutes prior to dressing, as occupational therapists have noted these reduce a child's hypersensitivities. For example, with toddlers, preschoolers, and young school-age children, you can roll them up in their weighted blanket on the bed and play the hot dog game, or give older children a massage. A more complete list of deep-pressure activities is provided in "Chapter 7: Sensory Diet."

b. Choose clothing that is soft, tagless, and seamless and has an encased elastic waist. Also, do not buy clothes with metal parts, heavy embroidery, or appliqué. Additionally, hand-me-down items and clothes from used clothing stores may work well as they are soft from frequent washing.

c. Check the inside of your child's shoes for dirt, sand, or other loose particles as this can send a sensory-defensive child into a meltdown quickly.

d. Collaboratively problem-solve when your child tells you that her clothes are "itchy" or do not feel good. Tights are an example of clothing that may be problematic for your child. A solution may be substituting cotton jersey leggings for tights to make wearing a skirt tolerable.

e. Let your child choose his clothing. This increases sensory tolerance, as the child will choose clothing that he finds comfortable.

f. Provide seamless undergarments to minimize irritation for sensitive children. You can find seamless socks and underwear at SmartKnit Kids at http://www.smartknitkids.com. Some sensory defensive children prefer socks that are slightly too small so they do not bunch up in their shoes.

g. Be open to your child's dressing needs regardless of weather. Some children will insist on wearing long sleeves and pants year-round to avoid sensations from air due to tactile hypersensitivity. Other children will eventually adapt to the outside temperature. For these children, a good strategy is to allow them to choose their clothing, but carry backup clothing for the moment reality hits them. For example, "Oh, you are sweating, here's a pair of shorts."

h. If you have one of those children who refuses to give up his sandals at the end of the summer, require him to wear gym shoes and socks all year unless you are going to the beach or pool.

i. Use silliness to encourage positive momentum. In his book *Playful Parenting*, Dr. Lawrence J. Cohen describes how he encouraged his daughter to dress using play.[15] He picked up two of her dolls and staged a silly disagreement between them; one doll insisted that his daughter could not dress herself, and the other insisted that she could. She giggled and dressed herself.

19. Miscellaneous Sensory Supports.
   a. Events
      - Consider having your child's birthday party at home with a small number of kids if your child is easily overstimulated. Avoid highly stimulating environments such as inflatable party places, arcades, and bowling alleys. If it's a friend's party and you think it could be overwhelming, plan to arrive halfway through the party. If a party could be potentially unmanageable, suggest your child have a playdate with the other child to celebrate that child's birthday. At holiday events, find a quiet, safe place to take your child should she become overstimulated.
      - If your child goes to a birthday party or holiday event and takes a seat on the periphery, observes the party and refuses to participate, she may be experiencing the "freeze" response. The overstimulation and social anxiety may be causing her to shut down, rendering her incapable of participation. Provide emotional support and allow her to continue observing the party if she desires.
   b. Movement Breaks
      - If you have a sensory craving kiddo, and your child must attend an event that requires sitting for a period, provide at least thirty to sixty minutes of organizing sensory input prior to the event. Sit in an aisle seat, if possible, so you can take your child out for an exercise break, if required. Incorporate deep-pressure activities into any exercise break to help regulate the child's nervous system.

Deep-pressure exercises have an effect on the nervous system that lasts up to two hours[16] If your event has chairs, you can bring along a resistive exercise band and attach it to the legs of a chair for your child to press her feet into and get deep-pressure input. Build in movement breaks wherever you can throughout your child's day. For example, during family meals, have your child help serve the food and clear the table afterward.

c. Avoid Overstimulation.

- If your child tends to get overstimulated easily, avoid malls, sporting events in stadiums, and any other places with a lot of people and congestion. When attending noisy events, take earplugs or earphones if your child is hypersensitive to noise. For children who are oversensitive to light, buy darkening curtains or shades.

- If noise and personal space are issues, have your child enter the school before or after the school bell, lineup, or cubby routine happens. Lunchrooms are generally overwhelming for a child with SPD due to the loud noise, crowd, and smells. You may need to request that the school find the quietest area of the lunchroom or an alternate room for your child to eat.

d. Night and Morning Strategies.

- Some children relax to a stargazer at bedtime. Stargazers project the night sky onto the ceiling and certain brands add floating clouds. Other children relax to slow, rhythmic rocking or swinging back and forth.

- A vibration massage mat underneath the child's waterproof mattress pad may help calm him at bedtime; mats that have an auto-off after twenty minutes are ideal. Massage mats can assist the child to go to sleep, go back to sleep upon waking, and self-regulate instead of going to the parents' bedroom during the night. In order to help a young child (2 years of age) find the "on" button upon waking in the night, some parents find it helpful to affix a puffy sticker to the "on" button.

- Sensory children will calm in a small, enclosed space for a litany of reasons. It visually enables them to negotiate the space around them more easily, serves to block out sensations that overwhelm them, and makes them feel safe. Some children feel safer sleeping on the ground and prefer sleeping bags or portable tents, especially children with gravitational insecurity. Gravitational insecurity may be consistently present or fluctuate along with the child's regulation level.

- Address sensory problems associated with high arousal to help your child slow her internal engine for sleep. Give the child plenty of opportunities for deep-touch pressure prior to bed. Then provide deep pressure through a weighted blanket or a sleeping bag full of stuffed animals if too young for a weighted blanket. Address auditory hypersensitivity with a white-noise machine or a fan, and all tactile hypersensitivity: cut out all tags, ensure there is no applique on the pajama shirt, and provide super soft fabric for both pajamas and sheets.

- Passive underresponders can benefit from parents singing an up-tempo song when entering the child's room, deep pressure while still in bed, alerting music, and sensory activities. Deep pressure in bed can be a massage or the hot dog game. Play alerting music and once out of bed, have your child jump on the mini-trampoline, hippity hop ball, or jump rope for at least thirty minutes. At breakfast, serve textures that are alerting to the child, such as crunchy, hard, thick, cold or hot foods. Stimulating flavors are sour, spicy and bitter. For example, you could serve bacon and toast (with spicy butter or jam) with lemon water. Any way you can incorporate spicy flavors into their breakfast meal will help alert the child. Throughout this process, use high affect and animated expression when speaking to him.

- Similar to the passive underresponder, the sensory craving child will benefit from deep pressure while still in bed. Once out of bed, interrupting games such as Mother May I? or Freeze will serve to slow down the action and impulses of this child.[17] Breakfast for the sensory craving child should include calming flavors such as sweet, salty and savory. Textures should include chewy, soft, thin, and silky. For example, a chewy bagel with sweet fruit would be calming. Room temperature foods are best for this child.

- Sensory overresponders sometimes have difficulty transitioning from a state of sleep to wakefulness. A progression wake-up clock is helpful for this child.[18] Deep pressure while still in bed will help transition the SOR child into the calm-alert state. Children with overresponsivity will benefit from the same type of breakfast as the sensory craver.

- For the child with postural disorder, a stool beneath her feet will provide stability while the child is eating. When dressing, help the child stand on one foot to put her pants on, providing less and less support over time.[19]

- If you have a sensory-defensive child, have your child dress *after* they have participated in a sensory activity for at least thirty minutes. If your child is not sensory-defensive but tends to run away when time to dress, try using positive behavioral momentum described in strategy #2a.

e. Travel

- If your child screams non-stop when put in a car seat be sure to engage her in deep-pressure/heavy work activities for twenty to thirty minutes prior to leaving. For example, you can have your child help pack and give her some books to carry to the car. This helps desensitize your child and put her in the calm-alert state. Dress her in her most comfortable clothing so she does not feel restrained by her clothing as well as the car seat.

  - Some sensory children suffer from motion sickness, which experts believe is due to conflicts in sensory input to the brain. If your child suffers from motion sickness, position the child in the middle seat so that he can look out the front window. Watching the passing scenery from the window seat can confirm his balance system's detection of motion and the mismatch that causes carsickness. Instruct the child to close his eyes while riding in the car and open the window for some fresh air. Opening the window helps most children with motion sickness, but not all. Contact your pediatrician to see if motion sickness medication is an option for your child.

- When booking flights, try to book first thing in the morning, before fatigue sets in, and when risks for flight delays are lowest. For longer trips, you may want to consider booking an itinerary with a stopover if your child has difficulty sitting for an extended period. Choose airline seats wisely. Aisles may not be ideal if your child is active or sensory-defensive, as bumps by the cart or passersby could send him spiraling into a meltdown. You can get information on the best and worst seats available on your specific flight at http://www.seatguru.com.

- Making sense of luggage restrictions can be quite a task. Obtain your airline's luggage requirements in advance so there are no delays upon arrival at the airport. Having correct information about luggage restrictions can reduce family stress. Do not wait in line if you can avoid it. Check in at home and print your boarding passes or use your smartphone.

- Give your child a big dose of deep-pressure activities prior to boarding the plane. For toddlers and preschoolers, consider playing tug-of-war, wall push-ups, wheelbarrow walks, or stretches. For school-age children, crab walks, bear crawls, wheelbarrow walks, wall/chair push-ups, or yoga stretches are beneficial. After you have completed deep-pressure activities, have the child sit under a weighted blanket or use a neck massager while waiting to board the plane.

f. Homework.

- A Movin' Sit blue seat wedge or a vibrating massage seat will often help the child stay seated. Using a weighted lap pad or weighted blanket while the child is seated will introduce deep pressure and help your child get into the calm-alert state. Provide chewing gum to the child as gum delivers proprioceptive input and is calming to your child's nervous system.

- If your child has trouble with homework, break it down into small sections and have her work on each section individually until it is completed. Another option is to break down homework into sections, and implement a sensory break after each section by having your child jump on the mini-trampoline or hop on the hippity-hop ball. While your child is jumping or hopping, you can have her practice multiplication tables, spelling, counting, or other memory work required for that day's homework.

- Prepare a permanent designated space where your child can do homework each day. Make this space a quiet area consisting of either a desk or a beanbag chair. Ensure this area is free of visual and auditory distractions.

The master plan in part two, while not exhaustive, combines many of the strategies above and covers some of the more common transitions. Hopefully, the strategies in the master plan will give you an idea of how to compose strategies for other transitions not covered in this chapter.

The Master Plan

This Master Plan combines all the strategies presented in part one and will help you guide your child through the toughest transitions. Below are some sample master plans.

Unexpected Transition

Should you encounter a situation where you cannot provide lead-time for your child to prepare herself (e.g., you get a call from school and have to go pick up your child's sick sibling), use the following strategies to counteract challenging behavior:

- Use the Time Timer clock and set it for at least 5 minutes.
- Go over exactly what you are going to do while the five minutes is elapsing on the Time Timer clock, e.g., get your coat, put your shoes on, etc.
- Connect emotionally with your child, as this will help to regulate your child.

- Have a mobile activity stashed in the car for the unexpected surprise.
- If your child is in the middle of an activity say, "What safe place would you like me to save it until we return?" Help designate a spot if your child cannot.
- Provide your child positive attention and praise following smooth transitions.

Transition from Play to Bedtime

- Implement the bedtime routine at the same time each evening.
- Structure the time between dinner and bedtime, and present it to the child in a relaxed and enjoyable manner.
- Include all steps of the bedtime routine on your child's transition board.
- Provide organizing sensory input prescribed by your child's occupational therapist. If your child doesn't have an OT, implement deep-pressure activities for at least thirty to sixty minutes prior to starting the bedtime routine.
- Slow, gentle, and rhythmic swinging or rocking helps to relax the child prior to bedtime.
- Your child's strongest attachment relationship (the person the child feels most comfortable with) should handle the bedtime routine.
- Give auditory warnings starting twenty minutes before the bedtime routine.
- Provide choices when possible.
- If your child is sensory-defensive or motorically challenged, see transition strategy #19 for tips on helping your child get dressed and feel comfortable in his pajamas.
- Most children are scared of the dark and require a nightlight.
- Help a child who is afraid of monsters by using Dr. Jodi Mindell's (http://sleepfoundation.org) monster spray strategy.

- Dr. Mindell further advises, "Play games in the dark, such as flash-light tag, or hide glow-in-the-dark items and do a treasure hunt in the dark."
- If your child has trouble going to bed, incorporate a bedtime scenario into her play such as one doll trying to put the other to bed.
- Let your child take a transitional object of her choice, such as a stuffed animal, favorite blanket, or pillow, to bed with her.
- Address auditory and tactile hypersensitivities to make her comfortable and slow her internal engine for sleep. See strategy #20(d) for tips.
- Spend at least five minutes emotionally connecting with your child. Some children like to discuss their worries once in their bed for a few minutes. If you have one of these children, you can use this time to connect emotionally with your child.
- Vibration massage mats underneath the child's waterproof mattress cover can be calming to some children and assist with going to sleep and staying asleep.
- A child who experiences gravitational insecurity, which can be consistently present or fluctuate based on the child's regulation levels, may avoid sleeping in her bed and prefer to sleep on the floor. Provide a tent or other enclosed space on the floor for this child.
- Many sensory children will calm in an enclosed space such as tent covering for the bed, floor tent, or sleeping bag.
- Some children relax when viewing a stargazer in their bed. Stargazers project the night sky on the child's bedroom ceiling.
- For young children who are still suffering from separation anxiety, empathize with, label and validate their emotions.
- If your child gets up and comes out of his room, grab his hand and quietly say, "It's bedtime," and escort your child back into his room and tuck him in.

- If your little one gets up too early and disrupts the household, try using My Tot Clock.
- When you are regulating your child externally, she can habituate to a routine. If this happens, adapt your approach by using a gradual routine. See 18 (g) above.
- Check with your child's pediatrician for further recommendations.
- Provide your child with positive attention and praise following smooth transitions.

The Morning Transition

- All components of your child's morning routine should be on your transition board.
- Pack lunch (if applicable) and lay out clothes the night before.
- Find at least five minutes to connect emotionally with your child.
- The order of your morning routine will depend on whether your child is sensory-defensive. See transition strategy #20(d), last bullet point, to determine your strategy.
- Strategies for getting your child with modulation disorder out of bed depend upon their profile. See strategy #20(d) above for tips.
- For a child with postural disorder, a stool underneath her feet at the breakfast table is often helpful to stabilize the child while eating.
- Provide organizing sensory input prescribed by your child's occupational therapist. If your child doesn't have an OT, implement deep-pressure activities; deep-pressure activities followed by swinging; going to school early and playing on the playground; or participation in a sport for at least thirty to sixty minutes.
- Provide verbal warnings of a forthcoming transition at least twenty minutes prior to the actual transition.

- Use the Time Timer clock, set at least ten minutes out, to warn of upcoming transitions.
- If your child is playing and you need to transition him to breakfast, you can call him to the breakfast table for a quick game.
- If your child has trouble dressing, see transition strategy #19 for tips on helping your child dress.
- Provide plenty of positive attention and praise to children when they complete transitions successfully.

After School and Homework Transition

- After school is an especially challenging time for parents. Ensure that the after-school transition is structured in the same manner each day, if possible. If this time between after school and bedtime varies by day due to extracurricular activities, include all the various activities on the child's transition board and preview it with the child.
- If your child is easily overstimulated, she could have trouble with all the chaos she experiences when the bell rings to mark the end of the school day. If so, pick up your child five minutes early to avoid this, as early pick up from school can make a significant difference.
- Implement the sensory diet prescribed by your child's occupational therapist. If your child does not have an OT, implement deep-pressure activities; deep-pressure activities followed by swinging; participation in an after-school sport; or a combination of an extracurricular activity and home-based movement for at least thirty to sixty minutes.
- Offer your child a snack; snacks can be mood changers. If you pick up your child from school, consider taking along a smoothie with a straw for your child to drink.
- Once your child is calm enough, try to talk to her about her day at school (this should be at some point after the sensory diet activity). Validate your child's feelings about homework.

- Prepare a permanent, designated spot where your child can do homework each day.
- If your child has trouble with homework, break it down into small sections and have her work on each section individually until it is completed. See transition strategy #20 (f) above for tips on dealing with homework.

Institutional Transitions

- Conduct informational meetings.
- Preview a new school by making a picture book of that school, and include personnel that will be interacting with your child. Often, you can get these pictures from the school social worker. If your child receives formal school support, then request the school psychologist or social worker provide a book for your child.
- Preview the school by visiting prior to the first day of class and playing on the school's playground during the summer.
- Take your child to meet her new teacher as early as possible. While there, request an outline of the day's activities so you can learn your child's future routine and the teacher's expectations of your child. A daily schedule is usually possible for children in preschool, kindergarten and early elementary where they have a more uniform daily schedule.
- Identify the location of the bathroom, lunchroom, and classroom while there, show your child where these rooms are located, and teach him the visual cues to find each of these places, if needed.
- Use the outline of the day's activities that you acquired from your child's teacher and develop a social story.
- Ask the child's teacher to preview school skills required such as lining up, circle time, snack time, and any other routines that may be new to your child.

- If noise and personal space are issues, have your child enter the school before or after the school bell, lineup, or cubby routines happen.
- If your child is reactive to the lunchroom, ask school personnel to seat your child in a separate room to eat.
- If your child is transitioning to kindergarten for the first time, reading your child books on this topic, recommended by your local librarian, is helpful.
- Answer all of your child's questions and address all concerns about their transition into kindergarten. Empathize with and validate the child's feelings. Share your story about transitioning into kindergarten.
- Start the school morning in a quiet, calm manner and have a predictable morning routine at home.
- Mark the time leading up to the first day of school by having your child place a sticker on each day of the calendar.
- Prepare your child for school breaks by using a calendar to mark the time leading to and ending breaks.
- Provide positive attention and praise to children following smooth transitions.

Permanent Good-bye Transition

- Purchase a calendar or make one with your child and mark off the days with stickers until the day your child will say good-bye to the person leaving.
- Discuss your child's feelings with her leading up to the final day at a level appropriate for her developmental stage. Empathize with and validate her feelings.
- Make a picture book including pictures of the fun things your child did with that person (make sure the person leaving is in

the pictures). Laminate the book and give it to your child so she can maintain the connection with the person after they leave.

- Be aware that underresponsive children can sometimes start processing a loss days or even weeks after the loss.
- Provide positive attention and praise to children following smooth transitions.

New Baby-Sitter Transition

- Discuss your child's preferences, strengths, and vulnerabilities, along with your values and approach to discipline, with the new caregiver. Share any recent special events or milestones that the babysitter can use to build a relationship with your child.
- Create a social story for your child about meeting the new baby-sitter.
- Read the social story to your child two to three times before the babysitter comes and subsequently discuss her feelings on her developmental level. Empathize with and validate his emotions.
- Make or purchase a calendar with your child and mark off the days with stickers until the new caregiver comes.
- Incorporate the caregiver visit on the child's transition board the day of the visit.
- Prior to the visit, implement the sensory diet prescribed by your child's occupational therapist. If your child does not have an OT, provide deep-pressure activities for at least thirty to sixty minutes.
- Start verbal warnings of the visit twenty minutes in advance.
- The day of the first visit, use the Time Timer and count down the last ten minutes until the visit.
- On the day of the visit, empathize with, label and validate her emotions.
- Introduce this new relationship gradually. See 18(f) above.

- Provide positive attention and praise to children following smooth transitions.

Playdate with New Child Transition

- Create a social story for your child.
- After reading a social story to your child, discuss her feelings about the impending playdate. Empathize with and validate her feelings.
- Make or purchase a calendar with your child and mark off the days with stickers until the child is going to meet the new friend.
- Put your child's favorite toys away for the playdate so that sharing will be easier.
- Facilitate a playdate based on the developmental level of your child.
- Preview negotiation skills with your child, delineated under transition strategy #5(g) above.
- Include relaxation activities in his schedule on the day prior to the playdate along with the sensory diet prescribed by your child's occupational therapist for at least thirty to sixty minutes. If your child does not have an OT, implement deep-pressure activities.
- The child should be accompanied by the person with whom she feels most comfortable, in order to reduce stress and maximize a sense of safety.
- Put the playdate on your child's transition board.
- Use auditory reminders starting twenty minutes prior to the playdate.
- Set the Time Timer ten minutes before the playdate starts.
- If your child is showings signs of overstimulation during the playdate, immediately switch the children to a slow-paced activity.
- Provide positive attention and praise to children following smooth transitions.

Holiday and Religious Service Transition

- Children with SPD have a particularly challenging time during the holidays because of the intense stimulation. Prepare your child for the holiday schedule in advance.
- Use daily calendars to mark the time leading up to and during holiday breaks from school.
- Adjust your transition boards to incorporate any special holiday gatherings, events, or religious services.
- Proactively discuss your child's feelings about holiday breaks from school as well as special events, family gatherings, and religious services during holiday breaks and other times of the year (such as Passover or Easter). Empathize with and validate your child's feelings.
- Prior to leaving for any religious service or holiday event, provide organizing sensory input prescribed by your child's occupational therapist. If your child does not have an OT, implement at least thirty to sixty minutes of deep-pressure activities.
- Start auditory warnings twenty minutes prior to departure.
- Set the Time Timer clock to count down the last ten minutes.
- If your child is auditory defensive, provide earplugs or headphones for noisy holiday events.
- Preview all specific activities related to events, services, or family gatherings.
- Prepare for food sensitivities, preview the menu in advance, and determine whether you need to bring along food for your child.
- If your child is sensory-defensive to clothing, allow your child to wear whatever is comfortable, regardless of the formality of the event.
- If the event location is unfamiliar to your child, try to visit the location in advance. Identify a quiet place at this location where you can take your child during periods of overstimulation.

- If possible, have your child avoid malls, sporting events, concerts, and other places with congested traffic during the holidays.
- It is difficult for some children with SPD to sit still for long periods of time, especially sensory cravers. Build in movement breaks wherever you can.
- Bring along transitional activities to keep your child busy during religious services or other holiday events.
- Give your young child a version of religious text with many pictures and few words rather than one with mostly words.
- Try not to break bedtime routines during the holidays. However, if it is necessary to break the routine, go over the changes with your child when you are previewing the day's schedule.
- Provide positive attention and praise to children following smooth transitions.

Traveling: Road Trip Transition

- Prepare a social story about the trip.
- Provide visuals such as photo albums, maps, and schedules to help your child understand where he is going and whom he will see.
- Make or purchase a calendar with your child and mark off the days with stickers or a marker until your departure.
- Pack a cooler with food and drink items that your child will need.
- Have a small bag or suitcase that your child packs with transitional items to bring on the trip.
- Bring transitional activities to keep your children occupied in the car.
- Start auditory warnings twenty minutes prior to departure.
- Set the Time Timer clock to count down the last ten minutes.
- Provide organizing sensory input prescribed by your child's occupational therapist. If your child does not have an OT, incorporate

deep-pressure activities for at least thirty to sixty minutes prior to departure. This is critical for the child that screams nonstop when put in a car seat.

- Be prepared for a toileting emergency in the event you are stuck in traffic.
- Stop along the way and take sensory breaks.
- If your child is an escape artist, consider getting covers for the buckles in the backseat. Switch on the child lock so your child cannot open the door from the inside.
- You can purchase clips or clamps that adjust the angle of the seatbelt or booster seats that will provide more height so the seatbelt hits them at the proper angle.
- If your child hates car seats, she should wear her most comfortable clothing so she does not feel restrained by her clothing as well as the car seat.
- If you have trouble getting your child into a car seat, give him something to keep his hands busy or have a video playing.
- Many children with SPD suffer from carsickness due to vestibular overresponsiveness. See transition strategy #20(e) for tips to combat carsickness.
- If your itinerary includes a national park or recreation area, your child may be eligible for a lifetime Access Pass. See Transition Strategy #20 for information on how to acquire one.

Traveling: Flight Trip Transition

- If you are taking a longer trip, you may want to consider booking a flight with a stopover.
- Try to book morning flights, when your child is the most relaxed and delays are the least likely.
- Choose the seat that is best for your child. The website http://www.seatguru.com describes seats on various airplanes.

- Read about airports and airplanes with your child.
- Show your child videos of airplanes.
- TSA offers a help line called TSA Cares for individuals with special needs. Call 1-855-787-2227 with questions about screening policies, procedures, and what to expect at the security checkpoint.
- Create a social story describing your trip.
- Preview the airport with your child by taking her there, if nearby.
- Ask whether your airport conducts mock flights.
- Make or purchase a calendar with your child and mark off the days with stickers or a marker until your departure.
- Check in and print your boarding pass at home or check in using your smartphone to reduce wait times.
- If your child is not averse to car seats, consider utilizing an FAA-approved car seat or purchasing the CARES harness restraint system, an FAA-approved product that turns the airplane seatbelt into a five-point harness.
- Take along a portable transitional activity kit.
- When you have the opportunity (usually after the cart has gone down the aisle), take your child for a walk up and down the aisle for a sensory movement break.
- Provide organizing sensory input prior to boarding the plane prescribed by your child's occupational therapist. If your child does not have an OT, implement at least thirty to sixty minutes of deep-pressure activities prior to boarding the plane.
- Manage ear pain on ascents and descents.

Summary

Structure, consistency, and emotional processing are indispensable in guiding your child through challenging transitions. It is important that you validate your child's feelings, as the absence of validation will escalate your child's behavior. Make sure all your routines are in place and consistent, such as morning routines, after-school routines, and bedtime routines.

This predictability will go a long way in resolving transition problems in sensory children. Inconsistent use of transition strategies will not achieve positive results; however, consistent implementation will make your family dynamic a more peaceful and happy one.

Ten

Emotions

In most *typical* children, the overall progression of controlling emotional reactions is comparable and related to brain maturation. Nevertheless, individual differences such as temperament contribute to variations. Emotional responses can be as diverse as children's personalities and will differ in intensity, longevity, and the behavioral responses they trigger. Different children may react to identical situations with disparate levels of emotional intensity. One child may fall down and cry inconsolably, while another may not cry at all.[1] Children with sensory processing disorder may show contrasting emotional responses depending upon the child's unique profile. One child may be overly sensitive demonstrating empathy out of proportion to the situation or experience emotional outbursts. Another sensory child will have little emotional response in situations that would elicit a significant response from typical children. For example, the child may show no visible signs of upset when terminating a relationship with a long-term caregiver. Still another child may fluctuate from one end of the continuum to the other exhibiting both limited emotional responses and overemotional responses depending upon their regulation level at the time.

Emotions encompass feelings, physiological reactions, and behavioral response patterns. A child's expression of feelings follows a developmental process, and sensory processing disorder can interfere with this process. Below are some potential developmental delays.

Potential Developmental Delays

- Co-regulation. The caregiver provides coregulation for the infant and engages the infant playfully. Some children with sensory overresponsivity may have difficulty utilizing their caregiver for emotional regulation if they suffer from significant tactile defensiveness. Picking up an upset infant to soothe him may result in more intense dysregulation as the child reacts to the touch of the caregiver. Occupational therapy can help to minimize or eradicate sensory defensiveness.

- Awareness of emotional states. A child depends on awareness of her physiological states and emotions to guide her thoughts and regulate emotions. Children who are underresponsive have a difficult time being aware of their own emotional states because a lot of sensation is required for these states to register.[2] For example, a child may not exhibit any pain upon injuring herself when typical children would. Similarly, the child may not recognize when they are feeling happy and will need an adult's help to recognize those positive feelings.

- Developing empathy. Some children with SPD are delayed in developing empathy. Once your child learns awareness of feeling states, you can help your child to develop empathy by modeling this skill and initiating reflective conversations around situations that require this skill. Suggestions for developing empathy are located below, under parental strategy five.

- Forming emotional ideas (emotional expression). Children develop ideas or thoughts around their wishes, needs and emotions and eventually learn to use words as symbols to represent them. For example, she will learn to say, "I want that toy," instead of just grabbing or pointing to the toy. You can determine whether your child is capable of expressing an emotional idea by asking the right question when your child gets her toy taken away by another child. If you ask, "How do you feel when that happens?" and he responds with "I'm going to hit or kick him!" he is not exhibiting evidence of an emotional idea. If instead, you get a response like "I feel mad!" and you ask him what he feels like doing when mad, and he replies with "I feel like hitting and kicking," then he can develop an emotional idea around a feeling[3]

- Pretend Play. When children play make-believe using emotional ideas, the ideas expressed are through the symbols of pretend play. When a child pretends that a mud pie is ice-cream cake, she is using the mud as a symbol to represent her idea of ice-cream cake. She draws upon previous sensory experiences with ice-cream cake to help her create an image of ice-cream cake in her mind. Typical children who have had numerous experiences can conceptualize multisensory ideas and use them effortlessly during their play. Sensory reactivity or motor planning problems will inhibit the child from having a vast array of experiences the child can draw upon, as she may lack sensory information from certain senses resulting in distorted or fragmented information.[4]

  The sensory child's anxiety may inhibit him from staying regulated around negative emotions such as aggression and fear in order to pretend play. For example, superheroes face fear-provoking situations and use aggression to overcome the adversary. The sensory child's anxiety inhibits him from staying regulated around these big and scary feelings and the child may respond by avoiding pretend play.

- Immaturity. The child with dyspraxia is often developmentally younger than her chronological age. She may be twelve years of age, but act eight years of age and prefer the company of younger children. She may seem immature compared to her peers.

Anxiety

Sensory processing disorder often results in challenging behavior. For instance, do you wonder why your sensory child displays disruptive behavior in public places, such as the playground, the mall, or a restaurant? What causes these children to "lose it" at times and have challenging behavior that appears to arrive spontaneously?

The primary culprit is anxiety. So what exactly is anxiety? "Anxiety is the experience of feeling nervous, worried, scared, or afraid, and it is the opposite of feeling relaxed."[5] Stress puts the child out of the optimal arousal level. The child may be restless and exhibit increased activity levels. Anxiety may bring about temporary motor planning deficits in the child with modulation disorder or magnify motor planning deficits in the motor-disordered child. Stress and anxiety may compromise short-term memory, attention, focus and concentration making it difficult for the child to learn. Anxiety may also amplify sensory and tactile defensiveness, resulting in fluctuating hypersensitivities; one day the child may tolerate a shirt she would not the next.[6] Social interactions suffer as their attention constantly diverts to their worries and away from social engagement.

Some children with SPD experience stress on a fluctuating basis with single events, tasks, or transitions triggering the response and others live in a constant state of stress. Challenging behavior may relate to a single event or to transitional peaks and valleys throughout the year. Single events may include a school assembly, substitute teacher, separation or divorce, termination of a long-term relationship, or a difficult motor planning task. Peak times usually coincide with the transition into and out of the school year, after-school transitions, breaks from school, or changing seasons. Children in a constant state of stress experience stress-fueled arousal and never fully land back in the resting state. It takes time to revert to the resting state after an adverse event. During this period, the child's sympathetic nervous system is still in an escalated state of alert. Therefore, multiple transitions and motor challenges may further activate their sympathetic nervous system, resulting in a continuous roller coaster with the child never fully landing back in the resting state. As a result, the child may experience elevated heart rate and blood pressure 24 hours a day.[7]

Some of the ways in which anxiety can affect a sensory child are below.

- The most common behavior associated with anxiety is avoidance.[8] Some sensory children will try to avoid situations that are challenging for them, such as constructional toys, pretend play, playground games, arts and crafts, and sports. The child may use cover-up strategies such as clowning around or not bothering with tasks when she fears failure, invent elaborate excuses, or go to great lengths to manipulate a situation to avert failure.
- Some children with SPD may have poor short-term memory of things they hear or see, or they may have memory deficits that fluctuate with their regulation level. When children experience anxiety, the child focuses his attention solely on his worries and his attention to tasks and associated short-term memory wanes.
- Children with SPD often suffer from low self-esteem and lack of self-confidence. Children with dyspraxia may avoid many typical play experiences, become shy, and afraid to try anything new. As a result, these children may become isolated, with few friends. Some sensory craving children are at high risk for social, emotional, and societal consequences of being labeled not just different, but dangerous, reckless, or anti-social. As a result, these children are at risk of expulsion from schools. These children may grow up thinking they are bad, when, in fact, they are just physiologically different. This may lead to low self-esteem and a lack of self-confidence.[9]
- It is very common for a sensory child to feel anxious during social interactions and they may respond with by running away, aggression, avoiding eye contact, turning their back, and not speaking to the new child. Younger children

do not have the cognitive ability to have organized thoughts attached to their feelings; for these children new social interactions just don't feel safe. Older children sense the threat of being scrutinized, judged, or embarrassed. They may experience irrational thoughts such as, "He won't like me," "He's going to laugh at me," or any other unfavorable reaction your child can think up. Some children with SPD struggle to read non-verbal cues and social nuances. Trouble interpreting these cues can make friendships difficult if the child incorrectly assesses another child's behavior. For example, if John turns his back on Joe to reach for the Legos, Joe may construe this as a snub and respond aggressively.

- Some children with SPD may have separation anxiety when it is no longer age-appropriate. Their feeling of loss during separations is more distorted and exaggerated than a typical child's because their unmodulated emotions. They may have irrational thoughts around the separation anxiety, such as, "Mommy or Daddy is never coming back." Unmodulated emotions manifest during temporary and permanent good-byes, going to bed, or even throwing away things such as old artwork, unused toys, etc.
- Defiant behavior is often a direct expression of anxiety and stress.[10] The anxiety can stem from transitions; tasks or activities that challenge their motor planning competency; or modulation challenges (e.g., being overwhelmed by sensations).
- Controlling Behaviors. Sensory children feel little control over a confusing, chaotic, and unpredictable world. In response, they may try to control everything in their environment, such as what clothes are worn, what activities are played, or what, where and when they eat. Children with motor planning deficits will often boss peers or adults around attempting to control an activity or task so that he can keep the requirements within his competency level. A preschool child may try to take particular toys away from

other children in order to create an environment that is within his proficiency level. Peers may rebuff the child's controlling and bossy behavior leaving the child feeling rejected and isolated.

- Stress Response. Anxiety may provoke physiological symptoms, behaviors such as hyperactivity and flight response, or the maximum fight response. Refer to chapter eight for more information on potential stress responses.

- Repetitive statements and behaviors occur when a child experiences stress and feels little control over his environment. The child's behavior may lessen the anxiety and provide an oasis of security in an otherwise chaotic and confusing world. During her transition into kindergarten, one child began constantly kissing her desk, floor, and walls. The repetitive behavior may be verbal such as when the child says the same thing over and over (e.g., "I want to go out, I want to go out, I want to go out"). Give the behavior meaning by leading the child's statement into another expressed statement.[11] For example, if it's too cold to go out, say, "I want to go out to the family room and play [with the child's favorite toy] or make [a craft such as a snowman].

- All children go through a fearful phase when they start differentiating fantasy and reality. When your child starts to use her imagination, she can picture a monster in her room. Sensory children may experience this phase more intensely and for a longer duration. A child's hypersensitivities may transform into irrational fears, e.g., a child who is overly sensitive to touch, he may be upset about holding the hand of another child during a game and later conceptualize that sensation as a hairy monster keen to crush her in her bed.[12]

- Compulsive Behaviors. Some children with dyspraxia may exhibit compulsive behaviors because they help to decrease anxiety. These behaviors may border on obsessive-compulsive behaviors with the child insistent upon ritualistic routines.

- Irrational fears and nightmares reflect recurring anxiety and often convert into scary foes in their dreams or irrational fears during the day. Irrational fears may include being afraid to be alone in a room or experiencing extreme fear of bugs, germs, thunderstorms, separation from loved ones in public places, or monsters lurking in her bedroom. Dealing with this temporary developmental stage often leaves parents feeling helpless as logic and reassurance fail to persuade their children. Providing lots of empathy and validation during this period will go a long way.

- Body Rocking. Typical and special needs children may occasionally body rock. Most typical children will engage in body rocking from six months to three years of age. Only five percent of typical children still body rock at five years of age and outgrow this behavior by school-age.[13] Children may body rock when overstimulated, frustrated, and fatigued or for relief of physical or emotional pain. There is no required treatment for body rocking, as most children with and without SPD will eventually outgrow this behavior. Parents should check for loosened hardware in the baby's crib or child's bed to ensure safety. Parents should allow their children to body rock when needed for self-regulation.
- Chewing Behaviors. These behaviors may help the child to alleviate stress and anxiety. Children with SPD may engage in nail and cuticle biting or chewing on non-edible objects such as shirtsleeves. You can help your child curb this behavior by substituting acceptable behaviors. You may provide chewelry such as a necklace or bracelet, chewy tubes, chewable pencil toppers, or other fun-shaped chewable objects available from special needs stores. Refer to Appendix A for a list of special needs stores. Check with your occupational therapist or mental health professional for more suggestions.
- Masturbation. Many children with SPD will engage in masturbation for the deep rhythmic proprioceptive pressure and tactile input, which is soothing to the nervous system. This behavior helps children to self-soothe and regulate their overstimulated nervous systems. The most effective way to redirect them is to

put a Koosh Ball in their pocket and, anytime they start to masturbate in an inappropriate place (outside the home), redirect them to their squeeze ball. If the child is at home, direct them to find a private place (e.g., their bedroom), where they may engage in this activity.

How do we start responding to our children in a well-planned and thoughtful way? These steps will help you consider their feelings and respond in a thoughtful and effective way. The most critical element is to respond to your children with love and empathy whenever they are in a state of emotional dysregulation.

Parental Regulation Strategies

Children learn self-regulation by imitating role models.[14] A critical variable for a sensory child's emotional regulation is love and empathy from a calm and supportive caregiver. Young children learn self-regulation by observing their parents' self-regulation. Therefore, when sensory children spin emotionally out of control, it is important for the parents to remain emotionally regulated, as the child will look to a trusted adult to help him with self-calming. Many parents are advised to ignore tantrums to avoid reinforcing the behavior. However, this strategy cannot be employed with sensory children. At the same time, parents should not overreact as responding emotionally to your child's dysregulation will only escalate her behavior. When you parent out of frustration and anger with a lot of yelling, you are responding reactively to her conduct. This is a behavior pattern easy to fall into when interacting with a sensory child, but it is counterproductive for both parent and child. She needs *you* to provide love and empathy, to be her "rock" when she melts down or becomes aggressive.

Most children are sensitive to your moods and feelings even if you are trying to hide them. If you are anxious and stressed, they may become anxious and stressed. In this way, their regulation levels are partially tied to your own. As a parent of a sensory child, you may inevitably "lose it" occasionally. Should this occur, use it as a teachable moment. Apologize to your child for whatever negative action you took in order to restore the emotional connection with your child, and explain the feelings that led you to behave that way. When you handle your own mistakes this way, you model appropriate behavior, which helps them to imitate this communication in the future.

Should you find that your family dynamic is in a constant state of stress or you are "losing" it with your child frequently, seek professional help for yourself, your sensory child, and your family. Sensory children's challenges can create marital strife, sibling resentment, and intolerable stress and anxiety within the household. Parents must be emotionally supported in order to support their child. In addition, participating in activities that provide stress relief such as running, yoga, strength training, Pilates, Thai Chi, massage, or quiet reflection can be great avenues for stress reduction.

Child Emotional Regulation Strategies

There are a number of strategies to help sensory children with their emotions.

1. Manage transitions. Use the transition strategies in chapter nine to manage stress and anxiety around transitions.
2. Provide stability. Provide consistency in the home environment. For example, consistent limit-setting, clear household rules, and predictable routines help children know what to expect. In turn, this helps them to maximize their sense of safety resulting in a calmer disposition. If children perceive their home environment as a predictable and stable environment, they can often better manage the unpredictable outside the home.
3. Model emotional regulation. Another contributing factor to your child's emotional regulation is exposure to adult's regulation levels. If you display emotional outbursts with a short temper and a lot of yelling, then your child is likely to display the same when

he is trying to manage his emotions. Children learn most by imitating the adults in their lives. Therefore, in order for children to manage their emotions, it is important that they observe their parents employing strategies for doing the same. For instance, you might say, "Remember when mom was trying to fix the oven door yesterday, and I got really frustrated and mad? When I get mad, I take a deep breath, count to three, and try to think of the best solution."

4. Use sensory diet. Deep-pressure activities are the most effective in altering arousal levels due to the modulating effect the proprioceptive (muscles and joints) system has over the vestibular (movement) system. Refer to chapter seven for more information. These activities will relieve the anxiety the child is holding in his muscles and joints and help the child to achieve a calm-alert state.

5. Express feelings. When your child is experiencing a particular emotion, label the emotion, which helps the child to connect her feelings and behavior. Another way to help your child learn feelings is to make an emotion book together drawing different emotions, or go through magazines and try to match the people's expressions to one of the emotions in the book. If your child is old enough to participate, play emotion charades. Create an appealing container (decorated box or cool hat), and put various emotions on separate pieces of paper. Have your child pick an emotion, act it out, and have the balance of the family members guess what it is! Teach your child that all expressions of emotions are normal, natural and unpreventable—even negative feelings—and there are various ways to express them One good way to teach your child to communicate emotions is to start with an "I feel" message. Start with "I feel" first, and then add in a description of the feeling such as "I feel angry." Lastly, add in why you are feeling that way such as "I feel angry because you will not share your bike. Share past experiences which mirror the child's

current event. For example, "I was scared when I started kinder-garten too."

6. Nurture empathy. Some underresponsive children need assis-tance in learning empathy. A child best learns empathy by ob-serving his parents' empathy and participating in reflective conversations around challenging situations that require this skill. Child development and behavioral specialist Betsy Brown-Braun suggests the following approach when your child is disappointed: "When your child's play-date gets canceled due to a friend's ill-ness, do you assuage his disappointment with an outing to the park? What if, instead, you modeled empathy by making a card or baking a batch of cookies for the sick playmate?"[15]

7. Teach children positive self-talk. When an emotion is experienced, there is often an underlying thought connected. These underlying thoughts are "self-talk." For example, a child may say "I'm such a loser" or "I might as well not bother." Parents can teach children to substitute with positive self-talk, which serves to help the child broaden his viewpoint of a situation, calm down and control his re-action. For example, when a child fails a task, she can stay calm by thinking to herself, "Everyone makes mistakes. I can calm down. No one is perfect and I will do better the next time."

8. Identify situations to problem-solve. Use situations that elicit the most frequent emotional outbursts as an opportunity to problem-solve. Role-play situations that typically trigger your child's anger, which helps them to control their future emotions. Review the problem, label the emotions involved, assess potential solutions, and examine consequences of each solution.

9. Reflective Listening and Validation. Reflective listening refers to the process of reflecting a person's feelings back to him in an empathic tone.[16] For example, "You're angry that the playdate had to end." Sometimes reflective listening is not sufficient when the child is expressing strong emotions. Validation takes the process one-step further, e.g., "I can understand why you

would be angry that the playdate had to end." When you say this, you are not agreeing with your child's feelings, but sending the message that you are listening and subsequently your child feels understood. In the absence of this validation, his emotions can become more intense as he tries to bring you around to his point of view. Validation is a cornerstone for diffusing tantrums and dismantling power struggles, encouraging interaction with your child, and helping your child label feeling states.

10. Manage a child's worries. If you have a child that cannot shut down the worries, teach your child the evolution of worry in an age-appropriate way; For example, our ancestors needed the worry alarm system to help alert them to dangers in the environment. Explain that sometimes our system sets off a false alarm, but this type of worry is reduced with some simple techniques. Discuss that feelings are not necessarily facts. Teach them to challenge their feelings by questioning whether the facts are true. For older children, guide them to collect evidence to support or negate the thought. Be sure to validate your child's feelings and use relaxation techniques to help reduce physical stress.

11. Restore the emotional connection. Sensory children can be challenging and caregivers may occasionally lose their tempers. Apologizing to your child and explaining the feelings that provoked your reaction models the right behavior, so when your child loses control in the future, he may react in the same manner. Not only is this situation a teachable moment to your child, but restoring the emotional connection with the child is fundamental for emotional regulation and mutual love.

12. Collaboratively problem-solve. Dr. Ross Greene's book *The Explosive Child* delineates an effective collaborative proactive solutions (CPS) approach. This approach is helpful with all children not just those with developmental delays. The approach involves communication and mutual respect between parent

and child and helps deal with inflexibility, noncompliance, verbal aggression, or physical aggression. The approach is for typical children six and older, as younger children do not have the cognitive and language skills to engage in CPS.

13. Use Praise. Praise your child any time he talks about his feelings instead of responding impulsively or aggressively. Explain what your child did well and how proud you are that she expressed her feelings appropriately. Be sure to praise children for handling their frustration without losing control of their emotions. "I am very proud that you let your cousin have a turn on the swing even though it was frustrating." Always praise your child when they maintain control in situations that involve mastery over frustrating or disappointing situations.

14. Utilize emotional scripts. Developing a successful emotional script involves validating the child's emotion with empathy and stating the limit. In cases where the child has committed an aggressive act, send the child to a time out (which cannot be their sensory retreat). In time out, the child should not have access to any toys, sensory items, or books. If there are items in time out that the child enjoys, this will reinforce the behavior. Sending the child to their retreat is acceptable and calms the child in situations where the child has not committed an aggressive act, but is escalating. The next step is parental modeling, in which the parent models how to resolve the conflict. When the child is calm, complete the last step by reviewing the problem, the inappropriate action taken, and acceptable future action. Below are common conflicts in the life of children developmentally younger than six.

If your child hits another child due to sharing, turn taking, or waiting:

- Validate emotion: "You really wanted a turn.... I can understand how not getting a turn made you mad."

- State limit: "But you can't hurt Suzie." Send your child to Time Out for one minute per year of age. After Time Out, the child may rejoin play without the toy that initiated the aggression.
- Model future problem-solving (review the problem): When your child is calm, say, "You really wanted a turn when playing with Suzie. And that made you angry, but we can't hit." What better choice could you have made? If your child can't generate an idea, supply one. You can coach your child on how to problem-solve similar situations in the future as well as to express emotions. Coach her to express her emotion by starting with an "I feel" message. I feel angry when Suzie won't give me a turn." Also, "next time, you can ask Suzie for a turn and if Suzie doesn't agree, get an adult's help. When your child comes to you for help, you can say, "Let's ask Suzie how much additional time she needs with that toy—maybe five or ten minutes?" Then tell Suzie she has five or ten minutes visible on the Time Timer clock and redirect your child to another toy until the time is up. Also, make sure to review consequences of different choices. For instance, you might say, "If you hit Suzie, then you won't get a turn." It is important to have this discussion the same day after your child calms.

Your child is jealous of time spent with a sibling and throws an object.

- Validate emotion: "Jack, I understand why you are jealous that I am spending a few minutes with your sister Suzie."
- State limit: "But you can't throw toys."
- Problem-solve (parental modeling): "I am here to spend time with you, too...How about we play your favorite game when I am done with Suzie?" At this point, if your child is too upset to problem-solve, say, "I see you don't feel good right now, but Mommy will help you." Take him to his calming spot, use a weighted blanket, and have him blow bubbles through a wand until he feels calm enough to rejoin play. At that time, try problem solving again.

- Model (review the problem): When your child is calm, say, "You really got jealous when I spent some time with Suzie, and that made you angry. It's hard to share, but we can't throw toys. Throwing toys can hurt people or the toy. Next time, you can tell me that you are jealous and want time with Mommy." It is important to have this discussion the same day after your child calms.

If your child is having a hard time leaving an activity/task prior to completion:

- Validate emotion: After you have implemented transition strategies (see chapter nine for a complete list), say, "I understand why you would be having a hard time leaving and feeling sad."
- State limit: "But we have to go."
- Problem-solve (parental modeling): "What safe place would you like me to put it until we return?" If your child can't think of one, make a suggestion.
- Model (review the problem): When your child is calm, say, "You really got sad when you had to leave before you were done, and that made you angry. It's so hard to leave when you didn't get to finish. Next time, you can tell me that you are sad that we have to go." It is important to have this discussion the same day after your child calms.

If your child gets overstimulated with another child and becomes aggressive:

- Validate emotion: "I see why you would be very excited to play with your friend Chloe."
- State limit: "But we can't push and shove." Your body is moving too quickly right now, and Daddy will help you slow down."
- Problem-solve (parental modeling): "Let's do [a favorite slow-paced activity]." You can slow down the play through slow-paced

activities. Sample activities include crafts such as beading, friendship bracelets, painting, drawing, Play-Doh, sand art, building toys such as Legos or blocks, or woodshop sets. For a child with significant fine motor problems, you can use Play-Doh or clay, sand, or felt boards with different characters and objects that the child can stick on to create a scene. If your child is too upset to engage in a slow-paced activity right away, take him to his calming spot until he is able to rejoin play; then implement a slow-paced activity.

- Model (review the problem): When your child is calm, say, "Sometimes when you play with friends, your engine starts running too quickly. When this happens, you can't hit and hurt your friends. That's when we need to slow it down, and, until you can slow it down on your own, Mommy will help you." It is important to have this discussion the same day after your child calms.

Emotional expression is one of the primary keys to self-regulation. This chapter has illuminated the many emotional challenges that sensory children face in their day-to-day lives. With patience, love, and empathy, parents can work with therapists to guide their children up the developmental ladder toward healthy emotional responses. Healthy reactions will promote social growth and foster self-esteem and self-confidence.

Eleven

Visual Dysfunction

Eyesight is not the only visual skill a child needs to succeed in school. Some of the many other necessary skills include eye teaming and focusing, eye movements and tracking, visual perception, and visual integration skills. These skills are required to succeed in reading, learning, sports, and daily life skills.

However, schools do not test for any of these skills. Schools have exclusively used the Snellen Acuity Test (the eye-chart test) to screen children's vision in school, but the test screens only for eyesight, leaving many children's vision disorders undetected. "Eyesight and vision are not synonymous," writes vision expert Patricia Lemer. Eyesight is the sharpness and clarity of the images seen by the eye, while vision is the ability to focus on, and interpret, the pictures seen. Research has shown that most children with special needs do not have eyesight problems, but many have visual dysfunction.[1] According to Jean Roberts, chief of the Medical Statistics Branch of the US Department of Health, Education, and Welfare, approximately one out of four children have an undiagnosed vision disorder, and these vision problems interfere with their ability to learn in school, play sports, and succeed socially.

The standard (or) distance Snellen test is inadequate as a solitary measure of vision because it only measures the clearness and sharpness of eyesight at a distance of twenty feet using a stationary target. Unfortunately, the ability to see a stationary object at twenty feet has little to do with how a child's vision will function in school activities. He must be able to do reading, writing, and math assignments placed approximately eleven to sixteen inches from his face. His visual efficiency in following moving objects or landscapes affects all sports, physical education, ball games, or riding a bicycle. The ability to judge distances and depth accurately affects his balance, large motor coordination, and perception of his environment. Therefore, a child can pass the Snellen test with 20/20 vision and have vision problems that affect his learning, participation in sports, and social interactions.

Symptoms of visual impairment vary from child to child. Children with vision impairments often demonstrate the same symptoms as children with ADD/ADHD as evidenced by recent studies.[2] As a result many children are misdiagnosed every year with ADD/ADHD. It is wise to seek a vision evaluation by a developmental optometrist if your child is diagnosed with ADD/ADHD.

Other children with visual impairment do not exhibit symptoms, as many vision problems have no obvious signs or symptoms. These children devise compensatory strategies that they use successfully for several years. For example, these children may exhibit task avoidance frequently. For instance, a child with poor visual memory may compensate by relying on her strong auditory skills. Children with high IQs are notorious for utilizing compensatory strategies and will be successful with these strategies until they reach higher-grades. These children may be able to demonstrate age-appropriate reading ability in the lower grades, when books help them follow stories through themes and pictures. In the higher-grades, books become more fact-based and less theme-based, with fewer pictures. This may result in difficulty reading and keeping pace with peers.

Children with undetected and untreated vision problems may face significant barriers in life that interfere with their ability to succeed. Quality vision care can break down these barriers and enable children to reach their highest potential. Because symptoms do not always manifest immediately and vary between children, it is imperative to have all aspects of your child's vision evaluated as soon as possible, regardless of whether your child has other existing diagnoses. Take your child to an eye doctor who measures efficiency of vision, as not all eye doctors do. The earlier a developmental optometrist diagnoses and treats a vision problem, the less it will negatively influence a child's development.

Vision problems are the fourth most prevalent disability in the United States. Considering that 80 percent of what children learn comes through visual information processing, this is some vital data.[3] The American Optometric Association recommends that infants and young children have comprehensive eye exams at ages six months, three years, and five years, and every two years thereafter, unless specific problems and risk factors exist, or as recommended by your child's pediatrician.[4]

Choosing a Doctor

What type of doctor do you need for a comprehensive visual evaluation? Two types of doctors evaluate pediatric vision: pediatric developmental optometrists and pediatric ophthalmologists. Both will conduct examinations, prescribe glasses, diagnose and treat eye disease, and evaluate how well people use their eyes together. However, they have different areas of expertise.

Ophthalmologists are medical doctors who followed college with eight years of medical training and provide the following services[5]

1. Vision services including eye exams, eyeglasses or contacts.
2. Diagnosis and treatment of eye diseases.
3. Eye surgery.

Board-certified developmental optometrists attend four years of optometry school after college and complete an additional two to three years of postgraduate training. They are required to complete clinical training and submit case studies before they can sit for their national boards. Once developmental optometrists complete their additional education and successfully pass the written and oral examinations, they are credentialed as fellows in the College of Optometrists in Vision Development, with the certification of FCOVD added to their professional title[6] Choose an optometrist for your child who is board certified.

Developmental optometrists are also known as *behavioral optometrists* because of their role in evaluating how vision affects behavior and performance. Developmental *optometrists* who work frequently with children are *pediatric optometrists.* Developmental optometrists do not perform eye surgery but are well educated in the functional and developmental aspects of vision. The Optometrist Network advises parents to ensure that a doctor evaluates their child for the following visual skills:

1. Acuity. An acuity test measures the clearness and sharpness of eyesight at a distance of twenty feet using a stationary target and near distance of sixteen inches from his face. This is the standard eye screening with the big "E" on the chart.

2. Eye Teaming. Eye teaming, or binocular vision, is a visual efficiency skill that allows both eyes to work together in a precise and coordinated way. Eye teaming allows sustained and single vision and is the basis for depth perception. The two most common eye-teaming problems are convergence insufficiency and convergence excess.

3. Oculomotility or tracking. Oculomotility is the patients' ability to control where they aim their eyes, which is a skill required for reading. Also measured is the ability to follow a moving target smoothly ("pursuits") and make eye jumps from one point to another ("saccades").

4. Accommodation or focusing. The optometrist evaluates the patient's ability to change focus rapidly and smoothly when looking from distance to near objects and back again, such as from the front of the classroom to the desk. In addition, the patient is tested for the ability to maintain clear focus at near ranges for an extended time without blur or fatigue, which is required for reading small print.

5. Stereopsis: Stereopsis is depth perception. Good depth perception is largely dependent upon binocular vision (eye teaming), which is the ability to use both eyes together in a precise and coordinated way.
6. Visual perception. Patients are analyzed to determine if they have developed the perceptual skill, they need to understand and analyze what they see, including, visual memory, form discrimination, visual closure, spatial relations, figure-ground relationships, and color vision.
7. Visual-motor integration or eye-hand-body coordination. The optometrist tests whether the patient's visual systems are efficiently transmitting information to the body's motor centers for good balance and coordination. The ability to transform images from a vertical to a horizontal plane (such as from the blackboard to the desk surface) is also tested.

Of the items above, just two—binocularity and acuity—are tested during a visit to an ophthalmologist; the others will be tested only at the developmental optometrist's office. If testing determines dysfunction in any of the remaining above areas, developmental optometrists will utilize lenses, prisms, and vision therapy to enhance and improve visual function.

Developmental optometrists treat the majority of learning-related vision problems, and their interventions often improve children's academic abilities. If your child's developmental optometrist diagnoses eye disease, he or she will refer you to an ophthalmologist in your area for treatment. Sometimes, an ophthalmologist and an optometrist will comanage a patient's condition. The ophthalmologist may operate on a patient's eyes and then rely on the optometrist for rehabilitation.

Questions to ask your potential optometrist:

1. Do you conduct standardized tests of tracking and visual processing?

2. Do you conduct a series of near-point tests utilizing dilation drops? The Optometric Professional Association states that eye examinations conducted entirely with the eyes dilated will seriously inhibit the capacity to diagnose visually related focusing problems, as the drugs used to dilate will temporarily paralyze the focusing muscles.[7]

3. Do you provide a customized vision report with individualized accommodations for the classroom?

4. Do you provide one-on-one, office-based vision therapy when necessary?

5. Is vision therapy based primarily on activity or on computer programs? (You want a doctor who provides activity-based therapy in addition to any computer programs.)

6. Will you call me back before the exam if I have questions?

Finding a Doctor

When choosing an optometrist, ensure the doctor is board-certified in vision therapy. You will see the initials FCOVD after his or her name.

You can search for a local eye doctor a number of ways. The College of Optometrists in Vision Development provides a list of doctors who have passed oral and written exams, demonstrating competence in vision therapy; you can contact the COVD at 1-888-268-3770 or at http://www.covd.org. You can also call 1-800-PAVE-988 to reach Parents Active in Vision Education (PAVE®). These parents will provide a list of developmental optometrists in your area, as well as information about symptoms. You can also locate a developmental optometrist at http://www.optometrists.org.

Vision Development

Both vision and the brain's use of visual information are learned skills. According to occupational therapist A. Jean Ayres, who developed sensory integration theory, the eyes and neck are the first body parts to develop control. Ayres further states that a baby's brain uses and interprets sensory information received from his inner ears, and eye and neck muscles. The baby utilizes this information in order to take a mental picture of what his eyes see and make sense of this information.[8] The College of Optometrists in Vision Development has a "Child Development Timeline" on their website, which is a wonderful vision development resource for parents. The strategies on the timeline range from birth to ages 4+ and located at http://www.covd.org/?page=Child_Timeline.

The Visual Dysfunction Signs and Symptoms Checklist delineate general symptoms associated with a wide array of visual performance disorders.

Visual Dysfunction Signs and Symptoms

Below is a general list of potential symptoms from the office of developmental optometrist Neil Margolis.[9]

Physical Symptoms

- Red, sore, or watery eyes
- Jerky eye movements
- One eye turning in or out
- Squinting, eye rubbing, or excessive blinking
- Blurred or double vision
- Head tilting when reading
- Closing/blocking one eye when reading
- Poor posture when reading
- Headaches, dizziness, or nausea after reading

Performance Symptoms

- Avoidance of near work (within ten inches of face)
- Frequent loss of place
- Omitting, inserting, or rereading letters or words

- Mixing up similar-looking words or letters. This is commonly mistaken for dyslexia. Instead, this visual perception problem often coexists with dyslexia.
- Letter or word reversals after the first grade
- Failure to recognize the same word used in multiple sentences in a row
- Poor reading comprehension
- Difficulty copying from the front of the classroom
- Poor handwriting; misaligned numbers
- Holding a book too close to the eyes
- Vocalizing when attempting to read silently
- Reading slowly
- Using finger as a marker
- Difficulty staying on the line, organizing spacing on page or between words when writing
- Experiencing text moving on the page
- Difficulty lining up math columns

The above physical and performance symptoms often result in behavioral challenges. The fatigue, frustration and stress these children experience often result in short tempers, frequent crying, and aggressive behavior. Their short attention spans often lead to a misdiagnosis of attention deficit disorder. One of the most prevalent indicators is a gap between the child's IQ and school performance. The inability to perform in school, sports and play activities commonly leads to low self-esteem and a lack of self-confidence.

Visual Performance

Visual performance is the ability of the visual information gathering system (VIGS) and the visual information processing system (VIPS) to operate quickly, effectively, and with no discomfort on both a conscious and a subconscious level. All parts of the human body are involved in the VIGS, which is a combination of eye acuity, eye teaming/binocular vision, eye focusing/accommodation, and eye tracking. The VIGS system is central in capturing the image transmitted to the brain and central nervous system.

In addition to the efficient visual skills we need to gather visual information, which is accomplished by the VIGS system, we also need to process and integrate the visual information obtained, which is a task completed by the VIPS system. Specifically, the VIPS system is responsible for visual discrimination, spatial dimensions, visual memory, whole-part relationships, visual-motor coordination, visual-auditory integration, and visual-vestibular integration. Discussed below are the components of both the VIGS and VIPS.

Acuity

Visual acuity, the component of vision most of us are familiar with, is an indication of the clarity of one's vision. The word "acuity" comes from the Latin word "acuitas," meaning sharpness. Acuity is measured by the Snellen Visual Acuity Test, which tests distance and near vision at specific distances. This eyesight test with the big *E* on the wall came into use over a hundred years ago. Since its inception, it has been widely used as the sole test to screen children's vision in school. Near acuity can also be tested using reduced Snellen charts held sixteen inches away from the eyes. The test is administered in the same manner as the twenty-foot test. When the chart is sixteen inches from the eyes, the patient reads the smallest line of print that he can see.

Therefore, while the Snellen test will provide an accurate indication of distance or near eyesight, it does not test for the seventeen other visual skills they need to succeed in reading, learning, sports, and in life.[10] Children with learning-related vision problems often pass the Snellen test, and their vision reported as normal. As a result, a child may continue through school with undetected poor vision that detracts from her learning potential. For example, she may have symptoms of eyestrain, headaches, fatigue, or even blurred vision, while reading or working on a computer, due to a focusing or eye-teaming problem.

In summary, acuity is only one part of vision and cannot be generalized to mean that someone has perfect vision—because along with our eyes, we rely on cooperation between our ocular motor muscles, senses, and brains to see.

Delayed Visual Development

Delayed visual development may affect a child academically, socially, athletically, and emotionally. These children's performance levels will lag behind those of typical peers. They may not meet school standards and may have significant trouble with reading or copying information from the front of the classroom. Parents often write off children's lack of athletic success as individual differences. Social activities often revolve around sports or games that require efficient vision and the visually delayed child may become socially isolated. Further contributing to their social isolation is the inappropriate behavior often exhibited by these children due to their disability. Emotionally, this delay may result in a lack of self-confidence and self-esteem. Rarely do these children outgrow this delayed development.

Treatment. Vision therapy provided by a developmental optometrist can accelerate a child's rate of visual development while diminishing the impacts of vision problems. Vision therapy is an individualized, supervised treatment program designed to correct many common visual deficiencies and is an effective nonsurgical treatment. Children with delayed visual development may exhibit the following symptoms:

Checklist of Delayed or Incomplete Visual Development Symptoms

- Delayed reading
- Emotional immaturity/lack of self-confidence
- Inappropriate behavior

- Poor motor coordination Short attention span/highly distractible
- Poor social interactions

Binocular Vision

Binocularity is the ability to maintain visual focus on an object with both eyes, creating a single visual image. Delineated below are the different types of binocular vision problems, such as eye teaming and focusing, eye movement and tracking, strabismus, and amblyopia.

Eye teaming and Focusing Problems

Focusing and eye teaming problems may manifest at any age due to changes in development, workload, or skill level. The focusing system within the eyes is called accommodation, and children with focusing difficulties are said to have accommodative dysfunction. Our eyes have an automatic focusing system, which adjusts the lens inside our eye in order to see clearly at all distances. When looking in the distance, up close, and far away again, the eyes quickly adapt in order to see clearly at any distance like an auto-focus camera.[11] A well- functioning accommodation system contributes to good reading comprehension.

Eye teaming is extremely important for everything we do, including reading, writing, arts and crafts, playing sports, and negotiating the space around us. Eye teaming is responsible for much of our depth perception which is the depth attained from the merging of two slightly different pictures seen in each eye into one 3D image.[12] In order for the eyes to work in tandem, they must be able to turn inward to focus on close images; this ability is called convergence. Two common types of eye teaming/convergence problems can cause double vision, intermittent blurred vision, headaches, fatigue, and avoidance of close work: convergence excess where the eyes turn in too much and convergence insufficiency where the eyes don't turn inward enough during focusing.

Convergence insufficiency is frequently misdiagnosed as ADD/ADHD. The inability of the two eyes to turn toward each other, or converge, causes reduced near-point (close-up) visual attention. Because a child must expend considerable effort to compensate for her convergence insufficiency, she will experience a shortened visual attention span, exhibit avoidance behaviors, or pay less attention to visual processing.[13] The reduced attention span is what causes a misdiagnosis of ADD/ADHD so often. The connection between eye teaming problems and attention-deficit disorder has been discovered by pediatric ophthalmologist Dr. David B. Granet. Dr. Granet's research found that children diagnosed with ADHD were three times more likely to have convergence insufficiency than peers' in the rest of the population.[14] Therefore, the medical establishment recommends that any child diagnosed with ADD or ADHD undergo a vision screening due to the high risk of misdiagnosis.

During reading, the two eyes must turn inward or converge at the proper distance so that they aim appropriately and fixate on words during reading. Because he has problems fixating, he may not land on the next word but a few words farther on in the text. As a result, he commonly omits or confuses small words. Most studies suggest that the more effort encompassed during reading, the lower the comprehension and associated performance.[15] Therefore, the child may avoid reading because of the level of difficulty involved. Confusing to parents is the child's refusal to read but desire to play electronic video games. As a result, parents typically assume that the child is simply not working hard enough or not paying attention in school. However, electronic games do not require a child to use the same close-focusing mechanisms that reading, writing, and copying necessitate. Movement on television or video games is easy for these children to follow but written words are not.[16]

Do not expect your child to tell you that his vision is not clear. He has no reference point to inform him that his vision differs from the vision of anyone else. Therefore, it is parental observation and subsequent examination from a developmental optometrist that will lead to a proper diagnosis and treatment.

Children with inadequate focusing and eye teaming problems often exhibit the symptoms listed in the below checklist.

Checklist of Focusing and Eye Teaming Problems

- Excessive time completing assignments/copying from blackboard
- Slow reading speed, frequent loss of place, and reduced comprehension
- Short attention span
- Motion sickness or vertigo
- Avoiding close work
- Eye strain or headaches
- Fatigue or drowsiness during the activity
- Blurred or double vision
- Moving, jumping, or floating words
- Rubbing, squinting, closing or covering an eye
- Poor sports performance; trouble catching balls or other objects in the air
- Misjudgment of physical distances; stumbles on uneven surfaces, stairs, curbs; bumps into doors or furniture
- Avoidance of tasks requiring depth perception (tasks that require hand-eye coordination)

While struggling to overcome eye teaming or focusing problems, some children find ways to avoid the bothersome tasks or compensate with adaptations to reduce their difficulties. Avoidance behaviors are very successful in disguising a vision problem because children refuse to do tasks or activities that are challenging, uncomfortable or tiring. Therefore, these children will show no visible symptoms.[17] In the absence of avoidance, physical adaptations may follow. The child may move the entire head to read instead of just the eyes, cover one eye to eliminate distorted or double vision, or hold a book very close to her eyes to compensate for poor vision. Without intervention, these physical adaptations can lead to either intermittent or continuous blurred vision due to focusing spasms. Temporary blurring may materialize as a rapid, intermittent blur or short period of continuous blur. Transient blur is frequently followed by a permanent reduction of distance clarity (i.e., near-sightedness/myopia), as the child's eyes gradually adapt to the excessive visual stress of close work. Her eyes may now be more comfortable during close work, but her distance vision is sacrificed in the process.

Treatment. In the case of virtually all eye teaming and focusing problems, vision therapy is the only way to treat the condition. The treatment program uses a combination of lenses, prisms, instruments, computers with special software programs, and variable-demand 3-D techniques. In some cases, glasses can treat the symptoms of a focusing dysfunction. However, this only treats the symptoms and does not resolve the underlying problem. Periodic optometric vision examinations can predict visual changes so that preventative steps are taken.

Eye Movement Control and Visual Tracking
Eye movements are necessary for everyday activities, such as playing sports and reading. In order to read efficiently, we need to be able to:

- Maintain focus on a word so that we can absorb and process information about it (fixation).
- Skip from one word to another accurately and quickly (saccades).
- Track and follow lines of print (pursuits).

Eye movement problems, also referred to as eye tracking problems, exist when one or both eyes do not move smoothly, accurately, and quickly across a line of print or from one object to another. Eye movement problems also include the inability to fixate, or lock one's eyes, onto a single target (such as a word on a printed page). Eye movement problems cause text to blur, jump, and skip.

The presence of vestibular dysfunction in a child with SPD will *always* result in eye movement difficulties. The vestibulo-ocular reflex (VOR) in the vestibular system allows us to maintain steady fixation over very short periods. One can compare the VOR to a photographer who must steady the camera (eyes) in order to produce a clear picture. If the photographer is unable to hold the camera (eyes) steady, then the picture will be blurry, even though the camera (eyes) is in perfect working order. The VOR has two parts: the translational (linear) part receives input from the otoliths in the inner ear, and the rotational (rotary) part receives input from the semicircular canals in the inner ear. The otoliths sense gravity, tilt, linear acceleration/deceleration, and the semicircular canals sense rotary acceleration/deceleration. Each semicircular canal and otolith organ neurologically yokes with a corresponding pair of extra ocular muscles located around the eyes. The inner ear organs and extra ocular muscles work in the same plane of action and are one system.[18abc]

These problems are often present very early in a child's vision development but it may not become problematic until a child is asked to read, copy and attend to tasks that require good eye movement control skills. Therefore, these problems are likely to present initially between kindergarten and fourth grade.

Reading requires the skill of fixation so that the reader can pause very briefly on each word before moving on to the next word. In other words, the eyes make a series of fixations looking from word to word when reading a line of print. A child with fixation problems will often skip lines, lose his place frequently, and misread words. He may also experience word or letter reversals, frequent rereading, comprehension loss, and trouble copying information from the front of the classroom. Eye tracking problems will also result in a child moving his entire head while reading instead of using his eyes to track print. These children may also hold books very close to their faces or bend over closer to a book on the table.

Poorly controlled eye movement's impact sports performance. Distance, speed, and timing are sacrificed, as the eyes must coordinate and focus accurately and efficiently in order to make the quick judgments required in sports; this often results in slow reaction times. These children will be highly distractible with short attention spans, as their attention diverts to their surroundings instead of on a book or other target. Often, children with eye movement, focusing, and eye-teaming dysfunctions are unfairly accused of "not paying attention" or being "lazy learners." Misdiagnosis of dyslexia, ADD/ADHD, or other learning disabilities often occurs.

Treatment. There are several sources of oculomotor deficiencies, and the diagnosis dictates the course of treatment. If the diagnosis is poor focusing, glasses are often prescribed; however, if the diagnosis is not poor focusing, vision therapy is recommended.

Vision therapy treatment will frequently result in significant improvement of the symptoms listed in the below checklist.

Checklist of Poor Visual Tracking and Eye Movement Control Symptoms

- Loss of place of words while reading, writing, or copying
- Misreading known words in text
- Use of a finger or marker when reading
- Word or letter reversals/poor reading comprehension
- Movement of the entire head while reading
- Short attention span
- Trouble judging distance and location in sports and play
- Slow reaction time and poor timing
- Poor handwriting
- Motion sensitivity or sickness

Strabismus (Wandering/Turned Eye)

Strabismus (wandering/turned eye) is an extreme problem of eye teaming in which the two eyes do not point to the same place at the same time. This condition occurs when one of the eyes turns in, out, up, or down. The four common types of strabismus are: (1) exotropia, when eyes turn out,

(2) esotropia, when eyes turn in, (3) hypertropia, when eyes turn up, and (4) hypotropia, when eyes turn down.

It is estimated that up to five percent of all children have some type or degree of strabismus.[19] Infants (birth to three months of age) may occasionally be observed crossing their eyes as their visual system is in its early developmental stage; this is considered normal. The vestibular system holds the eyes aligned from three to six months of age, until the visual system is mature enough to function. Vestibular dysfunction, including chronic ear infections (more than one per year) or effusion (fluid buildup without infection that can occur two weeks prior to an infection and two to three weeks after the infection), is thought to play a significant role in strabismus because of its function prenatally and in early development, which can result in poorly developed control of the eye muscles. In typical children six months and older, the eyes should function together and point in the same direction.

Parents detect the majority of strabismus cases based upon the child's appearance. A parent's primary concern may be the appearance of crossed eyes, while not understanding that strabismus also causes vision problems. Sometimes, weak eye muscles are mistakenly described to be causal in strabismus, when it is actually a correctible malfunction of the processing of visual information, in which the eyes and brain are getting their signals literally crossed.[20]

Double vision, ranging from moderate to severe, is a typical vision problem for people with strabismus until they adapt and start to suppress one eye or to alternate the suppression of eyes. This condition may be either constant (occurs all the time) or intermittent (occurring only at specific distances, during certain activities, or during stressful situations).

A constant strabismus rarely affects academic performance, whereas an intermittent strabismus is likely to compromise performance due to the child's inability to maintain single, clear vision while doing near work. In the absence of compensatory strategies, a child may exhibit any of the symptoms below. On the other hand, there may be no symptoms if the child utilizes compensatory strategies such as task avoidance.

Treatment. If the strabismus persists after prescribed lenses, vision therapy is most often the treatment of choice. Sometimes surgery is necessary, but only after a developmental optometrist evaluates the potential benefits of vision therapy. Surgery should have its outcome enhanced through vision therapy, both before and after the procedure. In this situation, an ophthalmologist and a developmental optometrist should comanage the treatment process.

Checklist of Signs and Symptoms of Strabismus

- Headaches
- Rapid fatigue, especially when reading or after school
- Head tilting
- Poor depth judgments in sports, resulting in difficulties catching a ball
- Avoidance of specific tasks
- Loss of place when reading
- Transpositions when copying from one source to another
- Crossing or wandering of one or both eyes
- Blur of one eye or double vision
- Reduction in vision (amblyopia)
- Hiding, covering, or squinting of one eye

Amblyopia (lazy eye)

Amblyopia, commonly called "lazy eye," is a condition in which a person has significantly poorer vision in one eye than the other, not correctable by glasses nor due to any identifiable eye disease. Most children with amblyopia perceive a blurred image from one eye (or occasionally both). There may be no obvious signs or symptoms of the problem, with little disruption in school performance in milder cases. In more severe cases, children may complain of blurry vision. In addition, these children may present with headaches, rapid fatigue, and slower reaction time in sports performance.

With amblyopia, the brain learns to ignore or suppress the image from the "weak" eye and process only the sharper image from the "strong" eye. The two most common causes of amblyopia are Strabismus and Anisometropia, a large difference in prescription between the two eyes. Typically, both of these conditions result in the visual cortex (the part of the brain used for critical vision) receiving a blurred image from the eye(s) that will become amblyopic.

In most cases, this condition is difficult to detect in infants and toddlers and has no apparent symptoms easily recognized by a parent. As the child ages, the condition will persist. Amblyopia can cause poor depth perception, making it difficult to watch a 3-D movie, read, drive a car, catch a ball, and play sports. Children with lazy eye may have problems focusing on detail, making spatial judgments, and detecting subtle contrast changes. Amblyopia, if untreated, may contribute to later onset of strabismus (eye turn).

Treatment. The most common form of treatment for amblyopia is the use of graded occlusion foils (like a partially see-through plastic wrap). Occlusion foils allow peripheral vision to function more normally while blurring the central acuity of the better-seeing eye to force the affected eye to focus. When the brain only has the "blurred" image on which to focus, the brain and visual system will learn how to process the image correctly.

Ophthalmologists or developmental optometrists can treat amblyopia with graded occlusion foils. However, vision therapy, or specific eye exercises used in conjunction with the graded occlusion foils, usually results in better and longer-lasting improvement than the simple passive use of the foils. Early detection of amblyopia is the key to successful treatment. However, even if caught later, vision therapy can greatly mitigate the impact of amblyopia in older children. Recent scientific research has disproven the long-held belief that doctors cannot help children with lazy eye, or amblyopia, after age seven. Parents should take their infant for screening in the first year of life for possible amblyopia.

See the below checklist for signs and symptoms of amblyopia and strabismus.

Checklist of Signs and Symptoms of Amblyopia

- Blur of one eye
- Poor eye tracking and focusing abilities
- Poor depth judgments
- Avoidance of specific tasks
- Spatial distortions
- Excessive squinting or closing of the eyes
- Headaches
- A crossing of one eye that will excessively turn toward the nose, which is typically the eye less used

Visual Perceptual Skills (Visual Discrimination)

Visual perception involves the ability to organize and interpret the images we see and give them meaning; this takes place within the brain. The eyes look, but the brain sees! Visual processing speed is how quickly the brain manages visual information. Visual integration is how we use the visual information perceived and integrate it with our other systems.

Visual information processing is the basis for a number of perceptual skills that include the following:

1. Figure ground: The ability to locate an object, shape, word, or letter against a busy background, as with individual letters and words presented on a page full of sentences and paragraphs, or objects in a picture such as in a "Find Waldo" book.
2. Form constancy: The capacity to visually discriminate the distinctive features of forms such as size, shape, pattern, position, and color, e.g., discriminating *e* from *c* or *r* from *n*. Form constancy also involves the ability to manipulate visual figures and recognize

them even when they are in a different orientation or format. This skill allows us to recognize the fancy script O of "Once upon a time" even if we have never seen that script, or to switch easily from plain print to cursive script without confusion.

3. Color processing: The ability to process all colors of light simultaneously is color processing. White light includes all the colors of light, and each color has a different wavelength, or frequency. Problems with color processing can cause images, such as the floor or words on a page, to appear to be moving.

4. Visual-spatial relations: The ability to determine the positions of objects in space and their relative positions to other objects is visual-spatial relations. Visual spatial deficits can affect a wide array of skills in a child.

   a. The child may have trouble judging distance between herself and other people or objects, or the relative position of one object to another. She may stand too close to people and seem bewildered, as if moving about in unfamiliar territory.

   b. She may have difficulty with understanding positional concepts, identifying body parts (her own or those in pictures), and imitating the movements of others.

   c. She may bump into objects or people, over- or underreach for objects, or struggle to put two Legos together.

   d. Have difficulty with reading, math, and copying. Reading and math are two subjects where an accurate understanding of spatial relationships is particularly important, as these subjects involve the use of symbols. Copying requires the child to judge the spatial layout of the page.

5. Visual Closure. The ability to perceive and integrate an object or symbol in its entirety and its relationship to the parts that make it up is visual closure. Activities such as dot-to-dot designs, filling in incomplete pictures, and jigsaw puzzles require visual closure skills. When children learn to read, they use phonetic awareness. Later in development, proficient readers look

at the whole word shape, which requires visual closure. Some children who struggle with whole/part relationships may only perceive the pieces, while others only see the whole. A ten-year-old child with significant visual-spatial problems may go with her mother to watch her brother play soccer. As the kids are playing soccer, she may ask, "Mom, why are these kids running up and down the field?" She lacks the visual-spatial capacity to see the bigger picture of the game they are actually playing. These children may also have trouble reading facial expressions, body posture, or hand gestures since they have trouble understanding how the parts fit the whole.

6. Visual memory. The ability to remember forms and sequences of forms (e.g., letters and words) and recognize them quickly when you see them again in print is visual memory. Visual memory is a particularly important skill for spelling sight words. It is also important in arithmetic and pretend play. Educationally, visual memory problems can interfere with a child's ability to consistently recognize letters, numbers, symbols, words, or pictures, making information learned one day unavailable the next.

Below is a checklist of symptoms that may indicate a visual perception problem.

Checklist of Symptoms Indicating Visual Perception Problems

- Confuses letters, numbers, or words
- Easily forgets letters, numbers, or words
- Reverses letters or numbers
- Confuses similar-looking words
- Makes errors copying
- Spells poorly

- Has poor reading comprehension
- Writes crookedly or with poor spacing
- Has difficulty following a sequence or directions
- Has problems telling time at age eight or older

Treatment. Vision therapy treats visual perception deficiencies and can significantly improve these skills.

Visual Integration Skills

None of our senses function in isolation; rather, they integrate with one another to give us an accurate understanding of the world around us. Discussed below are three specific types of visual integration processing: visual-auditory integration, visual-motor integration, and visual-vestibular integration.

1. Visual-auditory integration is the ability to match auditory information with visual information, such as interpreting nonverbal linguistic cues while watching a speaker's face or the ability to read music. Other examples are seeing a word and saying it aloud or hearing a word and writing it down. Children who are unable to integrate these inputs simultaneously may avoid eye contact when listening, need to have directions repeated all the time, be poor spellers, have trouble learning to read phonetically, and have difficulty relating symbols to their relevant sounds (e.g., not recognizing that the "ah" sound is related to the letter *a*).
2. Visual-motor integration is the ability to integrate vision and motor movement to produce adaptive responses. Children with visual-motor integration deficits may have difficulty with gross and fine motor movements.
   - Gross visual-motor movement difficulty may manifest when the child tries to kick a football or shoot a basketball.

These children may have a hard time orienting themselves in space, especially in relation to other people and objects. Adults label these children "clumsy" because they bump into things, place things on the edges of tables or counters, where they fall off, or "miss" their seats when they sit down. Visual gross motor integration deficits can interfere with virtually all areas of the child's life: social, academic, athletic, and pragmatic.

- Fine visual-motor movement difficulty affects a child's daily self-care, eating and drinking, playing with precision toys, writing, and organization on paper. In addition, fine visual-motor movement difficulties compromise the ability to copy information between a worksheet and a page of a book or between keyboard and computer screen.

3. Visual-vestibular integration is the basis of oculomotor abilities. A mismatch between the visual and vestibular systems could result in motion sensitivity (car- sickness), inability to read, problems with eye teaming and focusing, eye movement control and tracking, visual perception skills, or strabismus.

When children perceive or process visual information incorrectly, our other senses cannot integrate with the visual information. Instead of reinforcing our learning experiences, it distracts us and interferes with them. The inability to trust what we see significantly impedes our ability to function.

Visual Modulation Disorder
Visual modulation occurs when the brain makes automatic adjustments to regulate arousal to visual input. When there is dysfunction present, the child may be passively underresponsive, overresponsive, or sensory craving. Some children with SPD have mixed subtypes, meaning they will be underresponsive or overresponsive depending on situational context.

Overresponsive

Children with overresponsivity or visual defensiveness find visual sensations painful, disrupting, or upsetting. They overreact to visual input, such as light, moving objects, direct eye contact, or the multiple sources of visual stimulation in their environment. For instance, a toy with many pieces, rooms with clutter or busy walls, crowded places, or bright light from snow or sunshine. For someone with visual defensiveness, the whole world is so visually overwhelming that it is difficult to know where to look or what to focus on. The experience of visual defensiveness is comparable to having a severe headache, during which bright lights can be painful and seeing movement can be very disturbing.

Frustration with these visually overwhelming situations may result in tantrums, withdrawal, or flight responses. For example, a child may react by dumping the bin of toys on the floor and running away (flight response). The caregiver's strategy should be to avoid busy, crowded places or rooms with extensive clutter, whenever possible. When the child is playing with toys with many pieces, such as Legos or puzzles, the caregiver should provide just a few pieces at a time so the child does not become visually overwhelmed.

A child who is peripheral dominant due to visual-spatial attention shifting disorder, detailed in the section below, may also show overresponsive behaviors. This is because the primitive peripheral vision system serves as our vigilance system to alert us to signs of danger, so a very peripheral child can be overly responsive to visual change.

These behaviors are associated with visual defensiveness.

Checklist of Symptoms Indicating Visual Defensiveness

- Shields eyes to screen out sights, closes or covers one eye, squints, or hides in the shade
- Avoids bright lights and sunlight or the brightness from a snowstorm; keeps eyes covered with sunglasses or a hat

- Is uncomfortable with or overwhelmed by moving objects or people
- Has increased agitation, distraction, or "coping" behaviors, such as chewing, moving, or hiding, when in a room full of visual stimulation (such as the typical elementary classroom)
- Visually fixates on certain preferred objects to tune out other stimulation
- Ducks to try to avoid approaching objects, such as a ball or another child
- Withdraws from classroom participation and avoids group-movement activities
- Avoids direct eye contact
- Experiences headaches, nausea, or dizziness when using eyes

Underresponsive

There are two types of underresponsive children: passive underresponders and sensory craving underresponders. Both of them can have problems modulating visual sensations.

The passive underresponder (hyposensitive) notices stimuli much less than typical children and requires more stimulation than peers to register sensations required. As a result, the child may look directly at the blinding sun or a bright light. She may stare at objects or people's faces without noticing them or trip over objects in her path. Underresponsive children may need to touch or hold objects to learn what others learned simply by viewing the objects.

These symptoms are associated with visual underresponsiveness.

Checklist of Symptoms Indicating Visual Underresponsiveness

- Unaware of light/dark contrast, edges, and reflections
- Unaware of movement, often bumping into moving objects such as swings

- Responding late to visual information, such as obstacles in her path
- Touching or holding objects in order to gain information from them.

A sensory craving child also underresponds to visual sensory input. However, the difference between passive and sensory craving underresponsive children is that sensory craving children will seek out visual sensations and moving objects. They may constantly stare at objects that spin and move; flick objects close to their eyes; love fast moving, brightly colored TV shows; or be attracted to the brightest colors. Sensory craving kids need constant visual stimulation in order to register visual sensations.

These symptoms are associated with visual sensory craving.

Checklist of Symptoms Indicating Visual Sensory Craving

- Obsessing on objects that spin and move
- Drawn to fast-moving, brightly colored TV shows
- Staring at shiny, bright things such as rhinestones and sparkly objects

Visual-Spatial Attention Shifting

Visual-spatial attention shifting is the ability to shift attention appropriately between central processing (what is in front of you) and peripheral awareness (what is beside you) as required for typical awareness, interaction, and learning. Children with visual-spatial attention shifting disorder will be dominant either peripherally or centrally and engage in the associated activities obsessively.

Most children with visual-spatial attention shifting disorder are dominantly peripheral in their visual processing. The peripheral system answers the question, where is it? Peripheral processing, which is noncognitive (nonthinking), is a more primitive processing pathway responsible for maintaining vigilance (a constant state of alertness). The peripheral visual system detects movement and contrast in lighting and edges, and serves to orient individuals in space relative to their surroundings.

A minority of children with visual-spatial attention shifting disorder are dominantly central in their visual processing. Central processing, a sequential processing pathway, is a cognitive function used to identify detail, recognize features, and maintain attention and focus for learning. The central processing pathway answers the question, what is it?

Typical individuals shift between their peripheral and central processing systems smoothly, resulting in a dynamic and fluid change in the bias of attention between the two. Your current activity influences which system you are primarily using at any given time. If you are driving your car, you will primarily rely on peripheral vision to orient yourself and detect movement by other cars and people. If you are reading a book, you are using central processing to focus on what is in front of you. As activities or external demands change, an individual should be able to switch the bias of attention back and forth innately and effortlessly.

Individuals with visual-spatial attention shifting disorder are unable to create visual balance relative to the demand of the activity. They are either hypervigilant (excessively alert) to peripheral activity or hyperfocal (excessively focused) on the isolated activity. Children with either type of visual-spatial attention shifting disorder can lock into their particular type of processing, and this can progress into high myopia (nearsightedness).

Visual-spatial attention shifting disorder is most prevalent in kids who have Sensory Processing Disorder. Dr. Neal Margolis, FCOVD, who has been in practice for thirty years, indicates he has never treated a child with visual-spatial attention shifting disorder that did not have Sensory Processing Disorder. Therefore, a visual developmental screening for a child with Sensory Processing Disorder is imperative. In order for a child to develop appropriate interaction with the environment and achieve integration, visual-spatial attention shifting requires treatment.

Peripheral Dominance

A child may be showing a dominantly peripheral mode of processing if he:

- Appears to be looking at objects with his peripheral vision.
- Is very distracted by peripheral movement when he is expected to sustain central attention.
- Constantly watches spinning/moving objects or drops objects, often resulting in hyperfocal tunneling. See the "Hyperfocal Behaviors" checklist below for specific behaviors.
- Stares through his fingers at lights or looks at objects through his fingers while moving them back and forth.
- Frames the world with his fingers or hand to organize the space or to block peripheral vision stimuli.
- Runs back and forth while looking at the edges of toys or other objects with his side vision (he may get down and look at the edge of his train).
- May observe edges of toys with head sideways as he pushes them back and forth utilizing his side vision.

The peripheral system is the pathway that alerts us to movement, so when children are more biased toward this pathway, they are more easily distracted by movement. When asked to maintain attention and focus on a teacher, which requires appropriate central processing, a normally developing child would be able to attend with his central vision and ignore (i.e., filter out) nonrelevant peripheral vision distractions. However, a child who is predominantly peripheral cannot filter out these peripheral distractions and primarily focuses on the clutter, movement, or lighting changes in the classroom. In response, this child may try to self-regulate by getting up and moving around the classroom so that he can sustain his central attention on the teacher.

Additionally, the peripherally dominant child may stare through her fingers at light because she uses her peripheral system to detect contrast and may love to study the contrast between her fingers in the light. She may also enjoy looking at objects through her fingers as she moves her fingers back and forth because her peripheral system is physiologically tuned to movement. She may run back and forth and look at edges of objects because this stimulates her peripheral system through motion and contrast. She will also try to filter out peripheral vision distractions by framing the world with her fingers or hand or going somewhere that blocks out peripheral vision distractions, such as a tent or Lycra hammock.

The child's inability to filter out nonrelevant peripheral vision distractions increases her likelihood of using her dominant peripheral visual system to regulate her sensory system. She may respond to peripheral vision overload with tunneling of her entire visual field. When this triggers, she first becomes hypervigilant (excessively alert to peripheral distractions), gets overwhelmed, shuts down, and ultimately transitions to hyperfocal tunneling (tunnel vision on a moving, spinning, or dropping object). Through this hyperfocal tunneling, she is able to take charge of the sensory input rather than having to deal with the random sensory input of the surrounding world that she cannot control.

This hyperfocal tunneling also causes clumsiness because it prevents her from having the simultaneous awareness of her visual surroundings, (including what is in front of and beside her), that she needs during movement for effective spatial orientation. Lack of simultaneous awareness inhibits her ability to play team sports such as soccer, where she must be aware of her surrounding teammates and avoid bumping against others in passing.

It is common to witness hand-flapping or distal cupping (cupping the hand very rapidly) while a child is engaged in hyperfocal tunneling. This behavior typically occurs when children watch moving objects (real life or on-screen) or visualize moving objects in their minds. See the below table for more examples of hyperfocal behaviors.

Hyperfocal Behaviors

- Visually tracking toys, such as a marble run, trains rolling around a track, or cars going down an incline
- Rolling balls or toys down a slide or any inclined surface
- Pressing elevator buttons to watch the door open and close, watching automatic doors open and close, or fixating on escalators or revolving doors
- Flushing toilets to watch the spinning water
- Rolling the car windows up and down
- Tracking the sand pouring from the top of a sand wheel toy or pouring sand or water back and forth from one cup to another excessively
- Spinning or watching objects that spin, including fans, for excessive time periods
- Tracking bubbles obsessively after blowing them

Central Dominance

A child may be showing a dominantly central "tunneling" mode of processing if he:

- Shows excessive attention to fine detail to the extent that the child does not notice peripheral cues, such as a hand waving next to his face.
- Appears to be clumsy because he cannot orient himself effectively using peripheral or tunnel vision when moving around.
- May have a compulsive need to order things or toys by features or do things in sequential order.

Children, who are centrally dominant, will tunnel vision their entire field to one object across the room. As they move toward that object without the assistance of peripheral vision, they will trip over objects in their path. Therefore, centrally dominant children will appear clumsy.

Since the central pathway is sequential, order is very important to these children. Children complete everything sequentially and place objects in the proper order. They may spend an extraordinary amount of time lining things up on the floor in order by size, color or shape and may always complete a number, clock, or alphabet puzzle in sequential order. Movement and balance activities best help these children to engage peripheral awareness.

Treatment

Vision impairments associated with visual-spatial attention shifting disorder are treated with vision therapy, occupational therapy, or a combination of these.

Vision Therapy

Vision therapy is an individualized, supervised treatment program designed to correct visual-motor and/or perceptual-cognitive deficiencies and is an effective nonsurgical treatment for many common visual problems. The College of Optometrists in Vision Development (COVD) defines optometric vision therapy as a blend of medical, developmental, and behavioral therapies, which may include:

1. Pursuit and saccade therapy to improve the speed and accuracy of eye tracking movements.
2. Visual-perceptual therapy to enhance visual information processing.
3. Accommodative therapy to enhance focusing, stability, flexibility, and comfort.
4. Visual-spatial awareness therapy including laterality, directionality, and visual imagery.
5. Visual-vestibular therapy to integrate eye movements with balance.
6. Visual-auditory integration therapy.

7. Visual-motor therapy (eye-hand coordination) to develop visually guided movement.
8. Peripheral awareness therapy to enhance the use of vision as a simultaneous sense that synchronously receives and processes multiple inputs.
9. Visual attention therapy.
10. Orthoptics, the mechanics of eye movements. Although optometric vision therapy evolved from orthoptics, orthoptics is only one of many therapies that used in contemporary optometric vision therapy.

Vision therapy trains the entire visual system, which includes the eyes, brain, and body. It is important to understand that vision therapy is a form of neurological and perceptual training or rehabilitation. The patient's brain is trained to use the eyes to receive information effectively, process it quickly, and react appropriately.

What Is Involved in a Vision Therapy Program?
The College of Optometrists in Vision Development (COVD) describes a vision therapy program as a progressive hierarchy of arranged vision procedures prescribed to help patients develop or improve fundamental visual skills and abilities; improve visual comfort, ease, and efficiency; and change how a patient interprets visual information. Vision therapy is performed under a doctor's supervision and is customized to fit the visual needs of each patient. Therapy occurs during weekly or semiweekly in-office sessions of thirty minutes to one hour. The doctor often supplements office therapy with home exercises between office visits.

Vision Therapy Is Not Just Eye Exercises
Effective vision therapy requires an in-depth understanding of developmental milestones and the visual skills and visual concepts to advance learning to the next developmental level. Sufficient probing

and retesting in an interactive manner is necessary, to ensure that true learning and skill application toward goals is occurring. Toward this end, vision therapy uses various types of treatment devices, including some regulated medical devices.

7. Corrective lenses (regulated medical devices)
8. Therapeutic lenses (regulated medical devices)
9. Prism lenses (regulated medical devices)
10. Optical filters
11. Eye patches or occluders
12. Electronic targets with timing mechanisms
13. Computer software
14. Vestibular (balance) equipment
15. Visual-motor-sensory integration training devices

These treatment devices develop visual skills and endurance. During the final stages of therapy, the doctor reinforces and automates the patient's newly acquired visual skills through repetition and integration with motor and cognitive skills.

Occupational Therapy

Pediatric occupational therapy is skilled treatment aimed at maximizing infants and children's ability to achieve age-appropriate self-help, play, and learning skills. Using purposeful activities, including the tasks of daily life, it promotes the greatest possible degree of functional independence. Occupational therapists treat vestibular dysfunction, which is the root cause of oculomotor deficits; visual-spatial attention shifting disorder; and visual modulation disorders. It is important for your occupational therapist to work in concert with your child's developmental optometrist to achieve overall vision goals. In respect to this, your child's developmental optometrist may request your child's occupational therapist incorporate vision treatment goals into your child's occupational therapy sessions.

Summary

Vision problems can be subtle, with few outward signs of distress. While many affected children will exhibit symptoms from one of the checklists, your child may not exhibit any symptoms and still have vision impairment. Therefore, a checklist is not a reliable way to be certain that your child does not have vision problems.

Vision plays a critical role in learning, sports, and everyday life, making it imperative that every child receive a vision screening by a developmental optometrist as soon as possible. This screening could literally make the difference between academic success and failure. Remember, it is estimated that one in four children has an undetected vision problem. Do not let your child be one of those statistics!

Twelve

Auditory Dysfunction

S ome children with sensory processing disorder exhibit an auditory disorder. These children may have auditory processing disorder (APD), auditory modulation disorder, or both. Auditory processing disorder is also
referred to as central auditory processing disorder (CAPD). Below is a discussion of both of these disorders.

Auditory Modulation Disorder
Auditory modulation disorder is sensory modulation disorder in the auditory system.

Receptors in the inner ear pick up auditory information and send it to the
brain-stem auditory centers. The nuclei in the auditory centers process the
auditory stimuli, along with the vestibular, proprioceptive, and tactile information. The auditory organizing centers are very close to the visual processing centers in the brain, and the two exchange information. Like visual input,
some of the auditory impulses travel to lower parts of the brain for integration with other sensations and motor messages. The auditory information
then travels, integrating with other sensations along the way, finally arriving
in higher parts of the brain. If the auditory information does not intermingle
with other types of sensory information at each stage of the process, the
result is hypersensitivity to auditory sounds.

Auditory modulation disorder is an extreme sensitivity to certain
sounds that would not be particularly disturbing or distressing to other

people. Triggers may be high-frequency sounds, low-frequency sounds, or both high- and low-frequency sounds. In other words, the child may be sensitive to loud noises, gentle noises, or both. Modulation enables us to filter sensations, attend to those that are relevant, and screen out those that are irrelevant. In the case of auditory modulation disorder, the child's brain does not filter out the auditory information it should, and this elicits the body's pain response.

Behavioral reactions to disturbing sounds can range anywhere from mild annoyance, the "fight or flight" reaction, or a shift into sensory craving mode. When overresponsive children feel assaulted by sensory stimuli to which they are hypersensitive, they may respond by either trying to avoid the sensation or combatting the sensation. When the child goes into combat mode, he will become more active, agitated, and aggressive. He will shift into sensory craving mode producing the very loud noises that he dislikes and eliciting loud noises from others. Ultimately, this will overload the child further creating a vicious cycle.

Avoidance children might cover their ears, show signs of distress, and cry when encountering loud noises. He may show signs of fear and anxiety and will avoid the activities other children enjoy to avoid the trigger sounds. Noises generated by power tools, thunder, and fireworks typically distress children with auditory modulation disorder. Trips to the restroom can be scary, as loud toilets flush on their own and hand dryers echo in the room. Movies may be unbearable as the surround sound sets off an explosion in the child's head. The school bus may incite physical ailments such as tummy aches. Infants and young children may cry when they hear a loud sneeze. Supermarkets, school cafeterias, public transport, or the sound of someone's voice may elicit visible stress. These children usually cope better in a quiet and calm environment as noisy environments may lead to self-regulation difficulties.

Auditory defensive children might be acutely aware of other sounds that typical children would not consider disturbing, such as the sound of a clock ticking or a small creature scratching. Some children are acutely aware of certain low-intensity and low-volume sounds and might become disorganized, upset, or annoyed upon hearing them. Young children may not realize that sound is distressing them. Parents can raise their child's awareness level by verbalizing the problem. You can say, "Was that vacuum cleaner too loud for you?" or "Does the sound of the clock ticking hurt your ears?"

Children with auditory defensiveness may experience some or all of these symptoms:

- Are troubled by loud or unexpected noise or sounds.
- Frequently cover their ears or put fingers in their ears in response to sounds that other children do not find distressing.
- Are distracted by sounds others do not usually notice, such as ticking clocks or the humming of lights, refrigerators, fans, or heaters.
- Fear the sound of a flushing toilet (especially in public restrooms), vacuum, hairdryer, squeaky shoes, or a dog barking.
- Feel bothered by environmental sounds (e.g., lawn mowers, outside construction, or garbage trucks).
- Frequently ask people to stop making noise, talking, or singing.
- Run away, cry, and/or cover their ears in response to loud or unexpected sounds.
- Refuse to go to movie theaters, parades, skating rinks, musical concerts or avoid experiences that require them to be in loud environments.
- Decide whether they like certain people by the sound of their voices.

Occupational therapists or Speech/Language pathologists may diagnose auditory modulation disorder. Occupational or speech/language therapists often recommend therapeutic listening as the primary treatment for auditory modulation disorder. For severe auditory defensiveness, your audiologist may recommend noise-reducing earplugs for your child. Several types are available that can be custom fit to the listener's needs.

Auditory Processing Disorder

A child who remembers only the third step of a three-step direction, a boy who feels nauseous when in a noisy lunchroom, a child who hears the word sheep instead of ship, and a child who hears "tell me how a chair and couch are alike" instead of "tell me how a couch and chair are alike" may all be experiencing a condition called auditory processing disorder (APD).

The majority of these children will pass a standard hearing test easily and parents categorize their problems as "behavioral." As with vision, hearing is more complicated than a simple hearing test administered by your child's school. The school auditory screening confirms whether a child is able to detect the presence of pure tones of sound, known as peripheral hearing. Individuals with peripheral hearing loss sustain damage to the organs or nerve responsible for transmitting auditory information to the brain. Children with APD do not have damage to auditory organs or the auditory nerve. Instead, these children cannot *process* auditory information efficiently in the brain, which leads to difficulty recognizing and interpreting sounds, especially those of speech.

It is important to note that APD is not the result of other cognitive, language, or related disorders.[1] In addition, APD dysfunction may occur as a stand-alone disorder or may co-occur with other conditions such as attention deficit disorder, learning disabilities, developmental language disorders, or sensory processing disorder.[2] The diagnosis children with auditory disorders are most frequently mislabeled is attention deficit hyperactivity disorder. Individuals' with attention deficit hyperactivity disorder (ADHD) may well be poor listeners and have difficulty understanding or remembering verbal information; however, the actual neural processing of auditory input in the CNS is intact. Instead, the attention deficit impedes their ability to access or use the auditory information that is coming in.[3] Treatment techniques appropriate for an ADHD child will not be effective for a child suffering from auditory processing issues, who needs to develop specific auditory skills.

The impact of APD can range from mild to severe. Children with a milder degree of APD often go undiagnosed because teachers' comments, such as "has trouble following directions" and "doesn't take adequate notes in class," are classified as behavioral problems in school. In reality, these children cannot interpret the teacher's speech due to the background noise from their classmates. Because performance is affected by the noise level in many of these children's environments, they will sometimes understand the material presented to them in class one day and be completely baffled the next day.[4] A child with more severe symptoms will display significant speech-language problems as well as social and emotional difficulties.

Auditory Processing Disorder does not yet have an identified cause. Research suggests that it can be congenital (some people are born with it) or it can be acquired. Evidence suggests links to recurring middle ear infections, head injury or trauma.[5] Research is underway to try to understand the complex nature of human communication, a process with several components, including auditory processing. Human communication relies on taking in complicated perceptual information from the outside world through the senses and interpreting that information in a meaningful way. It also requires certain cognitive abilities, such as attention and memory. Scientists still do not understand exactly how auditory processes operate, interact, or malfunction in people with communication disorders.

Evaluation of APD

Diagnostic testing is appropriate for children six years and older (some audiologists require an age of seven). Screening for auditory processing difficulties is appropriate for listeners aged four to six years. Common complaints associated with APD include:

- Difficulty understanding in noise or trouble hearing in groups
- Difficulty following directions and/or needs frequent repetition
- Seems to hear but does not understand, needs frequent clarification/repetition

- History of ear infections/other otologic problems, history of neurologic problems
- Distractible, does not "listen," short attention span, poor focus/concentration
- Speech and language problems, weak memory skills
- Poor localization skills
- Problems in phonics, reading, spelling, written language
- Poor balance and motor coordination skills.

Definition of APD

Audiologists have not yet reached consensus on the definition of APD. Nevertheless, Dr. Jack Katz, head of the National Coalition of Auditory Disorders, states that audiologists have consensus on the points below:[6]

- There is a neurological basis.
- There is a breakdown in receiving, remembering, understanding, and using auditory information.
- The ability to hear is adequate.
- The ability to listen is impaired.

Below is a checklist of APD symptoms. Each child presents with a distinctive blend of difficulties often with one emerging more dominant. It is rare for a child to suffer in only one of the symptoms noted in the checklist. A child who displays any of the symptoms below is a candidate for APD testing. If auditory deficits are not identified and managed during early development, many children may have speech and language delays, academic problems, social challenges, and emotional problems.

General Symptoms of Auditory Processing Disorder

- Is easily distracted or unusually bothered by loud noises, sudden noises, or noises that do not bother other people (such as a toilet flushing).

- Has difficulty understanding speech in noisy environments.
- Behavior and performance improves in quieter settings.
- Has language difficulty (e.g., confuses syllable sequences and has problems developing vocabulary and understanding language).
- May hear wreath instead of reef.
- Has difficulty following directions, especially multistep.
- Exhibits poor listening skills and trouble understanding conversations.
- Struggles to focus and remember information presented orally.
- When asked a question, often says, "What?" or "Huh?" or asks you to repeat the question (this indicates the need for more time to process information).
- Has reading, spelling, comprehension, vocabulary, writing, or other speech-language difficulties.
- May exhibit language or speech delays.
- Exhibits trouble mastering social skills.
- Has difficulty with verbal (word) math problems.
- Struggles to recognize rhymes, or understand jokes, riddles or idioms.
- Has low academic performance.
- Exhibits behavior problems.
- Is disorganized or forgetful.
- Appears unable to hear or to ignore you.
- Seems unaware of the sources of sounds.
- Struggles to recognize the differences between sounds (e.g., whether they are near or far, angry or pleasant, or high or low voices).
- Cannot speak clearly enough to be understood.

So how do these auditory processing symptoms fit within a classification scheme for this disorder? Currently, there is no single theoretical model of APD that is universally accepted. However, the Bellis/Ferre model provides a framework based on both the underlying neurophysiology and the relationship between the different types of auditory processing disorders and associated language, learning, and communication difficulties. Terri Bellis is professor of audiology at the University of South Dakota and Jeanane Ferre of Oak Park, Illinois, is a private audiologist whose practice specializes in APD.

The three primary types of APD in the Bellis/Ferre model are:

- Auditory decoding deficit
- Prosodic deficit
- Auditory integration deficit

The two subtypes of APD in the Bellis/Ferre model are:

- Associative deficit
- Organization deficit

A brief description of each of these types is below.

Primary Types

Auditory Decoding Deficit

The following description of auditory decoding deficit is reprinted with permission from Dr. Jeanane Ferre and provides an excellent description of this type.

> Auditory decoding, the most common deficit area in children with APD, is the ability to analyze and extract fine auditory differences in the speech spectrum. These children process information inaccurately and slowly, but are often wrongly described as having a hearing deficiency.
>
> Difficulty extracting or discriminating the fine auditory differences in the speech spectrum places children at risk for listening difficulties when noise is present, in highly reverberant

environments (e.g., gym, lunchroom), when extra visual or contextual cues are not available, or when listening to someone who is soft-spoken or has a noticeable accent. Even under optimal listening conditions, the child's auditory system must work harder than normal to analyze incoming acoustic information. As acoustic or linguistic conditions deteriorate, the child will expend more and more energy just to process the acoustic information, leaving less energy for the higher-order processing required for associated thoughts, logic, memory, and attention. As auditory overload occurs, fatigue sets in, and overall listening comprehension deteriorates.

Inefficient decoding/discrimination may affect all types of language development, including acquisition of age-appropriate vocabulary, grammar (e.g., how to use plurals or verb tenses), or semantics (e.g., using multiple-meaning words or understanding *what, when,* and *where* questions). Poor discrimination may make it difficult for an individual to hear and subsequently learn differences between "have been," "has been," and "had been," for example. Similarly, if someone says "park," the child may hear "bark." This makes learning the meanings of different words very challenging, and reading and comprehension may be adversely affected. These children may struggle to follow directions, particularly in situations where material is unfamiliar, noise is present, or they cannot fall back on visual cues. They will also find it difficult to complete spelling tests in which the words to be spelled are presented as isolated words rather than in sentences.

In a typical classroom, children with APD may have trouble listening to the teacher due to the sounds of the playground, the humming of lights overhead, the traffic outside, and other classmates whispering behind them. Children with auditory decoding deficit often perplex parents' as "the most baffling aspect of this difficulty is that the vast majority of children with APD can hear even the faintest speech signals, but when listening to speech input in a dynamic auditory environment, they have difficulty understanding the message.[7] Auditory decoding deficit is the most common type of APD experienced in both children and adults.

Prosodic Deficit

Prosodic deficit, which may be more outwardly apparent than other types of auditory deficits, makes it difficult to discern the *intent* of communication rather than its content. The difficult skill areas for people with auditory decoding deficit are usually the areas of strength for people with prosodic deficit.

Children with prosodic deficit will not modulate their voices to reflect rhythm, tone, or stress and are unable to recognize such modulation in other people's voices. This may render them unable to understand humor, sarcasm, or expressions of emotional states. The lack of this fundamental communication skill results in social challenges for the child with prosodic deficit. Children with this auditory deficit will also have little understanding or skill in the area of music, art, or math.

In *When the Brain Can't Hear* (2002), Dr. Terri Bellis suggests that prosodic deficit may not be a true type of APD. She states people with prosodic deficit often have greater difficulty in non-auditory areas and is often a symptom, as opposed to the cause of, a person's functional problems. As a result, it may not be appropriate to apply the label APD, but rather consider prosodic deficit to be an auditory piece of a global, right-hemisphere dysfunction.[8] Until further research clarifies Dr. Bellis's thoughts on prosodic deficit, it will remain in the Bellis/Ferre theoretical model.

Auditory Integration Deficit

The final primary type is related to the left and right hemispheres interaction and communication with each other, preventing individuals from recognizing the relationship between pieces of information. A child with auditory integration deficit may have a problem when an adult expects her to listen to directions and then perform a physical task, such as in a physical education class. It would be easier for her to watch another person physically complete the activity and mimic the actions. Therefore, these children tend to wait for others to begin a task so they can gauge how to accomplish the task themselves. In addition, they often have problems understanding words as a whole; they read letter by letter resulting in poor spelling and word recognition. This leads to reading problems because we must read words as a whole to process written text rapidly.

Interhemispheric integration is required for a vast array of tasks and proficiencies; thus, symptoms of this problem differ significantly from one person to another. It is important to note that integration deficit may exemplify one feature of the person's global difficulties, and that a child's complete list of complaints should not be attributed solely to an auditory deficit.[9] As a result, it is important for her to complete language, cognitive, neurological, and any other evaluations recommended by her doctors or therapists in order to produce a comprehensive representation of the disorder(s).

Secondary Profiles

Associative Deficit

Associative deficit profile is an auditory manifestation of a language processing disorder. People with associative deficit often have difficulty with a variety of receptive language abilities including semantics, or the meaning of speech. A person with associative deficit may have good sound discrimination but poor whole-word recognition. If a child repeats verbal directions verbatim, he may have little comprehension of the message. He may not understand complex sentences and higher-level linguistic forms, such as passive voice (sentence where the subject is being acted upon instead of the subject acting, making readers work harder to interpret the intended meaning of the sentence), compound sentences (sentences with two independent clauses), and those that include various forms of temporal (before, after, first, then), spatial (on, under, within), and related concepts. Children with associative deficit may perform adequately in school until they reach third grade, when the linguistic demands increase markedly.

Organization Deficit

Organization Deficit involves areas of the brain responsible for assisting in the execution of a response to verbal information. People with organization deficit receive auditory signals successfully but cannot organize or sequence the information in a meaningful way to enable an appropriate response, often resulting in an expressive language disorder. This sequencing deficit often permeates the child globally, affecting many cognitive and motor abilities, such as language, physical organization, keeping study notes in order, motor planning, and gross/fine motor tasks.

An organizational deficit may also negatively affect a child's ability to generate responses to direct, verbally presented questions or multi-step directions. These children usually fare better when adults present instructions in writing. Similar to other APD types, a hallmark symptom of organization deficit is severe difficulty hearing in noisy environments. Finally, organization deficit frequently coexists with (or is an associated symptom of) higher-order executive function disorders such as ADHD.

Diagnosing Auditory Processing Disorder

Children with APD exhibit a variety of listening challenges that span from understanding speech in noisy environments to academic difficulties. Therefore, a multidisciplinary team approach is vital to completely assess and comprehend the problems demonstrated by children with APD.[10] A pediatrician can help eliminate possible diseases that can cause similar symptoms as APD; an educational professional may provide information on the child's academic performance; a psychologist may evaluate cognitive functions; a speech-language pathologist will provide information regarding the listener's comprehension and usage of auditory information. Speech-language pathologists, psychologists, and educational professionals use assessment tools that can provide helpful insights into the listener's auditory performance in a variety of contexts, but they cannot diagnose APD. Audiologists are the only professionals that possess the diagnostic tools to diagnose this disorder. However, because audiologists can treat auditory processing disorder and speech-language pathologists focus on speech-language, it is common for them to work in concert to treat your child.

During assessment, an audiologist administers well-controlled tasks specifically sensitive to disorders of listening. During APD testing, the child enters a soundproof booth, the audiologist pipes in words or other signals and the child responds by repetition. The audiologist will test with and without background noise. Another means of testing auditory pathways, electrophysiology, provides information on how well the nerves in the auditory system fire in synchrony. However, because not all types of APD result in asynchrony of neural firing, many cases cannot be detected with sole electrophysiologic testing. Speak to your audiologist about the appropriate age to test for APD, as some audiologists will require an age of six and others seven or eight. This age variation is due to the pronounced inconsistency in brain function in young children that sometimes renders test interpretation impossible.[11]

By working together, the APD assessment team can develop an accurate picture of the listener's strengths and weaknesses related to using verbal information. This, in turn, leads to the development of deficit-specific treatment and management strategies that maximize both intervention resources and positive outcomes for the listener.

If your child is having problems in school, speech-language and psychological tests may be available as part of an educational evaluation to determine eligibility for special education services. If not, start by speaking with the Individualized Education Plan Coordinator to learn whether these assessments are obtainable through the school district free of charge. If the educational team (which often consists of the school psychologist, school occupational therapist, school speech-language pathologist, and child's teacher) does not feel that such testing is warranted for your child, or the school district does not provide such testing, you may need to pursue these assessments on your own through local professionals. Once the educational team obtains this baseline information, they can determine whether a central auditory processing evaluation is necessary, and refer you to a pediatric audiologist trained in APD evaluations. For information regarding audiologists with specialized APD training in your area, you may wish to contact the American Speech-Language-Hearing Association (1-800-638-8255 or www.asha.org), the American Academy of Audiology (1-800-AAA-2336 or www.audiology.org), or the National Coalition for Auditory Processing Disorders, Inc.

(www.ncapd.org). Make sure that an identified audiologist lists central auditory processing disorder as an area of expertise. A physician's referral is not necessary for an audiologist to assess hearing, but your insurance company may require it for reimbursement purposes. Some insurance companies do not reimburse for APD testing, so check with your health insurance company prior to pursuing an evaluation.

Treatment and Accommodations

Treatment for children with auditory modulation disorder revolves around therapeutic listening described below. Treatment for children with auditory processing disorder is highly individualized according to the type of auditory deficit. There are several options for treatment, and some of these are home-based and others require children to attend therapy sessions in school or a local clinic. The end-result of therapy may also be variable by child with some children completely eradicating the disorder and others maintaining some residual deficit throughout their lifetime. Where your child falls upon this treatment spectrum cannot be determined in advance, but with quality treatment, children can make significant gains. Your audiologist and occupational therapist will recommend the appropriate avenue based upon your child's profile. In addition, parents and professionals can implement several accommodations in the school and home setting to assist the child. Treatment methods and accommodations for home and school settings in use today are delineated below.

Treatment for Auditory Modulation Disorder

Occupational therapists Sheila Frick, OTR/L and Colleen Hacker, OTR/L developed Therapeutic Listening, which is an innovative program for providing high-quality auditory input within the context of sensory integrative treatment. Sensory integration treatment goals are to enhance sensory processing through the vestibular, proprioceptive, and tactile senses. The incorporation of sound into sensory integration treatment has been effective in recent clinical practice. Today, most experts would agree that the auditory system is a vital link in sensory integration treatment.[12]

Therapeutic listening's emphasis is on blending sound intervention strategies with vestibular, proprioceptive, core development, and breathe activities in order to sustain good posture, balance, motor skills and self-regulation. For information on research related to Therapeutic Listening, see http://www.vitallinks.net/pages/Evidence-Based-Brief-on-Effectiveness-of-Therapeutic-Listening.php

Treatment for Auditory Processing Disorder

Earobics. Earobics provides a research based, comprehensive reading intervention program that helps improve reading proficiency, reading skills, and reading comprehension. This computer-based program offers games to improve listening skills required for reading success. Earobics can be useful for children with auditory decoding deficit and offers a home-based version. For information on research studies that support the efficacy of this treatment method, visit http://www.ies.ed.gov/ncee/wwc/interventionreport.aspx?sid=158

FastForWord (FFW). This computer-based program's games increase auditory processing speed and work on auditory memory and sequencing. In short, FFW trains the auditory system to process the sounds of speech more efficiently. FFW is effective for those who have auditory decoding deficit. FastForWord must be purchased through a provider such as an audiologist or speech-language therapist. For more information on research studies that support the efficacy of this treatment method, go to http://www.ies.ed.gov/ncee/wwc/interventionreport.aspx?sid=173

Lindamood Phoneme Sequencing (LiPS) Program. The Lindamood Phoneme Sequencing (LiPS) Program teaches and improves phonemic awareness in children and adults. LiPS instruction directly applies phonemic awareness to the identification and sequencing of sounds in words. Students in the LiPS program move through a series of steps to learn the connection between mouth movements and the sounds of language. This kinesthetic feedback enables them to verify the identity and sequence of sounds within words and to become self-correcting in reading, spelling, and speech. The program was originally called the ADD Program (Auditory Discrimination in Depth). Research shows marked reductions in the incidence of reading failure when LiPS instruction is provided. The research base supporting LiPS efficacy is strong. For research information on this treatment program, visit http://www.ies.ed.gov/ncee/wwc/interventionreport.aspx?sid=173

Occupational therapy. Severe CAPD often interferes with the child's vestibular system development. Specifically, CAPD affects timing, rhythm, and balance to varying degrees. Occupational therapy can help to mitigate these issues.

The above list, while not exhaustive, describes some treatment methods in use today.

Management of APD in Home and School Settings

Following are strategies for managing central auditory processing disorder in the home and school settings.

Home Setting

- Delivering instructions. Instructions should be simple, no more than three at a time. When delivering multistep instructions to your child, alert your child to the total number of steps you are going to give (e.g., "I want you to do three things") and then "tag" items with words such as *first, last, before, after,* etc., and insert brief (one-to-two-second) pauses between items to enhance processing. Make sure your child comprehends the instructions by asking the child to repeat them back to you.

- Speaking and listening. Stand still facing your child and speak clearly, with a moderate rate. Keep language to a minimum when speaking to your child, as the child will be unable to follow lengthy communication. Give your child a longer response time, well beyond what might be typical, when asking questions. Do not rush the child when she is trying to process thoughts and communicate. Also, remember to give your child listening breaks at regular intervals throughout the day. The frequency of the breaks will depend upon the profile of the child.

- Visual cues. Do not expect your child to process auditory information if your household is noisy from multiple kids playing, TV, video games, or household appliances. Use visual or written cues in tandem with auditory cues (e.g., the Time Timer, a transition board to aid the child in understanding the daily schedule, written instructions, and closed captioning during TV or video programs). Cues should play to your child's strengths (e.g., if your child is a good reader, provide written instructions).

- Quiet space. Place your child in a quiet area away from auditory distractions such as other siblings, household appliances, telephones, and doors when doing seated work. Some children may need to wear earplugs.

- Environmental modifications. Make proper environmental modifications as needed. For example, install carpets and rugs over tile or wooden floors. Attach felt on the bottom of chairs to help reduce the overall noise level of the home.

- Oral sensory input. Chewing gum, sour candies, gummy worms, taffy, sucking on water bottles, or drinks with a straw (such as smoothies), all help to increase auditory concentration.
- Games and activities. Play games and activities helpful in strengthening auditory processing skills such as games for sound awareness: phoneme, word-chain, rhyming, or same and different games. Type in the game (such as word-chain) into your browser and many free on-line games will come up. A good game for developing auditory discrimination skills at home is to hide a music box or ticking clock and ask the child to find it. When outdoors, make an animal sound and have your child find you or play Marco Polo in the pool. You can work on auditory attending by clapping your hands or beating a drum and asking your child to repeat the pattern.
- Home programs and apps. Your audiologist may recommend home computer programs or apps to assist your child's auditory development as needed.

School Setting

Depending upon the specific type of APD diagnosed, the following modifications and accommodations are available options.

- Classroom placement. Teachers should place children with auditory processing disorder with quieter peers, as they need as little background noise as possible. Therefore, teachers should exclude any child with CAPD from classrooms with excessive talking or movement by other kids.
- Seating. The child needs to be seated near and facing the speaker. Ensure a clear line of vision and adequate lighting on the speaker's face. Some children perform best from the front row and others may need the visual cue of the person in front of or beside them. Avoid settings that are noisy or reverberant. Avoid seating near open doors, windows and pencil sharpeners.

- Gain attention and use clear speech. Always gain the child's attention before giving directions or initiating class instruction. Speak at a slightly reduced rate and slightly louder volume to improve acoustic signal clarity.
- Delivering instructions. See the information under home setting on delivering instructions. Encourage the child to indicate when they do not understand instructions. Also, provide written instructions on the classroom board in addition to auditory instructions.
- Repetition. Repeat auditory information as needed with associated visual cues and/or demonstrations.
- Task dissection. Breaking lengthy tasks into smaller, easier-to-process segments will assist the child with APD in processing the information.
- Optimization of the learning environment. Create a multisensory, hands-on, experiential learning environment with information presented in a well-structured, systematic, and logical fashion.
- Visual cues. Visual aids can significantly assist children with auditory deficits as many of these children have visual processing strength.
- Provision of oral sensory input. The student should have access to a water bottle or chewing gum as these help to increase auditory concentration.
- Provision of "thinking time" for all students. Insert a waiting time of up to ten seconds before allowing any student to respond. Do not rush a child with APD who is trying to communicate a thought, as they need time to process thoughts and organize responses.
- Exam accommodations. Limit oral exams, allow extended time for tests, and use a separate, quiet environment for testing.
- Environmental modifications. Placing rugs on floors and felt pads on the bottoms of chairs and table legs, along with the use of a cork bulletin board are effective in reducing extraneous background noise and reverberation in the classroom. In addition, using fabric to cover hard surfaces to increase sound absorption and reduce sound reflections is also helpful.

- Provision of "listening breaks." Teachers should implement listening breaks throughout the day to minimize auditory overload. The frequency of the breaks will depend upon the profile of the child.
- Use of assistive technology. A personal FM system consists of a student wearing an earpiece and the teacher wearing a headpiece microphone, improving the sound-to-noise ratio and enabling the student to pick up auditory information adequately. Alternative strategies include getting study notes from an organized friend or using a tape recorder with reduced-speed playback.
- Computer programs. Students can also learn to visualize auditory information through a reading or spelling program (such as Lindamood Bell Visualizing and Verbalizing® or Cast-A-Spell).

Summary

Children can make significant progress in developing auditory skills by following prescribed treatment from an audiologist who specializes in central auditory processing disorder. The time invested is well worth the effort!

Thirteen

Diagnosis and Treatment

Diagnosis

How do you know when to seek a screening for your child? Your child needs to be screened when adverse behavior occurs with more frequency, intensity, and duration than typical children and when it negatively affects your child and your family's daily life. There are many red flags to indicate that a child has disordered sensory processing. While there is no single indicator, any of these in combination suggests that sensory processing should be evaluated, especially if the indicator is typical of the child the majority of the time.

- Attention problems—fixating (excessively focused), perseverating (to repeat insistently), distractibility.
- Difficulty maintaining an optimal alert state—hyperactivity or hypoactivity (lethargic).
- Avoidance of touch or movement.
- Self-stimulation, especially when it is persistent and interferes with the ability to do other things. Sensory-craving children demonstrate many self-stimulating behaviors.
- Stereotypic behaviors (e.g., hand flapping/distal cupping, spinning or lining up objects).
- Rigidity, inflexibility, or difficulty tolerating or adjusting to even routine changes that are a natural part of daily living.

- Unpredictable emotional explosions.
- Disregard of, or impaired ability to interact with others, even a familiar person who provides routine daily care.
- Difficulty catching on, giving the appearance of trying hard but just not quite "getting it."

Diagnosis of SPD usually begins with an intake appointment. At this appointment, an occupational therapist will review the child's developmental history, historical tests, and presenting problems.

Some clinics may perform a screening as a next step or proceed straight to an assessment, if presenting problems are significant. A screening is a professional observation for atypical childhood development. You will fill out one or more parent checklists and a developmental history to supplement the observations of the evaluators. Providers will screen your child for SPD through distinguishable behaviors not biological means. There is no biological test such as a blood draw or brain scan to detect sensory processing disorder. The presence of SPD is determined by observing social, emotional, motor and attention behaviors.[1]

If screening identifies differences to warrant further evaluation, an assessment will follow. An assessment for SPD may involve standardized testing, detailed clinical observations, and parent and teacher feedback. The assessment process may also include a general health and physical evaluation, speech/language evaluation, psychological evaluation, and possibly referral to medical or other specialists if professionals identify a specific problem area. As mentioned previously, if the child's presenting problems are significant, the clinic may advise parents to proceed with a formal assessment and skip the screening stage.

A formal assessment by an occupational therapist with advanced training in SPD, resulting in a Sensory Integration Praxis Test (SIPT) certification, is essential to determine whether the observed behaviors are the result of sensory issues or other problems. An accurate assessment is critical as appropriate intervention relies upon the diagnosis. The therapist who completes the assessment is not necessarily the therapist who will treat your child. At the conclusion of the assessment, the evaluating therapist will sit down with you and review the results. The clinic will next assign your child's treating therapist. Meet and interview your child's treating therapist in advance to ensure the right fit for you and your child.

The process will involve few steps if you live in a rural area. There may be one occupational therapist available, or you may have to travel to obtain an assessment from a SIPT-certified therapist. Should the results indicate that your child would benefit from therapy the evaluating therapist may assemble a treatment plan that provides guidelines for your local treating therapist.

So what does a formal assessment entail? Evaluation of sensory modulation and sensory-based motor disorder utilize different tools. Assessment of pure modulation disorders, and referrals for occupational therapy, are based on clinical observations, caregiver reports, and developmental and sensory history.[2] While there is no standardized diagnostic test to identify sensory modulation disorder to date, most clinicians who have been practicing for a number of years are very astute in their clinical observation and identification of this disorder.

There are several standardized diagnostic tests that measure motor function and sensory discrimination, which may result in a diagnosis of dyspraxia and/or postural disorder. One of these is the SIPT, created and standardized through the work of A. Jean Ayres, the founder of sensory integration, SPD theories and treatment techniques. The SIPT is standardized for children aged four to eight; other assessments will be used for those who do not fall in this age range. Examples of other assessments include the Miller Assessment for Preschoolers (MAP), Miller Function and Participation Scales (MFUN), Bayley Scales (birth to four), Bruininks-Oseretsky Test of Motor Proficiency, Movement Assessment Battery for Children (Movement ABC-2), the Peabody Developmental Motor Scales, the DeGangi-Berk, and the Goal Oriented Assessment of Life Skills (GOAL).

Some children with sensory-based motor disorders can be challenging to diagnose due to personal and environmental factors. Recognition and diagnosis of this disorder depends not only on the severity of the motor disorder but also on the demands of the environment, social acceptability, tolerance of errors and the child's ability to cope emotionally.[3] In other words, if the child's environment does not require significant motor planning, there is a lot of acceptance and tolerance of errors, or the child has a great ability to cope emotionally with his shortcomings, recognition and diagnosis may be delayed until the child's motor planning and execution have been overtaxed. Children who learn motor actions well enough to automate them no longer involve motor planning. Thus, the child with dyspraxia doing familiar, learned things among peers does not stand out as different; he seems just the same as the others. It is only when new or unfamiliar tasks are involved that differences might become apparent—but even then, his dyspraxia may not be evident unless the observer knows what to look for, because a child with dyspraxia quickly learns compensatory strategies and techniques to cover his inabilities. This is why it is important to seek out an occupational therapist with advanced SPD training to evaluate your child.

Occupational therapists, speech-language therapists, physical therapists, or psychologists tests different skills. However, all assessments must include signs and symptoms of dyspraxia based on the child's age and stage of development. Professionals should share their findings with one another to gain an accurate, complete picture as a team.

Treatment

"Treatment for SPD is a fun, play-based intervention that takes place in a sensory-rich environment....Private clinics and practices, hospital outpatient departments, and university occupational therapy programs are typical places where treatment for SPD may be found."[4] Treatment for SPD is anchored by pediatric occupational therapy with a sensory integrative approach that may be supplemented with other therapies as required by your child's distinct profile. A sensory integrative approach is one that is holistic; it treats the entire body encompassing all the senses.[5] Treatment provides a rich multisensory environment in which the therapist designs interventions that promote integration of the senses. Other professionals such as physical therapists, speech and language therapists, mental health professionals, developmental optometrists, and audiologists may be involved in your child's therapy. The ideal situation is to receive treatment from a multidisciplinary clinic that can provide all or most of these services. This enables your child's team to communicate and collaborate to provide the best intervention tailored to your child's unique profile. That said, sensory clinics are not available in all areas, or the services may be limited at your local sensory clinic. If this is the case, you may need to seek out individual providers and facilitate meetings with your child's treating team so they can work in concert toward the established goals. Your child's therapists may suggest additional therapies such as playgroups and complimentary therapies. Playgroups are designed to address a range of individual needs as well as foster social development. Listening therapy, Wilbarger brushing protocol, craniosacral therapy, or hippotherapy (equine therapy) are examples of some complimentary therapies.

So what exactly is occupational therapy? Occupational therapy assists people to participate in doing what they want and need to do through the therapeutic practice of occupations (everyday activities).[6] The occupation of a child includes developing motor skills, crawling, walking, playing, eating, learning, socializing, paying attention, dressing, leisure skills, writing, reading, sports...the list is endless on what "occupations" a child needs to learn. Occupational therapy focuses on how to help a child achieve all the skills needed to be the best they can be!

Occupational therapists working with children are educated on the stages of childhood development and the appropriate milestones in a child's physical, mental, and behavioral growth.[7]

A pediatric occupational therapist can:

- Evaluate the child's level of performance in critical developmental areas.
- Observe the child's home and school environments and determine modifications to promote optimal development.
- Develop a plan of treatment in coordination with other health-care professionals who are treating the child.
- Develop age-appropriate self-care routines and habits, play skills, and social skills.
- Recommend adaptive equipment to facilitate the development of age-appropriate abilities.

An occupational therapist cannot provide a SPD diagnosis for insurance purposes. Your child's pediatrician must provide the diagnosis; therefore, it is important for your pediatrician to collaborate with your child's occupational therapist to generate the most accurate diagnosis. There are two different models of occupational therapy. One is the medical model of occupational therapy administered in a medical setting. The other is an educational model of occupational therapy, which the child may receive through his school.

These two models are not synonymous. Occupational therapists in the schools use their expertise to assist children in preparation and performance of learning and school-related tasks, which helps them to succeed as students.[8] They accomplish this through environmental modifications (such as preferential seating, providing incline or slant boards for writing, etc.), behavior management, and incorporating sensory breaks (these breaks may involve jumping on a mini-trampoline or using other sensory equipment to help positively alter the child's arousal level). The occupational therapy intervention provided by the school does not promote integration or long-term regulation in the child. These are goals of medical occupational therapy.

Medical occupational therapy goals for children are always on developing automatic and appropriate responses to sensation so that daily occupations can be competently performed and social participation fostered.[9] Developing automatic and appropriate responses to sensations can only be achieved through integration of the senses. Integration is a very different concept than sensory stimulation. When working on sensory integration, occupational therapists help your child take in sensory information and process it around a novel task (motor planning), and help her to understand and manage these experiences. For example, if a child has motor planning problems, the therapist may use a game that requires multi-step sequencing, providing the appropriate support to help the child achieve success. This child may play the game in a big gym full of sensorimotor activities. Each of these activities provides different levels of vestibular, proprioceptive, tactile, and visual input for him. Once a task is learned, the therapist will conceive a new, more challenging task for the child. Therapy transpires through the medium of play in pediatric occupational therapy. Play is internally motivating for the child and therapy is most effective facilitated in the child's natural occupation. Occupational therapy in the school setting does not provide the necessary therapy through play and will not help the child overcome their developmental delays. Instead, the school occupational therapist helps the child to manage their disabilities in order to perform school-related tasks. Therefore, occupational therapy provided in the school setting cannot replace private occupational therapy. Should the child require services in the school setting, this should be in addition to, and not in place of, medical therapy.

Often confusing to parents is why sensory children require specialized therapy since play naturally provides the *typical* child with the sensory experiences his brain needs and allows him to respond in a meaningful way.[10] Why does not playing on the playground, participating in sports, or general play develop and organize a sensory child's brain? Playground swinging is sensory stimulation not sensory integration. Sensory stimulation often results in improved regulation, which is why occupational therapists recommend swings as part of a sensory diet. In order to facilitate integration, the child must swing while participating in a meaningful task. For instance, the child throws beanbags through a target while she swings. This activity forces her brain to organize sensory information from several origins, analyze the information, organize a response, monitor its success or failure, benefit from feedback, and refine further adaptive responses.... In addition, therapy sessions must challenge the child in order to effectively facilitate integration.[11] This type of occupational therapy promotes integration.

Sports such as swimming, gymnastics, or ice skating are great adjunct activities but cannot replace occupational therapy. These sports are all based on repetitive movements and do not provide the myriad opportunities for the child to motor plan new movements. While participating in these activities are great avenues for developing regulation, muscle strength, stabilization, bilateral coordination (using both sides of the body together), social interaction and muscle tone, doing so will not facilitate sensory integration. Nor will it help your child to be flexible and adaptable when motor planning.

Other types of play do not promote the necessary integration to overcome the child's developmental delays as neurological problems prevent him from processing the sensations from his own play. Therefore, he cannot play in a manner that is integrating for him nor produce adaptive responses. For example, a typical child who is pretending to be a server, taking your order, walking to pick up the order and delivering the order is integrating auditory, visual, vestibular, proprioceptive, and tactile sensations as she is playing out this theme. Children with SPD cannot play in this integrating manner due to sensory reactivity and motor planning challenges. For instance, a child with motor planning challenges may be unable to sequence through the steps required to play out this theme.

Therefore, the sensory child requires a multisensory highly specialized environment with customized activities to present the "just-right" challenge. Researchers found occupational therapy mitigates sensory challenges in autistic children, scientifically supporting occupational therapy as an effective treatment for children with SPD.[12]

Role of the Family in Treatment

Effective treatment for SPD should also be family centered. Parents and therapists form a partnership during treatment. "Parents identify priorities and act as the experts on their child...Together, the family and the therapists collaborate to develop the best possible program that reflects the family's culture, needs, and values."[13] Parents play the biggest role in assessment by sharing the ways the disorder affects the child, themselves, and the family. In addition, parents play a large role in facilitating daily therapeutic routines, teaching life skills (dressing, cleaning teeth, and bathing), calming and soothing their child (coregulators), and engaging with their child on a daily basis. Parents are there every day with their child and those are moments that parents can capitalize on in a way that nobody else can.[14] As a result, "the nurturing, love, and commitment of a family cannot be replaced by any array of services."[15] The first challenge of a family with a child with developmental concerns is to understand what options are available. Below is age specific information on how to locate help for your child.

Finding an Occupational Therapist

Children under Age Three

Should you notice that your child is lagging behind developmentally and your child is under the age of three, then your child may be eligible for the Birth to 3 Program if you are a United States citizen. The Birth to 3 Program is a federally mandated program (Part C of the Individuals with Disabilities Education Act—IDEA) to support families of children with delays or disabilities under the age of three. Early intervention is the process of providing services and support to young children believed to have an established condition. There are three qualifying circumstances: (1) those evaluated and determined to have a diagnosed physical or mental condition with a high probability of a resulting developmental delay; (2) an existing delay; (3) a child who is at-risk of developing a delay or special need that may affect their development or interfere with their education.

How does my child qualify for the Birth to 3 Program?
States have discretion in setting the criteria for child eligibility, including whether or not to serve at risk children. As a result, definitions of eligibility may vary significantly from state to state. States also differ concerning which state agency has been designated "lead agency" for the Part C program.

In order to find Birth to 3 contact information for your state, visit the Early Childhood Technical Assistance Center at http://ectacenter.org/contact/ptccoord.asp and click on your state. Next, click the Refer Website link, and fill in your county for provider listings. If the aforementioned link does not work (because they have modified the website), then go to http://www.etaccenter.org, click the tab C at the top of the page, and scroll to the bottom of the page labeled, Part C Contacts, and click, State Part C Program Coordinators List. Click on your state and, click the Refer Website link, and fill in your county to receive a list of providers. Select the office or provider closest to you and contact that office to start the process of obtaining a developmental screening or evaluation.

If your child qualifies for the Birth to 3 Program, you will be assigned a service coordinator who will organize the requisite services for your child. Your coordinator will provide you with the information to get started in the program. Some states have a parental cost-share system, in which parents deemed financially able must share in the cost of early intervention services for their children. In addition, if your child is eligible for Medicaid or any other state programs, the state will request that you apply.

You will have to advocate for your child if the program in your state does not operate as described above. According to one occupational therapist, her state communicates that developmental therapists will address all their needs and replace other therapies. This is definitely not the case. Developmental therapists do not have training or licenses in occupational therapy or speech-language therapy. In addition, the waiting time for services in this state is extraordinarily long. If this is the situation in your state, first see if you qualify for Medicaid. If so, Medicaid covers occupational therapy, speech-language therapy and developmental therapy and requires only a pediatrician's prescription. You can arrange your child's services for early intervention if you do not qualify for Medicaid. Check with your local hospital and contact occupational therapists and/or speech-language therapists to see if they participate in early intervention services. Of course, private therapy is an option for children under three if your family insurance policy covers the therapy and the expense is affordable for the family.

Do not delay this process, as the young brain is highly malleable due to rapid neurological growth. As a result, these precious early years offer a window of opportunity optimal for learning and treatment. This does not mean that older children and adults cannot benefit from treatment. "Adults and older children may progress more slowly in treatment than young children because brain plasticity diminishes through life, but improvement is achievable at any stage of life with effective therapeutic intervention."[16] The earlier you start treatment, the better the outcome.

Children Ages Three and Over
You will need to find a multidisciplinary clinic in your area if your child is three or older. A multidisciplinary clinic consists of several therapists who practice different disciplines, such as occupational therapists, speech-language therapists, physical therapists, mental health professionals, etc. Some areas do not have multidisciplinary clinics. Locate an occupational therapist in your area if there is not a multidisciplinary clinic available. Not any occupational therapist will suffice; the occupational therapist should use a sensory integrative framework for treatment.

One resource to find a private occupational therapist is to check the database on Dr. Lucy Jane Miller's website http://www.SPDfoundation.net. Dr. Miller's SPD treatment directory helps parents and caregivers locate professionals experienced in working with children with SPD. The directory is free for both professionals and caregivers. Currently, this database is limited as not all professionals are registered. You may also inquire at your local hospital whether they provide occupational thera-py using a sensory integrative framework. Family and friends can be a great resource for referrals as well.

The Impact of Treatment

What improvements can you expect to see from treatment? You may see the following changes in your child if you follow the treatment program prescribed by your child's therapists:

- Improved attention, participation, and learning
- Improvements in arousal state
- Increase in flexibility and cooperativeness, which positively af-fects social life (as the child becomes able to accept peers' ideas for play more easily, take turns, and share) and family dynamics as the child cooperates with parents and siblings more easily.
- Enhanced fine motor control (e.g., increased legibility in handwriting)
- Better gross motor control (e.g., couldn't ride a bike prior but can post treatment)
- Faster processing speed (e.g., can respond to verbal requests more quickly and can complete timed tests at school in a reason-able time frame)
- Improved social interactions with peers (better able to develop empathy, read non-verbal cues and social nuances, negotiate and keep up with peers play)
- Increased independence in functional activities (dressing, bath-ing, eating, etc.)
- Decreased fear and anxiety
- Increased ability to navigate transitions successfully
- Less defiant and aggressive behavior
- Greater ability to have fun and experience joy
- Motor planning improvements (e.g., trying new activities and learning to do old activities in a new way)

Treatment can make an enormous difference in sensory children's daily lives and help them to function at higher levels socially, emotionally, and academically. Most importantly, as soon as you feel that something is not quite right with your child, seek help immediately.

Appendix A

Formal School Support

Public schools offer three tiers of support: An Individualized Education Plan (IEP), a 504c Plan, or a Response to Intervention (RTI). Below is a description of each of these:

The Individualized Educational Plan (IEP) is a federal plan or program developed to make sure that a child who has a disability identified under the law and attending an elementary or secondary educational institution receives specialized instruction and related services. To receive an IEP and be served by special education, a child must demonstrate two legal criteria: (1) she has at least one of the thirteen disabilities listed in IDEA (the Individuals with Disabilities Education Act), which includes learning disabilities and attention disorders, and (2) as a result of the disability, she needs special education to make progress in school and benefit from the general education program. Parents of sensory children need to understand that in order to qualify for an IEP, the child must have a significant discrepancy between IQ and school performance. This means that a child with an average IQ or higher must be underperforming academically in order to qualify with a learning disability.

The 504c Plan is for children who do not require specialized instruction or have one of the thirteen disabilities listed in IDEA. The 504c Plan is a plan developed to help children who have a physical or mental impairment that substantially limits at least one major life activity, such as walking, seeing, learning, speaking, listening, reading, writing, breathing, working, or caring for oneself, and are attending an elementary or secondary educational institution. Under a 504c plan, children receive accommodations that will ensure their academic success and access to the learning environment. For example, children with a 504c plan may get built-in "sensory breaks" during their school day or special accommodations within the classroom.

Response to Intervention (RTI) program is another option in the public school system today. In 2004, when Congress reauthorized IDEA, the law was changed. Historically, IDEA required schools to take into account the discrepancy between achievement and intellectual ability to identify children with a specific learning disability. Now, a child does not have to show a big discrepancy between her IQ and her performance to qualify for formal school support. Many children with SPD are smart children who can perform academically but have difficulty getting through their days due to anxiety, resulting in behavior problems in school, at home, or both. The resulting Response to Intervention program is sometimes called a "pyramid of intervention." The goal of RTIs is to reach children quickly without requiring them to fit into the categories allowed by an IEP. The school starts by trying an intervention to help the child. If one intervention doesn't work, they try another. If interventions fail, then the child will undergo an evaluation to determine the specific disability and qualify for a 504c or an IEP.

When working in concert with school personnel, the process should be a collaborative effort with your requested accommodations for your child resulting in an easier school day for teacher, school, and child. Therefore, present your requests as strategies to support and help all parties involved.

Appendix B

Information on Sensory Processing Disorder and Treatment

Early Childhood Technical Assistance Center (ectacenter.org/contact/ptccoord.asp). This website will provide information on the lead agency managing the early intervention program in your state, and associated contact information.

STAR Center (SPDStar.org). The STAR Center is a treatment and research center owned by Dr. Lucy J. Miller. This website presents information such as symptoms, general facts, treatment, research and education on sensory processing disorder.

SPD Treatment Directory (spdstar.org/treatment-directory). This directory includes occupational therapists, speech-language therapists, physical therapists, physicians, mental health providers, eye care providers, dentists, and educators with a special interest in SPD. The directory also list facilities and community resources nationwide.

SPD University (spduniversity.spdstar.org). A rich set of e-learning courses, symposia, webinars, as well as, links to related resources on sensory processing disorder and associated issues.

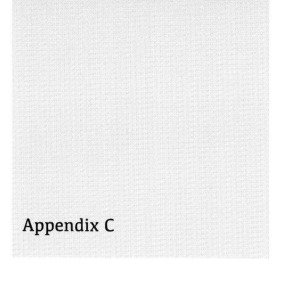

Appendix C

Books and Equipment

Ayres, Jean A. *Sensory Integration and the Child.* 3rd ed. Los Angeles: Western Psychological Services, 2008.

Baker, Bruce L. and Alan J. Brightman. *Steps to Independence: Teaching Everyday Skills to Children with Special Needs.* 4th ed. Baltimore, Maryland: Brookes Publishing, 2004.

Bellis, Teri James. *When the Brain Can't Hear: Unraveling the Mystery of Auditory Processing Disorder.* New York: Atria Books, 2002.

Bialer, Doreit S. and Lucy Jane Miller. *No Longer a Secret.* Arlington, Texas: Sensory World, 2011.

Biel, Lindsey and Nancy Peske. *Raising a Sensory Smart Child: The Definitive Handbook for Helping Your Child with Sensory Integration Issues.* New York: Penguin Books, 2009.

Cohen, Lawrence J. *Playful Parenting.* New York: Ballantine Books, 2001.

Cohen, Lawrence J. *The Opposite of Worry: The Playful Parenting Approach to Childhood Anxieties and Fears.* New York: Ballantine Books, 2013.

Delaney, Tara. *101 Games and Activities for Children with Autism, Asperger's and Sensory Processing.* Columbus, Ohio: McGraw-Hill Education, 2009.

Greene, Ross W. *The Explosive Child: A New Approach for Understanding and Parenting Easily Frustrated, Chronically Inflexible Children.* 4th ed. New York: HarperCollins, 2010.

Harvey, Pat and Jeanine A. Penzo. *Parenting a Child Who Has Intense Emotions: Dialectical Behavior Therapy Skills to Help Your Child Regulate Emotional Outbursts and Aggressive Behaviors.* Oakland, California: New Harbinger, 2009.

Heller, Sharon. *Too Loud, Too Bright, Too Fast, Too Tight: What to Do If You Are Sensory Defensive in An Overstimulating World.* New York: HarperCollins, 2003.

Koomar, Jane, Carol Kranowitz, Stacey Szklut, Lynn Balzer-Martin, Elizabeth Haber, and Deanna Iris Sava. *Questions Teachers Ask About Sensory Integration: Forms, Checklists, and Practical Tools for Teachers.* 3rd ed. Arlington, Texas: Future Horizons, 2007.

Kranowitz, Carol Stock. *The Out-of- Sync Child has Fun: Activities for Kids with Sensory Processing Disorder.* Revised Edition. New York: Perigee Books, 2006.

Kranowitz, Carol Stock. *The Out-of- Sync Child: Recognizing and Coping with Sensory Processing Disorder.* Revised Edition. New York: Perigee Books, 2006.

Kurckina, Mary Sheedy. *Kids, Parents, and Power Struggles.* New York: HarperCollins, 2001.

MacKenzie, Robert J. *Setting Limits With Your Strong-Willed Child: Eliminating Conflict by Establishing Clear, Firm, and Respectful Boundaries.* New York: Harmony, 2013.

Miller, Lucy Jane. *Sensational Kids: Hope and Help for Children with Sensory Processing Disorder.* 2nd ed. New York: Penguin Group, 2014.

Murray-Slutsky, Carolyn and Betty A. Paris. *Is It Sensory or Is It Behavior?* Austin, Texas: Hammill Institute on Disabilities, 2005.

Siegel, Daniel J. and Mary Hartzell. *Parenting from the Inside Out.* New York: Penguin Group, 2014.

Siegel, Daniel J. *The Whole-Brain Child.* New York: Bantam Books, 2012.

Voss, Angie. *The Survival Guide for Travelling With A Sensory Kiddo.* Lexington, Kentucky: CreateSpace Independent Publishing, 2012.

Weissbluth, Marc. *Healthy Sleep Habits, Happy Child.* New York: Ballantine Books, 2003.

Yack, Ellen, Paula Aquilla, and Shirley Sutton. *Building Bridges through Sensory Integration.* 2nd ed. Las Vegas, Nevada: Sensory Resources, 2004.

Equipment and Products

Integrations (store.schoolspecialty.com). Several catalogs of sensory equipment for home, school, and therapeutic settings.

Achievement Products for Children (achievement-products.com). A catalog of sensory equipment and accessories.

Chewigem.com (chewigem.com). Chewigem provides stylish and functional chewelry.

Different Roads (difflearn.com). Although this company serves the autistic community, many of the products are appropriate for children with SPD. Available products include visual aids, timers, manipulatives, a limited selection of fine and gross motor products, and social skills games (including feelings games).

eSpecial Needs (especialneeds.com). A catalog of adaptive equipment and various special needs resources.

Fun and function (funandfunction.com). A catalog offering hundreds of sensory equipment and accessories for home and school.

Mayer Johnson (mayer-johnson.com). Offers Boardmaker software, assistive technology and other special needs products for the home and classroom.

Playaway Toy Company (playawaytoy.com). This company provides indoor play equipment for at-home fun.

Pocket Full of Therapy (pfot.com). This company provides parents, teachers, and occupational therapists with a wide selection of developmental sensory toys, games, equipment, and books for promoting fine-, gross-, and oral-motor development.

Sensory Edge (sensoryedge.com). A product line for home, school, and therapeutic settings.

Southpaw Enterprises (southpawenterprises.com). A wide variety of sensory equipment for home, school, and therapeutic environments.

The Therapy Shoppe (TherapyShoppe.com). This company specializes in sensory integration products, special needs toys, oral motor tools, and occupational therapy supplies.

Therapro (therapro.com). Therapro offers a wide variety of products for occupational therapists, speech-language therapists, physical therapists, educators, and parents.

Therapy Works. (alertprogram.com). Offers *How Does Your Engine Run? A Leader's Guide to the Alert Program for Self- Regulation.*

Social Thinking. (socialthinking.com). Offers *The Zones of Regulation: A Curriculum Designed to Foster Self-Regulation and Emotional Control* program.

Weighted Blankets

The catalogs mentioned above carry weighted blankets with the exception of Chewigem, Different Roads, Playaway Toy Company, Therapy Works and Social Thinking. In addition, you can check Amazon, Etsy or E-Bay. You can also learn how to make your own by visiting E-how, mamasmiles. com, or Pinterest. The below sites are dedicated blanket sites.

Dreamcatcher Weighted Blankets (weightedblanket.net). Dreamcatchers offers pre-made and custom order blankets in several sizes a wide variety of fabric selections.

Mosaic Weighted Blankets (mosaicweightedblankets.com). Mosaic offers a nice selection of various sizes and fabrics. Choose pre-made or custom order.

Peace Weighted Blankets (peaceweightedproducts.com). Peace offers a selection of blankets from twin to full size in assorted fabrics. These blankets are pre-made or custom order.

SensaCalm (sensacalm.com). Sensacalm offers a selection of blankets in differing sizes and various fabrics. Choose from pre-made or custom order.

The Magic Blanket (beanblanket.com). Magic blanket offers a selection of blankets in diverse sizes and fabrics. Choose from in-stock or custom order.

Weighted Blankets Plus (weightedblanketsplus.com). This site offers a weighted blanket in a queen size as well as smaller options. Blankets are pre-made or custom order with a variety of fabric options available.

Charts for Sleep Schedule and Milestones

American Speech and Hearing Association (http://www.asha.org/public/speech/development/chart/). This chart represents the age at which most children will accomplish speech milestones.

The National Sleep Foundation provides guidelines on children and sleep at http://sleepfoundation.org/how-sleep-works/how-much-sleep-do-we-really-need. Refer to Parents.com for a summary chart that includes wake/sleep hours including naps based on the National Sleep Foundation's guidelines. The chart may be found at Parents.com, "Baby and Children Sleep Chart." http://www.parents.com/baby/sleep/basics/age-by-age-guide /.

The Centers for Disease Control and Prevention has developmental milestone checklists that can be found here http://www.cdc.gov/ncbddd/actearly/milestones/

College of Optometrists in Vision Development (covd.org/?page= Child_Timeline). This timeline provides visual developmental milestones by age as well as parental strategies to help your child develop his vision.

Clocks

My Tot Clock (mytotclock.com). This is an all-in-one clock that changes colors to teach little ones when to sleep (blue) and when it's ok to wake (yellow), plays lullabies, bedtime stories, fun wake music, white noise, night light and much more.

Time Timer. The Time Timer can be found at any of the websites listed under "Equipment and Products" above with the exception of Chewigem, Playaway Toy Company, and Sensory Edge.

Clothing

Stride Rite (http://www.striderite.com). You can find seamless socks on this website.

World's Softest (http://www.worldssoftest.com). This company makes one product-soft socks!

SmartKnitKids (smartknitkids.com). Seamless socks, underwear, and t-shirts.

Kozie Clothes (kozieclothes.com). Kozie Clothes offers apparel and products with soft fabrics, no tags and inverted seams. This company also offers weighted clothing, compression clothing, and weighted vests.

Therapro (therapro.com). This company offers a wide variety of products for occupational therapists, speech therapists, physical therapists, educators, and parents. In their clothing category, Therapro offers shirts, socks and pants that are soft, seamless and designed for those with tactile hypersensitivities. Therapro also offers compression shirts and other clothing with weight options.

Funandfunction (funandfunction.com). Fun and Function offers products for special needs parents and therapists. Clothing selections offered include soft, seamless, tagless dresses, leggings, pants, tees and socks designed for children with tactile hypersensitivities. Fun and Function also offers a compression vest section with various graphics printed on them.

No Netz (nonetz.com). No Netz offers bathing suits for men and boys with no lining or net. For children with tactile hypersensitivity, the lining in bathing suits can cause skin irritation and chaffing.

Miscellaneous Resources

A Sensory Life (asensorylife.com/sensory-retreats.html). This is occupational therapist Angie Voss's website and contains a lot of good information, including a litany of sensory retreat ideas.

Lakeshore Learning (lakeshorelearning.com). This company supplies educational toys for parents and teachers. You can find the "ice cream parlor game" here.

Natural Candy Store (naturalcandystore.com). You can find natural and organic candy here free of artificial colorings and flavorings.

Your Therapy Source (yourtherapysource.com/visualperceptual.html). Offers books and activities for teachers, parents, and therapists to incorporate sensory motor activities into the child's day or therapy session. Many of their books are available in electronic and printed format. This website has great visual perceptual games and activities.

Writing Help Sources.If your child has significant trouble with writing, writing tools utilized by occupational therapists can be found at http://therapro.com, http://therapyshoppe.com, or http://achievement-products.com, or http://store.schoolspecialty.com You can find writing tools, handwriting practice sheets that have raised lines or other qualities that assist the child, or slanted boards. Pencil grips are also helpful for some children; a sampler pack is available at http://funandfunction.com

Relaxation

Yoga for the Special Child (specialyoga.com). Yoga for the Special Child is a multi-level comprehensive Program of Yoga techniques designed to enhance the natural development of children with special needs developed by Sonia Sumar. Licensed practitioners are listed on this site. In addition, you can find the book written by Sonia Sumar: Yoga for the Special Child: A Therapeutic Approach for Infants and Children with Down Syndrome, Cerebral Palsy, Autism Spectrum Disorders and Learning Disabilities, 2007 on Amazon.

Inner Health Studio (innerhealthstudio.com). This website is owned by an occupational therapist and offers coping skills information including stress, anxiety and relaxation. You can find relaxation scripts to use with your child on this website.

Teacher Supply Stores

Bright Hub Education (brighthubeducation.com). If your child is vision impaired, has postural disorder or ADHD, then a writing slant board may be beneficial in the classroom. Bright Hub Education has a good section on explaining the benefits of these boards and the various types available at http://www.brighthubeducation.com/special-ed-inclusion-strategies/76678-about-adjustable-writing-slant-boards/

Teachers Pay Teachers (teacherspayteachers.com). This website has some good resources you can browse. For children with auditory discrimination, this website has the game "Sound Bingo" which will help improve auditory discrimination skills. Just type in Sound Bingo in the search box when you get to the main menu of teacherspayteachers or use the direct link provided in Chapter 5: Sensory Discrimination Disorder under parental strategies for auditory discrimination.

Really Good Stuff (reallygoodstuff.com). For children who need help reading due to visual discrimination challenges, Really Good Stuff offers the E.Z.C. Reading Strips that highlight text as the child is reading.

Travel

Federal Aviation Administration-Child Safety on Airplanes (http://www.faa.gov/ passengers/fly_children/crs for parental information on flying with children).

Federal Aviation Administration-Information for Operators (http://www.faa. gov/other_visit/aviation_industry/airline_operators/airline_safety/info/). This website contains information provided to the airline operators on airline safety. Located here are airline safety rules on flying with children.

United States Geological Survey (http://store.usgs.gov/pass/access. html). If your itinerary includes a national park or recreation area, your child may be eligible for a lifetime Access Pass. You can acquire information about who qualifies for the lifetime Access Pass on this website.

SeatGuru (http://www.seatguru.com). This website provides seat maps, comparison charts and advice when travelling by air.

Communication Aids

There is a diverse selection of visual aids ranging in price. Some resources are free and others are fee-based services. In addition to the below resources, check the catalogs above and Pinterest for communication pictures. Of course, you can draw pictures of the day's activities as well; even stick figures will suffice.

Mayer Johnson (mayer-johnson.com). Mayer Johnson offers several versions of Boardmaker, the leading software of picture communication symbols among educators. Mayer Johnson now offers a personal version for individual use that offers all the features and flexibility of the institutional version, and is available in multiple languages.

Do2Learn (do2learn.com). Do2learn provides social skills and behavioral regulation activities and guidance, learning songs and games, communication cards, academic material, and transition guides for employment and life skills. The communication cards are helpful in putting together a transition board for your child.

Mrs. Riley (mrsriley.com). This site offers communication cards for parents, teachers and professionals. Download existing cards or you can customize your own.

Gateways (jgateways.org). Gateways provides support services, resources, on-going coaching and professional development to Jewish special needs children in Jewish Day School Programs and provides a Sunday program for Jewish special needs children ages 5-17 with moderate to severe disabilities. This website offers resources around Jewish holidays and special events such as Passover, Shabbat, Purim, Hanukkah, Bar/Bat Mitzvah preparation including communication cards. Also offered is the Gateways Haggadah, which utilizes over 150 communication symbols to help a special needs child understand Passover.

Previewing Aids

Sensory Stories (sensorystories.com). Sensory stories are for children with sensory overresponsivity and have built-in calming strategies to help the child deal with everyday events. You can purchase them at http://www. therapro.com.

Social Stories. Social stories were originally invented by Carol Gray. You can find *The New Social Story Book* by Carol Gray and Tony Attwood on amazon.com. You can also make your own social stories by taking digital pictures of your child, adding text and laminating. There is also an app called StoryMaker from Handhold Adpative for iPhone or iPad platforms.

References

Books

1. Ahn, Roianne R., Lucy Jane Miller, Sharon Milberger and Daniel N. McIntosh. "Prevalence of Parents' Perceptions of Sensory Processing Disorders Among Kindergarten Children." *The American Journal of Occupational Therapy 58*, no.3 (May/June 2004): 287-293.

2. Arnwine, Bonnie. *Starting Sensory Integration Therapy.* 2nd ed. Arlington, Texas: Future Horizons, 2007.

3. Auer, Christopher R. and Susan L. Blumberg. *Parenting a Child with Sensory Processing Disorder: A Family Guide to Understanding & Supporting Your Sensory-Sensitive Child.* Oakland California: New Harbinger Publications, 2006.

4. Ayres, Jean A. *Sensory Integration and the Child.* 3rd ed. Los Angeles: Western Psychological Services, 2008

5. Baker, Jed. *No More Meltdowns: Positive Strategies for Managing and Preventing Out-Of-Control Behavior.* Arlington, Texas: Future Horizons, 2008.

6. Barbas, Helen, Basilis Zikopoulos and Clare Timbie. "Sensory Pathways and Emotional Context for Action in Primate Prefrontal Cortex." *Biological Psychiatry* (2010) doi: 10.1016/j.biopsych.2010.08.008

7. Bellis, Teri James. *When the Brain Can't Hear: Unraveling the Mystery of Auditory Processing Disorder.* New York: Atria Books, 2002.

8. Ben-Sasson, Ben A., A.S. Carter and M.J. Briggs-Gowan. "Sensory Over-Responsivity in Elementary School: Prevalence and Social-Emotional Correlates." *Journal Abnormal Child Psychology* 37 (2009): 705-716.

9. Ben-Sasson, Ben A., T.W. Soto, A.E. Heberle, A.S. Carter and M.J. Briggs-Gowan. "Early and Concurrent Features of ADHD and Sensory Over-Responsivity Symptom Clusters." *Journal of Attention Disorders* (August 4, 2014) ISSN:10870547.

10. Berns, Roberta M. *Child, Family, School, Community Socialization and Support.* 8th ed. Belmont, CA: Wadsworth Cengage Learning, 2010.

11. Bialer, Doreit S. and Lucy Jane Miller. *No Longer A Secret.* Arlington, Texas: Sensory World, 2011.

12. Biel, Lindsey and Nancy Peske. *Raising a Sensory Smart Child: The Definitive Handbook for Helping Your Child with Sensory Integration Issues.* New York: Penguin Books, 2009.

13. Blair, Clancy and Adele Diamond. "Biological processes in prevention and intervention: The promotion of self-regulation as a means of preventing school failure." *Developmental Psychopathology* 20, no.3 (2008): 899-911.

14. Brock, Eide and Fernette Eide. *The Mislabeled Child.* New York: Hyperion, 2006.

15. Bundy, Anita C., Shelly J. Lane, and Elizabeth A. Murray. *Sensory Integration Theory and Practice.* 2nd ed. Philadelphia: F.A. Davis Company, 2002.

16. Carr, Janet and Roberta Shepherd. *Movement Science.* Gaithersburg, Maryland: Aspen Publishers, 2000.

17. Case-Smith, Jane and Jane Clifford O'Brien. *Occupational Therapy for Children and Adolescents.* 7th ed. Philadelphia: Mosby, 2014.

18. Cermak, Sharon A. and Dawne Larkin. *Developmental Coordination Disorder.* Clifton Park, New York: Delmar Cengage Learning, 2002.

19. Chansky, Tamar E. *Freeing Your Child From Anxiety: Powerful, Practical Solutions to Overcome Your Child's Fears, Worries, and Phobias.* New York: Broadway Books, 2004.

20. Chermak, Gail D. and Frank E. Musiek. "Managing Central Auditory Processing Disorders in Children and Youth." *American Journal of Audiology.* (July 1992): 61:65.

21. Cohen, Lawrence J. *Playful Parenting.* New York: Ballantine Books, 2001.

22. Cohen, Lawrence J. *The Opposite of Worry: The Playful Parenting Approach to Childhood Anxieties and Fears.* New York: Ballantine Books, 2013.

23. Davies, Douglas. *Child Development.* 3rd ed. New York: Guilford Press, 2011.

24. Davies, Patricia and William J. Gavin. "Validating the Diagnosis of Sensory Processing Disorders Using EGG Technology." *The American Journal of Occupational Therapy* 61, no.2 (March/April 2007): 176-189.

25. DeGangi, Georgia. *Pediatric Disorders of Regulation in Affect and Behavior: A Therapist's Guide to Assessment and Treatment.* San Diego, California: Academic Press, 2000.

26. DelCarmen-Wiggins, Rebecca and Alice Carter. *Handbook of Infant, Toddler, Preschool Mental Health Assessment.* London: Oxford University Press, 2004.

27. Goldsmith, H.H., C.A. Van Hulle, C.L. Arneson, J.E. Schreiber and M.A. Gernsbacher. "A Population-Based Twin Study of Parentally Reported Tactile and Auditory Defensiveness in Young Children." *Journal of Abnormal Child Psychology* 34, no.3 (June 2006): 393-407.

28. Gray, Carol and Abbie Leigh White. *My Social Stories Book.* 17th ed. Philadelphia: Jessica Kingsley Publishers, 2006.

29. Greene, Ross W. *Lost at School: Why Our Kids with Behavioral Challenges Are Falling Through the Cracks and How We Can Help Them.* New York: Scribner, 2008.

30. Greene, Ross W. *The Explosive Child: A New Approach for Understanding and Parenting Easily Frustrated, Chronically Inflexible Children.* 4th ed. New York: HarperCollins, 2010.

31. Greenspan, Stanley and Nancy Breslau Lewis. *Building Healthy Minds: The Six Experiences that Create Intelligence and Emotional Growth in Babies and Young Children.* New York: Da Capo Press, 2000.

32. Greenspan, Stanley and Serena Wieder. *The Child with Special Needs.* New York: Da Capo Press, 1998.

33. Greenspan, Stanley I. and Ira Glovinsky. *Children and Babies with Mood Swings: New Insights for Parents and Professionals.* Bethesda, Maryland: Interdisciplinary Council on Developmental and Learning Disorders, 2007.

34. Greenspan, Stanley I. *Playground Politics: Understanding the Emotional Life of Your School-Age Child.* New York: Da Capo Press, 1994.

35. Gupta, Ravi, Deepak Goel, Mohan Dhyani and Manish Mittal. "Head Banging Persisting During Adolescence: A Case with Polysomnographic Findings." *Journal of Neuroscience in Rural Practice* 5, no.4 (October-December 2014): 405-408.

36. Harvey, Pat and Jeanine A. Penzo. *Parenting a Child Who Has Intense Emotions: Dialectical Behavior Therapy Skills to Help Your Child Regulate Emotional Outbursts and Aggressive Behaviors.* Oakland, California: New Harbinger, 2009.

37. Held, Richard and Alan Hein. "Movement-Produced Stimulation in the Development of Visually Guided Behavior." *Journal of Comparative and Physiological Psychology* 56, no.5, (1963): 872-876.

38. Heller, Sharon. *Too Loud, Too Bright, Too Fast, Too Tight: What to Do If You Are Sensory Defensive in an Overstimulating World.* New York: HarperCollins, 2003.

39. Hickman, Lois and Rebecca E. Hutchins. *EyeGames: Easy and Fun Visual Exercises.* 3rd ed. Arlington, Texas: Sensory World, 2010.

40. Interdisciplinary Council on Developmental and Learning Disorders. *Diagnostic Manual for Infancy and Early Childhood.* Bethesda, MD: Interdisciplinary Council on Developmental and Learning Disorders, 2005.

41. Interdisciplinary Council on Developmental and Learning Disorders. *Clinical Practice Guidelines.* Bethesda, MD: Interdisciplinary Council on Developmental and Learning Disorders, 2000.

42. Jung-Beeman, Mark. "Bilateral brain processes for comprehending natural language." *TRENDS in Cognitive Science* 9, no. 11 (November 2005): 512-518.

43. Kirby, Amanda and Sharon Drew. *Guide to Dyspraxia and Developmental Coordination Disorders.* New York: David Fulton Publishers, 2003.

44. Kurcinka, Mary Sheedy. *Raising Your Spirited Child: A Guide for Parents Whose Child is More Intense, Sensitive, Perceptive, Persistent, and Energetic.* 3rd ed. New York: HarperCollins, 2006.

45. Kurckina, Mary Sheedy. *Kids, Parents, and Power Struggles.* New York: HarperCollins, 2001.

46. Kurtz, Lisa A. *Understanding Motor Skills in Children with Dyspraxia, ADHD, Autism, and Other Learning Disabilities.* Philadelphia: Jessica Kingsley Publishers, 2008.

47. Lane, Shelly J., Stacey Reynolds and Leroy Thacker. "Sensory Over-Responsivity and ADHD: Differentiating Using Electrodermal Responses, Cortisol, and Anxiety." *Frontiers in Integrative Neuroscience* 4, no.8 (2010) doi:10.3389/fnint.2010.00008

48. Lewis, Michael, Jeannette M. Haviland-Jones and Lisa Feldman Barrett. *Handbook of Emotions.* 3rd ed. New York: The Guilford Press, 2010.

49. Lewis, Michael and Linda Michalson. *Children's Emotions and Moods: Developmental Theory and Measurement.* New York: Plenum Press, 1983.

50. MacKenzie, Robert J. *Setting Limits with Your Strong-Willed Child: Eliminating Conflict by Establishing Clear, Firm, and Respectful Boundaries.* New York: Harmony, 2013.

51. Miller, Lucy Jane. *Sensational Kids: Hope and Help for Children with Sensory Processing Disorder.* 2nd ed. New York: Penguin Group, 2014.

52. Morris, Kathleen. *Insights into Sensory Issues for Professionals.* Arlington, Texas: Sensory World, 2010.

53. Murray-Slutsky, Carolyn and Betty A. Paris. *Exploring the Spectrum of Autism and Pervasive Developmental Disorders.* Austin, Texas: Hammill Institute on Disabilities, 2000.

54. Murray-Slutsky, Carolyn and Betty A. Paris. *Is It Sensory or Is It Behavior?* Austin, Texas: Hammill Institute on Disabilities, 2005.

55. Myles, Brenda Smith, Melissa L. Trautman, and Ronda L. Schelvan. *The Hidden Curriculum: Practical Solutions for Understanding Unstated Rules in Social Situations.* Shawnee Mission, Kansas: Autism Asperger Publishing Company, 2004.

56. Nicholasen, Michelle and Barbara O'Neal. *I Brake for Meltdowns: How to Handle the Most Exasperating Behavior of Your 2-to5 Year-old.* Philadelphia: Da Capo Press, 2008.

57. Owen, Julia P., Elysa J. Marco, Shivani Desai, Emily Fourie, Julia Harris, et.al. "Abnormal White Matter Microstructure in Children with Sensory Processing Disorders." *NeuroImage:* 2 (2013): 844-853.

58. Portwood, Madeleine. *Developmental Dyspraxia.* 2nd ed. London: David Fulton Publishers, 2000.

59. Reebye Pratibha and Aileen Stalker. *Understanding Regulation Disorders of Sensory Processing in Children: Management Strategies for Parents and Professionals.* Philadelphia: Jessica Kingsley Publishers, 2008.

60. Ripley, Kate, Bob Daines and Jenny Barrett. *Dyspraxia: A Guide for Teachers and Parents.* 2nd ed. New York: Routledge, 2007.

61. Royeen, Charlotte B. and Aimee J. Luebben. *Sensory Integration: A Compendium of Leading Scholarship.* Bethesda, Maryland: AOTA Press, 2009.

62. Schaaf, Roseann C., Teal Benevides, Ema Imperatore Blanche, Barbara A. Brett-Green, Janice P. Burke, et.al. "Parasympathetic Functions in Children with Sensory Processing Disorder." *Frontiers in Integrative Neuroscience* 4, no.4 (March 2010): 1-11.

63. Schoen, Sarah A., Lucy J. Miller and Jillian C. Sullivan. "Measurement in Sensory Modulation: The Sensory Processing Scale Assessment." *The American Journal of Occupational Therapy* 68, no.5 (September/October 2014): 522-530.

64. Schoen, Sarah A., Lucy J. Miller and Kathy E. Green. "Pilot Study of the Sensory Over-Responsivity Scales: Assessment and Inventory."

The American Journal of Occupational Therapy 62 no.4 (July/August 2008): 393-406.

65. Shumway-Cook, Anne and Marjorie H. Woollacott. *Motor Control.* 4th ed. Baltimore: Wolters Kluwer, 2012.

66. Siegel, Daniel J. and Mary Hartzell. *Parenting from the Inside Out.* New York: Penguin Group, 2014.

67. Siegel, Daniel J. *The Whole-Brained Child.* New York: Bantam Books, 2012.

68. Stadtler, Ann C., Peter A. Gorski and T. Berry Brazelton. "Toilet Training Methods, Clinical Interventions and Recommendations." *Pediatrics* 103 Supplement 3 (June 1999): 1359-1361.

69. Turecki, Stanley and Leslie Tonner. *The Difficult Child.* 2nd ed. New York: Bantam Books, 2000.

70. Voss, Angie. *The Survival Guide for Travelling with A Sensory Kiddo.* Lexington, Kentucky: CreateSpace Independent Publishing, 2012.

71. Voss, Angie. *Understanding Your Child's Sensory Signals* Lexington, Kentucky: CreateSpace Independent Publishing, 2011.

72. Weissbluth, Marc. *Healthy Sleep Habits, Happy Child.* New York: Ballantine Books, 2003.

73. Williamson, Gordon and Marie E. Anzalone. *Sensory Integration and Self-Regulation in Infants and Toddlers* Zero to Three, 2001.

74. Zucker, Bonnie. *Anxiety-Free Kids.* Waco, Texas: Prufrock Press, 2009.

Notes

Chapter 1: Overview of Sensory Processing Disorder

1. Miller, Lucy Jane. "About SPD." SPD Foundation. Accessed June 8, 2014, http://spdfoundation.net/about-sensory-processing-disorder.html

2. Murray-Slutsky, Carolyn and Betty Paris. Is It Sensory or Is It Behavior? Workshop. Arlington Heights, Illinois, 2011.

3. Miller, Lucy J. "What Is SPD?" Sensory Therapies and Research Center. Accessed June 3, 2014. http://spdstar.org/what-is-spd/

4. Ayres, Jean A. *Sensory Integration and the Child.* Los Angeles: Western Psychological Services, 2005.

5. Case-Smith, Jane and Jane Clifford O'Brien. *Occupational Therapy for Children and Adolescents.* 7th ed. St. Louis, Missouri: Mosby, 2015.

6. SPD Foundation. "Research." Accessed June 8, 2014. http://www.spdfoundation.net/research/collaborations/

7. Ahn, Roianne R., Lucy J. Miller, Sharon Milberger, and Daniel N. McIntosh. May/June, 2004. "Prevalence of Parents' Perceptions of Sensory Processing Disorders Among Kindergarten Children." *American Journal of Occupational Therapy* 58, no. 3 (May 2004): 287-93.

8. Miller, Lucy J. *Sensational Kids: Hope and Help for Children with Sensory Processing Disorder.* 2nd ed. New York: Penguin Group, 2014.

9. Bundy, Anita C., Shelly J. Lane, and Elizabeth A. Murray. *Sensory Integration: Theory and Practice, "Glossary."* 2nd ed. Philadelphia: F. A. Davis, 2002.

10. Case-Smith, Jane and Jane Clifford O'Brien. *Occupational Therapy for Children and Adolescents.* 7th ed. St. Louis, Missouri: Mosby, 2015.

11. See note 4 above.

12. See note 9 above.

13. Craig, Bud. "Interoception: the sense of the physiological condition of the body." *Current Opinion in Neurobiology* 13, no. 4 (August 2003): 500-05.

14. Miller, Lucy Jane, Marie E. Anzalone, Shelly J. Lane, Sharon A. Cermak, and Elizabeth T. Osten. "Concept evolution in sensory integration: A proposed nosology for diagnosis." *American Journal of Occupational Therapy,* 61 (2007): 135-140.

Chapter Two: Sensory Modulation Disorder

1. Ayres, A. Jean. *Sensory Integration and the Child.* Los Angeles: Western Psychological Services, 1979.

2. Case-Smith, Jane and Jane Clifford O'Brian. *Occupational Therapy for Children and Adolescents.* 7th ed. St. Louis, Missouri: Mosby, 2015.

3. DeGangi, Georgia. *Pediatric Disorders of Regulation in Affect and Behavior: A Therapist's Guide to Assessment and Treatment.* San Diego: Academic Press, 2000.

4. Murray-Slutsky, Carolyn, and Betty Paris. *Exploring the Spectrum of Autism and Pervasive Developmental Disorders.* Austin, TX: Hammill Institute on Disabilities, 2000.

5. Murray-Slutsky, Carrie and Betty A. Paris. "Is It Sensory or Is It Behavior Workshop." Arlington Heights, Illinois, 2011.

6. Miller, Lucy J. *Sensational Kids: Hope and Help for Children with Sensory Processing Disorder.* 2nd ed. New York: Penguin Group, 2014.

7. Brout, Jennifer Jo. "How to Help an Over-Responsive Child." New York Metro Parents. Accessed April, 2015. http://www.nymetroparents.com/article/How-to-Help-an-Over-Responsive-Child

8. See note 2 above.

9. Ibid.

10. Schoen, S. A., L. J. Miller, and K. E. Green. "Pilot Study of the Sensory Overresponsivity Scales: Assessment and Inventory." *American Journal of Occupational Therapy* 62 (2008): 393-406.

11. Miller, Lucy J. *A Sensible Approach to Sensory Processing Disorder: Sensory Over-Responsivity.* Video Course #1102, 1:19, SPD University.

12. Collins, Britt and Lucy J. Miller. "Sensory Overresponsivity." *Autism Asperger's Digest.* (January/February 2012): 13.

13. Heller, Sharon. *Too Loud Too Bright Too Fast Too Tight.* New York: HarperCollins, 2002.

14. See note 5 above.

15. See note 11 above.

16. Interdisciplinary Council on Developmental and Learning Disorders. *Diagnostic Manual for Infancy and Early Childhood.* Bethesda, MD: Interdisciplinary Council on Developmental and Learning Disorders, 2005.

17. See note 11 above.

18. See note 13 above.

19. See note 11 above.

20. Ibid.

21. Miller, Lucy J. *A Sensible Approach to Sensory Processing Disorder: Sensory Under-Responsivity.* Video Course #1103, 1:19, SPD University.

22. Reebye, Pratibha and Aileen Stalker. *Understanding Regulation Disorders of Sensory Processing in Children: Management Strategies for Parents and Professionals.* Philadelphia: Jessica Kingsley Publishers, 2008.

23. See note 6 above.

24. See note 16 above.

25. Williamson, Gordon G. and Marie E. Anzalone. *Sensory Integration and Self- Regulation in Infants and Toddlers: Helping Very Young Children Interact with Their Environment.* Washington, D.C.: Zero to Three, 2001.

26. See note 21 above.

27. See note 22 above.

28. See note 21 above.

29. Ibid.

30. See note 16 above.

31. Collins, Britt and Lucy J. Miller. "Sensory Underresponsivity." *Autism Asperger's Digest.* (March/April 2012): 45.

32. See note 16 above.

33. Osten, Beth and Emily Hildner. "Self-Regulation in Young Children." (Parents Educational Lecture, Beth Osten and Associates, Skokie, IL, 2010).

34. See note 5 above.

35. Ibid.

36. See note 16 above.

37. See note 5 above.

38. Miller, Lucy J. *A Sensible Approach to Sensory Processing Disorder: Sensory Craving.* Video Course #1104, 1:19, SPD University.

39. Schoen, Sarah A. *A Sensible Approach to Sensory Processing Disorder: Praxis and Dyspraxia.* Video Course #1106, 1:00, SPD University.

40. Aquila, Paula. *Sensory Strategies to Improve Communication, Social Skills, and Behavior.* DVD. Future Horizons, 2009.

41. Ayres, Jean A. *Sensory Integration and the Child.* Los Angeles: Western Psychological Services, 2005.

42. See note 5 above.

43. See note 6 above.

44. See note 38 above.

45. Ibid.

46. Ibid.

47. See note 16 above.

Chapter 3: Sensory-Based Motor Disorder-Dyspraxia

1. Beth Osten (Owner Beth Osten & Associates, Skokie, IL), in discussion, February 2, 2015.

2. Bundy, Anita C., Shelly J. Lane, and Elizabeth A. Murray. *Sensory Integration: Theory and Practice.* 2nd ed. Philadelphia: F. A. Davis, 2002.

3. Interdisciplinary Council on Developmental and Learning Disorders. *Clinical Practice Guidelines.* Bethesda, MD: Interdisciplinary Council on Developmental and Learning Disorders, 2000.

4. Ayres, Jean. "Learning Disabilities and the Vestibular System." *Journal of Learning Disabilities,* 11 (1978): 18-29.

5. See note 3 above.

6. Ayres, Jean A. *Sensory Integration and the Child.* CA: Western Psychological Services, 2005.

7. Losse, A., S. E. Henderson, D. Elliman, et.al. "Clumsiness in Children: Do They Grow Out of It? A 10-year Follow-Up Study." *Developmental Medicine & Child Neurology* 33 no.1 (1991): 55–68.

8. Gallahue, David L. *Motor Ability in Children.* New York: Wiley and Sons, 1985.

9. Miller, Lucy J. *Sensational Kids: Hope and Help for Children with Sensory Processing Disorder.* 2nd ed. New York: Penguin Group, 2014.

10. American Psychiatric Association: *Diagnostic and Statistical Manual of Mental Disorders,* 5th ed. Arlington, VA: American Psychiatric Association, 2013.

11. Richardson, Dr. Alexandra J., and D. Phil Oxon. "The Potential Role of Fatty Acids in Developmental Dyspraxia—Can Dietary Supplementation Help?" *Dyspraxia Foundation Professional Journal* 1 (2002):30-52.

12. Murray-Slutsky, Carolyn, and Betty Paris. *Exploring the Spectrum of Autism and Pervasive Developmental Disorders.* Austin, TX: Hammill Institute on Disabilities, 2000.

13. Radomski, Mary Vining and Catherine A. Trombly. *Occupational Therapy for Physical Dysfunction.* 7th ed. Latham, California: Lippincott, Williams & Wilkins, 2013.

14. See note 12 above.

15. Ibid, 12.

16. Schoen, Sarah A. *A Sensible Approach to Sensory Processing Disorder: Praxis and Dyspraxia.* Video Course #1106, 1:00, SPD University.

17. Case-Smith, Jane and Jane Clifford O'Brian. *Occupational Therapy for Children and Adolescents.* 7th ed. St. Louis, Missouri: Mosby, 2015.

18. See note 3 above.

19. See note 16 above.

20. Ibid.

21. See note 6 above.

22. See note 2 above.

23. See note 16 above.

24. See note 12 above.

25. See note 16 above.

26. See note 2 above.

27. Eingal, Tali and Yuval Nativ. *Maya's Fun Week: A Fine Motor Adventure.* Stillwater, Wisconson: Pileated Press, 2012.

28. See note 12 above.

29. Edwards, Marissa. "Help your Child Develop the "Crossing the Midline" Skill. North Shore Pediatric Therapy, April 18, 2011. http://

nspt4kids.com/parenting/help-your-child-develop-the-crossing-the-midline-skill/.

30. Murray-Slutsky, Carrie and Betty A. Paris. "Is It Sensory or Is It Behavior? Workshop." Arlington Heights, Illinois, 2011.

31. Schott, Danette. "Last is First in Backward Chaining." *Special-Ism.com.* Accessed April 25, 2015. http://special-ism.com/last-is-first-in-backward-chaining/.

32. See note 31 above.

Chapter 4: Sensory-Based Motor Disorder-Postural Disorder

1. Bundy, Anita C., Shelly J. Lane, and Elizabeth A. Murray. *Sensory Integration: Theory and Practice.* 2nd ed. Philadelphia: F. A. Davis, 2002.

2. Miller, Lucy J. *Sensational Kids: Hope and Help for Children with Sensory Processing Disorder.* 2nd ed. New York: Penguin Group, 2014.

3. Murray-Slutsky, Carolyn, and Betty Paris. *Exploring the Spectrum of Autism and Pervasive Developmental Disorders.* Austin, TX: Hammill Institute on Disabilities, 2000.

4. Collins, Britt and Lucy J. Miller. "Sensory-Based Motor Disorders: Postural Disorder." *Autism Asperger's Digest.* (July/August 2012): 47.

5. See note 1 above.

6. Ayres, Jean A. *Sensory Integration and the Child.* CA: Western Psychological Services, 2005.

7. Interdisciplinary Council on Developmental and Learning Disorders. *Clinical Practice Guidelines.* Bethesda, MD: Interdisciplinary Council on Developmental and Learning Disorders, 2000.

8. See note 6 above.

9. See note 3 above.

10. *See note 4 above.*

11. Ibid.

12. See note 6 above.

13. See note 2 above.

14. See note 4 above.

15. Ibid.

16. Mosby's Medical Dictionary. 8th ed. Elsevier, 2009.

17. Kawar, Mary J., and Sheila M. Frick. *Astronaut Training: A Sound Activated Vestibular-Visual Protocol.* Madison, WI: Vital Sounds, 2005.

18. Ibid.

19. Edwards, Marissa. "Help your Child Develop the "Crossing the Midline" Skill. North Shore Pediatric Therapy, April 18, 2011. http://nspt4kids.com/parenting/help-your-child-develop-the-crossing-the-midline-skill/.

20. See note 1 above.

21. See note 4 above.

22. Ibid.

23. Ibid.

Chapter 5: Sensory Discrimination Disorder

1. Miller, Lucy J. "What Is SPD?" Sensory Therapies and Research Center. Accessed June 3, 2014. http://spdstar.org/what-is-spd/

2. Miller, Lucy J. and Carol Kranowitz. *A Sensible Approach to Sensory Processing Disorder: Overview of all Types.* Video Course #1101, 1:10, SPD University.

3. Interdisciplinary Council on Developmental and Learning Disorders. *Diagnostic Manual for Infancy and Early Childhood.* Bethesda, MD: Interdisciplinary Council on Developmental and Learning Disorders, 2005.

4. Bundy, Anita C., Shelly J. Lane, and Elizabeth A. Murray. *Sensory Integration: Theory and Practice.* 2nd ed. Philadelphia: F. A. Davis, 2002.

5. Ibid.

6. Ibid.

7. Allen, Renee. *A Sensible Approach to Sensory Processing Disorder: Sensory Discrimination Disorder.* Video Course #1107, 1:00, SPD University.

8. Ibid.

9. Ibid.

10. Ibid.

11. Ibid.

12. Ayres

13. See note 7 above.

Chapter 6: Internal Regulation

1. American Academy of Pediatrics. "It's Potty Time!" *Healthy Children Magazine,* Fall 2008. https://healthychildren.org/English/ages-stages/toddler/toilet-training/Pages/Its-Potty-Time.aspx.

2. Osten, Beth. "Potty Training." (Parents Educational Lecture, Beth Osten and Associates, Skokie, IL, 2010).

3. Murray-Slutsky, Carrie and Betty A. Paris. *Is It Sensory or Is It Behavior?* Texas: Hammill Institute on Disabilities, 2005.

4. Murray-Slutsky, Carolyn, and Betty Paris. *Exploring the Spectrum of Autism and Pervasive Developmental Disorders.* Austin, TX: Hammill Institute on Disabilities, 2000.

5. American Academy of Allergy Asthma & Immunology. "Food Allergy." Accessed January 10, 2015. http://www.aaaai.org/conditions-and-treatments/conditions-dictionary/food-allergies.aspx.

6. American Academy of Allergy Asthma & Immunology. "Food Allergy: Tips to Remember." Accessed January 10, 2015. http://www.aaaai.org/conditions-and-treatments/library/at-a-glance/food-allergy.aspx.

7. Richardson, Alexandra J. and D. Phil Oxon. "The potential role of fatty acids in developmental dyspraxia-can dietary supplementation help?" *The Dyspraxia Foundation Professional Journal.* (June 2002): 30-52. (b) Richardson, Alexandra J. and M.A. Ross. "Fatty Acid metabolism in neurodevelopmental disorder: a new perspective on associations between attention-deficit/hyperactivity disorder, dyslexia, dyspraxia and the autistic spectrum." *Prostaglandins, Leukotrienes and Essential Fatty Acids.* 63 (2000): 1-9. (c) Richardson, Alexandra J. "Omega-3 fatty acids in ADHD and related neurodevelopmental disorders." *International Review of Psychiatry* 18 no.2 (April 2006): 155-172.

8. Montgomery, Paul, Jennifer R. Burton, Richard P. Sewell, Thees F. Spreckelsen, Alexandra J. Richardson. "Low Blood Long Chain Omega-3 Fatty Acids in UK Children Are Associated with Poor Cognitive Performance and Behavior: A Cross-Sectional Analysis from the DOLAB Study." *PLOS ONE* 8 no.6 (June 24, 2013): e66697. Doi: 10.1371/journal.pone.0066697.

9. Richardson, Alexandra J. and D. Phil Oxon. "The potential role of fatty acids in developmental dyspraxia-can dietary supplementation help?" *The Dyspraxia Foundation Professional Journal.* (June 2002): 30-52.

Chapter 7: Sensory Diet

1. Murray-Slutsky, Carrie and Betty A. Paris. Is It Sensory or Is It Behavior? Workshop. Arlington Heights, Illinois, 2011.

2. Ayres, Jean A. *Sensory Integration and the Child.* CA: Western Psychological Services, 2005.

3. Ibid.

4. Collins, Britt and Lucy J. Miller. "Sensory Underresponsivity." *Autism Asperger's Digest.* (March/April 2012): 45.

5. Murray-Slutsky, Carolyn, and Betty Paris. *Exploring the Spectrum of Autism and Pervasive Developmental Disorders.* Austin, TX: Hammill Institute on Disabilities, 2000.

6. Ibid.

7. See note 1 above.

8. Ibid.

9. Clopton, Heidi (Owner and Director of Center for Development), in discussion, October, 2014.

10. Ibid.

11. Hacker, Bonnie. "8 Fun Oral Sensory Activities to Improve Your Child's Regulation." *Special-Ism.com.* Accessed April 14, 2015. http://special-ism.com/eight-fun-oral-sensory-activities-to-improve-your-childs-regulation/.

Chapter 8: Aggression, Meltdowns and Defiant Behavior

1. Galinsky, Ellen. *Mind in the Making: The Seven Essential Life Skills Every Child Needs.* New York: HarperCollins, 2010.

2. Greene, Ross W. *The Explosive Child: A New Approach for Understanding and Parenting Easily Frustrated, Chronically Inflexible Children.* 4th ed. New York: HarperCollins, 2010.

3. Greenspan, Stanley and Serena Wieder. *The Child with Special Needs.* New York: Da Capo Press, 1998.

4. See note 2 above.

5. James, Katherine, Lucy Jane Miller, Roseanne Schaaf, Darci M. Nielsen, and Sarah A. Schoen. "Phenotypes within sensory modulation dysfunction." *Comprehensive Psychiatry.* 52 (2011): 715-724.

6. Florez, Ida. "Developing Young Children's Self-Regulation through Everyday Experiences." *Young Children* 66 no.4 (2011): 46-47.

7. Miller, Lucy J. *Sensational Kids: Hope and Help for Children with Sensory Processing Disorder.* 2nd ed. New York: Penguin Group, 2014.

8. American Speech-Language Hearing Association. "Speech, Language and Swallowing." Accessed June 3, 2014. http://www.asha.org/public/speech/

9. Beth Osten (Owner Beth Osten & Associates, Skokie, IL), in discussion, February 2, 2015.

10. Bundy, Anita C., Shelly J. Lane, and Elizabeth A. Murray. *Sensory Integration: Theory and Practice.* 2nd ed. Philadelphia: F. A. Davis, 2002.

11. Ibid.

12. Ibid.

13. SPD Foundation. "About SPD: Ten Fundamental Facts About SPD." Accessed March 8, 2014. http://www.spdfoundation.net/about-sensory-processing-disorder/facts/

14. Ibid.

15. American Academy of Pediatrics. "Temper Tantrums: A Normal Part of Growing Up." *Patient Education Handout.* Accessed September 19, 2015. http://www.patiented.solutions.aap.org.

16. Murray-Slutsky, Carrie and Betty A. Paris. Is It Sensory or Is It Behavior? Workshop. Arlington Heights, Illinois, 2011.

17. Murray-Slutsky, Carrie and Betty A. Paris. *Is It Sensory or Is It Behavior?* Texas: Hammill Institute on Disabilities, 2005.

18. Minnesota Association for Children's Mental Health. "Regulation Disorder of Sensory Processing Disorder," *Early Childhood Mental Health Fact Sheet.* Accessed March 8, 2014.

19. See note 3 above.

20. Mackenzie, Robert J. *Setting Limits with Your Strong-Willed Child.* 2nd ed. New York: Three Rivers Press, 2013.

21. See note 3 above.

Chapter 9: Transitions

1. Miller, Lucy J. *Sensational Kids: Hope and Help for Children with Sensory Processing Disorder.* New York: Penguin Group, 2014.

2. Miller, Lucy J. *A Sensible Approach to Sensory Processing Disorder: Sensory Under-Responsivity.* Video Course #1103, 1:19, SPD University.

3. Ibid.

4. Ayres, Jean A. *Developmental Dyspraxia and Adult-Onset Apraxia.* Torrance, CA: Sensory Integration International, 1985.

5. Bridley, Alexis and Sytsma Jordan. "Child Routines Moderate Daily Hassles and Children's Psychological Adjustment." *Children's Health.* 41 (2012):129-144. DOI: 10.1080/02739615.2012.657040

6. Aquilla, Paula. *Sensory Strategies to Improve Communication, Social Skills, and Behavior.* DVD. Future Horizons, 2009.

7. Mindell, Dr. Jodi. "Children and Bedtime Fears and Nightmares." National Sleep Foundation. Accessed January 10, 2014. http://sleepfoundation.org/ask-the-expert/children-and-bedtime-fears-and-nightmares

8. Ibid.

9. Cohen, Lawrence. *Playful Parenting.* New York: Ballantine Books, 2001.

10. Greenspan, Stanley and Serena Wieder. *The Child with Special Needs.* New York: Da Capo Press, 1998.

11. Voss, Angie. *The Survival Guide for Travelling with a Sensory Kiddo.* CreateSpace Independent Publishing, 2012.

12. See note 6 above.

13. Murray-Slutsky, Carrie and Betty A. Paris. *Is It Sensory or Is It Behavior?* Texas: Hammill Institute on Disabilities, 2005.

14. Ibid.

15. See note 9 above.

16. See note 13 above.

17. Collins, Britt and Lucy J. Miller. "Focus on Sensory Craving." *Autism Asperger's Digest.* (May/June 2012): 16-17.

18. Collins, Britt and Lucy J. Miller. "Sensory Overresponsivity." *Autism Asperger's Digest.* (January/February 2012): 13.

19. Collins, Britt and Lucy J. Miller. "Sensory-Based Motor Disorders: Postural Disorder." *Autism Asperger's Digest.* (July/August 2012): 47.

Chapter 10: Emotions

1. Harvey, Pat and Jeanine A. Penzo. *Parenting a Child Who Has Intense Emotions.* Oakland, CA: New Harbinger Publications, 2009.

2. Miller, Lucy J. *A Sensible Approach to Sensory Processing Disorder: Sensory Under-Responsivity.* Video Course #1103, 1:19, SPD University.

3. Greenspan, Stanley and Serena Wieder. *The Child with Special Needs.* New York: Da Capo Press, 1998.

4. Ibid.

5. Cohen, Lawrence J. *The Opposite of Worry: The Playful Parenting Approach to Childhood Anxieties and Fears.* 2013.

6. Murray-Slutsky, Carrie and Betty A. Paris. Is It Sensory or Is It Behavior? Workshop. Arlington Heights, Illinois, 2011.

7. Miller, Lucy J. *Sensational Kids: Hope and Help for Children with Sensory Processing Disorder.* 2nd ed. New York: Penguin Group, 2014.

8. See note 5 above.

9.   Miller, Lucy J. *A Sensible Approach to Sensory Processing Disorder: Sensory Craving.* Video Course #104, 2:01, SPD University.

10. Kurcinka, Mary Sheedy. *Kids, Parents, and Power Struggles.* New York: Harper Collins, 2001.

11. See note 3 above.

12. Ibid.

13. Cleveland Clinic. "Head Banging and Body Rocking?" Accessed June 23, 2014. http://my.clevelandclinic.org/childrens-hospital/Home/health-info/diseases-conditions/hic_sleep_in_your_babys_first_year/hic_head_banging_and_body_rocking

14. Berns, Roberta M. *Child, Family, School, Community: Socialization and Support.* Belmont, CA: Wadsworth, 2013.

15. Brown-Braun, Betsy. "Circle the Wagons: How Children Learn to Express Empathy." *Huffington Post.* May 3, 2013. http://www.huffingtonpost.com/betsy-brown-braun/how-children-learn-empathy_b_3175943.html

16. Hartnett, Tim. "Validating Feelings: Helping People to Feel Understood." Accessed February 23, 2015. http://santacruztherapist.net/Articles.html

Chapter 11: Visual Dysfunction

1.   Lemer, Patricia. "Choosing an Eye Doctor." *New Developments* 3 no.4 (1998): 1.

2. DeCarlo, Dawn K., Ellen Bowman, Cara Monroe, Robert Kline, Gerald McGwin, Jr., and Cynthia Owsley. "Prevalence of attention-defict/ hyperactivity disorder among children with vision impairment." *Journal of American Association for Pediatric Ophthalmology and Strabismus* 18 No. 1 (2014):10-4. (b) Granet, David B. December 2005. "The Relationship between Convergence Insufficiency and ADHD." *Strabismus* 13 no.4 (2005): 163-68.

3. College of Optometrists in Vision Development. "Vision and Learning." Accessed April 10, 2014. http://www.covd.org/?page=Vision_Learning

4. American Optometric Association. "Recommended Eye Examination Frequency for Pediatric Patients and Adults." Accessed January 8, 2015. http://www.aoa.org/patients-and-public/caring-for-your-vision/comprehensive-eye-and-vision-examination/recommended-examination-frequency-for-pediatric-patients-and-adults?sso=y

5. EyeSmart. "What is an Opthamologist?" Accessed January 10, 2015. http://www.geteyesmart.org/eyesmart/living/what-is-an-ophthalmologist.cfm

6. College of Optometrists in Vision Development. "Certification." Accessed September 2009. http://www.covd.org/?page=Certification

7. Optometrist Network. "Learning and Vision." Accessed January 20, 2015, www.children-special-needs.org/vision_therapy/esophoria_reading

8. Ayres, Jean A. *Sensory Integration and the Child.* CA: Western Psychological Services, 2005.

9. Margolis, Neil and Paul J. Lederer. "Intake Questionnaire." Accessed October 24, 2010.

10. College of Optometrists in Vision Development. "17 Visual Skills." Accessed January 15, 2015. http://www.covd.org/?page=Visual_Skill s&hhSearchTerms=%2217+and+visual+and+skills%22

11. College of Optometrists in Vision Development. "Focusing." Accessed January 15, 2015. http://www.covd.org/?page=Focusing

12. College of Optometrists in Vision Development. "3D and Stereo Vision." Accessed January 15, 2015. http://www.covd. org/?page=3D_Stereo_Vision

13. Margolis, Neil. (Developmental Optometrist and Owner of Lederer and Margolis), in discussion, September 2009.

14. Granet, David B. December 2005. "The Relationship between Convergence Insufficiency and ADHD." *Strabismus* 13, no.4 (2005): 163-68.

15. Getz, Donald J. "Vision and Learning." Optometrist's Network. Accessed January 20, 2015. http://www.children-special-needs.org/ vision_therapy/esophoria_reading_pf.html

16. Bernstein Center for Visual Development. "Eye Focusing Problems, Accommodative Dysfunction." Accessed December 20, 2014, http:// www.bernsteincenterforvisualperformance.com/eye-focusing-prob- lems-accommodative-dysfunction

17. Oregon Optometric Physicians Association Children's Vision Committee. *"The Effects of Vision on Learning and School*

Performance." Milwaukie, OR: Oregon Optometric Physicians Association, 2000.

18. (a) Clopton, Jason. "Balanced Vision: How the Visual and Vestibular Systems Interact." Handout. Undated.   (b) Ayres, Jean A. *Sensory Integration and the Child.* CA: Western Psychological Services, 2005.   (c) Vestibular Disorders Association. "Vision Challenges with Vestibular Disorders." Accessed January 25, 2015.   http://vestibular.org/sites/default/files/page_files/Vision%20Challenges.pdf

19. Optometrist Network, "What is Strabismus?" Accessed January 20, 2015. http://www.strabismus.org/

20. Bernstein Center for Visual Development. "Strabismus, Crossed Eye, Wall-Eye." Accessed December 20, 2014. http://www.bernsteincenterforvisualperformance.com/strabismus-cross-eye-wall-eye

Chapter 12: Auditory Dysfunction

1. Bellis, Teri James.   "Understanding Auditory Processing Disorders in Children."   American Speech-Language Hearing Association. Accessed December 10, 2014.   http://www.asha.org/public/hearing/Understanding-Auditory-Processing-Disorders-in-Children/

2. Bundy, Anita C., Shelly J. Lane, and Elizabeth A. Murray. *Sensory Integration: Theory and Practice.* 2nd ed. Philadelphia: F. A. Davis, 2002.

3. See note 1 above.

4. APD Foundation. "Auditory Processing Disorder Fact Sheet." Accessed December 10, 2014. http://theapdfoundation.org/further-reading

5. Ibid.

6. Katz, Jack. "What is APD?" *National Coalition of Auditory Disorders.* Accessed August 3, 2014. http://www.ncapd.org/What_is_APD_.html

7. See note 2 above.

8. Bellis, Teri James. *When the Brain Can't Hear.* New York: Atria Books, 2002.

9. Ibid.

10. See note 1 above.

11. Ibid.

12. Frick, Sheila. "Therapeutic Listening Fact Sheet." Vital Sounds, Undated.

Chapter 13: Diagnosis and Treatment

1. Miller, Lucy J. *A Sensible Approach to Sensory Processing Disorder: Overview of all Types.* Video Course #1101, 1:10, SPD University.

2. Dunn Winnie. *Sensory Profile.* San Antonio, TX: Psychological Corporation, 1999.
   Johnson-Ecker, Cheryl. L and Diane L. Parham. The evaluation of sensory processing: A validity study using contrasting groups. *American Journal of Occupational Therapy.* 54, (September/October 2000):494–503.

3. Gubbay, Sasson S. *The Clumsy Child.* London: W.B. Saunders, 1975.

4. See note 1 above.

5. Ayres, Jean A. *Sensory Integration and the Child.* CA: Western Psychological Services, 2005.

6. American Occupational Therapy Association. "What is Occupational Therapy?" Accessed April 24, 2014. http://www.aota.org/About-Occupational-Therapy

7. American Occupational Therapy Association. "Child Development." Accessed April 24, 2014. http://www.aota.org/About-Occupational-Therapy/Patients-

8. American Occupational Therapy Association. "Occupational Therapy in School Settings." *School-Based Occupational Therapy Fact Sheets.* Accessed April 28, 2014. http://www.aota.org/About-Occupational-Therapy/Professionals/CV/School.aspx

9. Miller, Lucy J. *"Occupational Therapy for Children."* SPD Foundation. Accessed April 28, 2014. http://www.spdfoundation.net/treatment/ot/

10. See note 5 above.

11. Murray-Slutsky, Carrie and Betty A. Paris. Is It Sensory or Is It Behavior? Workshop. Arlington Heights, Illinois, 2011.

12. Schaaf, Roseann C., Teal Benevides, Zoe Mailloux, Patricia Faller, et.al. 2013. "An Intervention for Sensory Difficulties in Children with

Autism: A Randomized Trial." *Journal of Autism and Developmental Disorders* 10, no.1007 (2013).

13. Miller, Lucy J. "Treatment." SPD Foundation. Accessed April 8, 2014. http://www.spdfoundation.net/index.php/treatment

14. Rogers, S.J., L. Vismara, A.L. Wagner, C. McCormick, G. Young, and S. Ozonoff. "Autism Treatment in the First Year of Life: A Pilot Study of Infant Start, a Parent-Implemented Intervention for Symptomatic Infants." *Journal of Autism and Developmental Disorders.* 44, no.12 (December 2014): 2981-2995.

15. Wisconsin Department of Health Services. "Birth to Three Program-Guiding Principles." Accessed April 16, 2014. https://www.dhs.wisconsin.gov/birthto3/principles.htm /

16. Miller, Lucy J. "Occupational Therapy for Adults" SPD Foundation. Accessed April 8, 2014. http://www.spdfoundation.net/treatment/ot/

18271885R00211

Printed in Poland
by Amazon Fulfillment
Poland Sp. z o.o., Wrocław